Globalizing democracy

MANCHESTER
UNIVERSITY PRESS

PERSPECTIVES ON DEMOCRATIZATION

The series presents critical texts on democratization processes and democratic theory. Written in an accessible style the books are theoretically informed and empirically rich, and examine issues critical to the establishment, extension and deepening of democracy in different political systems and contexts. Important examples of successful democratization processes, as well as reasons why experiments in democratic government fail, are some of the issues analyzed in the series. The books in the series make an important contribution to the ongoing debates about democracy, good governance and democratization.

SHIRIN M. RAI AND WYN GRANT   series editors

already published

Funding democratization
PETER BURNELL AND ALAN WARE   (editors)

Democratization in the South
ROBIN LUCKHAM AND GORDON WHITE   (editors)

forthcoming titles

Democratization in Latin America
GERALDINE LIEVESLEY

Globalizing democracy
Power, legitimacy and the interpretation of democratic ideas

KATHERINE FIERLBECK

MANCHESTER UNIVERSITY PRESS
Manchester and New York

distributed exclusively in the USA by St. Martin's Press

Published by Manchester University Press
Oxford Road, Manchester M13 9NR, UK
and Room 400, 175 Fifth Avenue, New York, NY 10010, USA

Distributed exclusively in the USA by
St. Martin's Press, Inc., 175 Fifth Avenue, New York,
NY 10010, USA

Distributed exclusively in Canada by
UBC Press, University of British Columbia, 6344 Memorial Road,
Vancouver, BC, Canada V6T 1Z2

British Library Cataloguing-in-Publication Data
A catalogue record for this book is available from the British Library

Library of Congress Cataloging-in-Publication Data applied for

ISBN 0 7190 4995 4 *hardback*

First published 1998

05 04 03 02 01 00 99 98   10 9 8 7 6 5 4 3 2 1

Typeset in 9.5/12pt Trump Medieval
by Servis Filmsetting Ltd, Manchester
Printed in Great Britain
by Bookcraft (Bath) Ltd, Midsomer Norton

Contents

FOR GORDON

Acknowledgements

The study of democratization in developing states increasingly involves not only the encyclopaedic knowledge of how indefinite numbers of polities work (required of comparativists as a matter of course) but also the ability to evalute the normative claims of democratic theory which most of these polities hold. As one more comfortable in the latter field than in the former, I am indebted to all of my colleagues for their interest and for their insight both outside of and within the realm of political theory; and for providing invaluable assistance regardless of whether they have agreed with the direction of my arguments or not. These especially include Louise Carbert, Gil Winham, Denis Stairs, Tim Shaw, Peter Aucoin, Florian Bail, and John E. MacKinnon. Fred Deveaux and Caitilin Mongey were inexhaustible and fearless research assistants; and Paulette Chaisson showed endless patience for my secretarial demands. My husband was infinitely supportive, and managed to soothe myself, our newborn, and the computer in our crankier moments. And, finally, I should like to mention a debt of gratitude to Shirin Rai, whose intellectual and editorial expertise were always offered with her usual common sense and good humour.

Portions of chapters 3, 4, and 5 were previously published in the *Canadian Journal of Development Studies*, 15(2), 1994 and *Canadian Journal of Political Science*, 29(1), 1996.

Introduction

If there is such a thing as 'moral progress', then the most obvious manifestation of it is the spirited diffusion of democratic ideals around the globe. But while the effervescence of democracy seems on the surface to be real enough, there is less agreement on whether it constitutes progress and, more testily, whether such progress as there is is necessarily moral. As the globalization of democracy becomes increasingly palpable, the political obstacles to its achievement become overshadowed by more vexing questions concerning the very nature of democracy itself; and the line between strategic and normative concerns, so much clearer (and more rancorous) during the Cold War, has collapsed as suddenly and unexpectedly as the Berlin Wall, leaving development theorists scrabbling in the rubble. Too much attention has been focused in the Cold War period upon the political impediments and expedients that have (or have not) resulted in the establishment of 'democratic' structures; and too little effort has been made to examine how the idea of democracy itself affects the political context within which it takes root.

This book examines some of the philosophical and theoretical debates underlying the 'democratic project' which increasingly dominates the field of comparative development. The first concern presented here is normative (and, to a certain degree, epistemological): as democracy becomes more widely accepted as the political currency of legitimacy, the more broadly it is defined. But as agreement decreases regarding what, precisely, democracy is, the less we are able to evaluate how it is working, or indeed whether it is working at all. What are the philosophical justifications presented for such an expansion of interpretation, and what are the political reasons underlying it? The second issue is causal: what are the claims being made regarding how best to secure a democratic system in developing states? To what extent do our beliefs and expectations of how political relations ought to be governed distort our understanding of how putatively democratic societies do in fact emerge; and, conversely, to what extent does our understanding of how democracy manifests itself temper our conception of what it ought to be?

The overarching argument presented in this book is that the claims of culture, identity, and nation are being pushed too far, and that the idea of democracy cannot make any sense unless it is firmly grounded upon at least a minimal amount of 'neutrality'. This is because the fundamental attraction of democracy is that it permits the diffusion of power within a relatively ordered social environment: thus, if certain actors within any given society retain for themselves the ability to define what is or is not open for collective decision-making (e.g., the protection of certain cultural traits or the unchallengeable protection of private property rights), then democracy simply cannot function as an effective mechanism to diffuse power, and it becomes a meaningless reflection of its original purpose.

This book is *not* about the virtues of democracies *vis-à-vis* non-democracies *per se*. While it is quite arguable that there are certain beneficial aspects to authoritarian or traditional rule in many cases, the more substantial debate amongst contemporary actors is not whether they ought to be democracies or not, but whether the type of democracy they claim to represent ought to be respected, and why. The political issues revolve around the question of 'who has the right to judge others' conceptions of legitimate authority?', and are tied very closely to epistemological issues of voice and right which have surfaced so dramatically at the end of the twentieth century, and which vociferously challenge the modern conceptions of political sovereignty established by western states in the past three or four centuries.

The first chapter addresses the recent explosion of theories of democratization and globalization within the discipline of political science, particularly within the fields of comparative development and international relations. This chapter is intended to show how 'democracy' has too quickly become, both academically and politically, all things to all people: it represents a philosophical ideal, a political strategy, and an instrument of economic well-being. It is expected to promote popular participation, stabilize weak regimes, give citizens a sense of meaning, meet individuals' material needs, empower women, add vibrancy to a society, encourage tolerance, and strengthen a sense of national solidarity. There are bound to be disappointments. We must evaluate contemporary appeals to democracy more critically in order to salvage a limited amount of credibility in the idea before an epistemological inflation irremediably devalues the term.

Chapter 2 takes a closer look at some philosophical debates underlying democracy in order to explain why it has evolved into such an ambiguous concept. A significant source of our current confusion is that democracy can be viewed both as a tantalizing ideal, and as a system of limits. One of the most powerful and evocative justifications grounding liberal democracy, for example, is the account of human beings as responsible individuals. This depiction of responsibility reflects both spiritually gratifying and deeply cynical views about what is meant in 'being human'. On the one hand, the nature of 'humanity' implies a quality worthy of respect; a fundamental dignity that sets human beings apart from other sentient creatures. This sense of dignity is largely derived from the recognition that adult human beings are self-governing creatures; we make decisions based upon an understanding of the implications of our chosen action. That individuals can stand on principle despite onerous consequences is a theme underlying the most enduring and powerful Greek tragedies, Shakespearean dramas, and Dickensian novels; the suffering endured by the protagonists as a result of difficult decisions in adverse circumstances defines what we understand as the noblest qualities of being human.

On a more brutally political level, however, the concept of 'responsibility' also underlies the legitimacy of official punishment. The recognition that human beings could be troublesome and dangerous in a way animals could not, for example, led the early liberal theorist Thomas Hobbes to argue that securing individuals' own consent was the most effective means of controlling destabilizing social behaviour. 'Consent' as the basis of legitimate political authority thus has its roots in two quite disparate views. The first is that human autonomy ought to be respected because it is through the capacity to make decisions about our lives that we mature and develop into fully human individuals. The second is that we can enjoy freedoms only because (and only insofar as) we recognize that we will be punished if we transgress the limits of acceptable political behaviour. This ambivalence concerning precisely what we wish democracy to achieve underlies much of the confusion and ambiguity apparent in contemporary accounts of democratization and development.

But the most potent debate within democratic theory has become the extent to which the traditional liberal conception of democracy grounded upon principles of personal autonomy and political liberty ought to be expanded both to shake its culturally-specific heritage and to mitigate the consequences of social fragmentation, alienation, and exclusion that many claim stem from the legacy of pronounced individualism. Chapter 3 surveys the arguments supporting the expansion of 'democracy' from its individualistic orientations to an account more able to accommodate the concerns and aspirations of groups. Upon what principles and arguments are such accounts based; and why do they reject ideas that many view as the axioms which most boldly define modernity? In response to the arguments presented in Chapter 3, Chapter 4 offers critical assessments of these new trends in democratic theory. How philosophically coherent are these accounts? How well do they achieve the objectives they set for themselves? And, most importantly, is the drive to expand democracy in this direction, on balance, worth the political costs it is likely to entail?

Chapters 5 and 6 examine the political contexts within which debates about democratization are centred. Two of the most significant variables influencing the development of democracy are the role of (international) capital, and the role of 'civil society' (in relation to the state). It was the development of the modern state which facilitated the emergence of democracy in Europe: the new theory of sovereignty underlying the nascent state system rested on 'a shared conception of legitimation, supported by the entirety of the commonwealth, and precluding the privileging of any constituent component (the prince, the aristocracy, the people) of the political regime' (Hont 1994: 184). Yet the very idea of popular sovereignty was, paradoxically, initially presented as a means of limiting the voice of the common citizen: 'It is important to recognize that the idea of the modern state was constructed, painstakingly and purposefully, above all by Jean Bodin and Thomas Hobbes, for the express purpose of denying that any given population, any people, had either the capacity or the right to act together for themselves, either independently of or against their sovereign' (Dunn 1992: 247). The role of the state in contemporary development theory is no less ambivalent. It is the state which is expected to protect the interests of its citizens from the increasingly severe effects of transnational market relations; yet 'the problem of artificially created nation-states' imposed by European imperialist states is also seen as contributing to the ungovernability of many African countries (Nyang'oro 1992: 23). A strong state is necessary to promote the interests of the weak against the powerful: the interests of women against men, of the economically marginalized against the entrepreneurs, of minority cultures against the dominant ethnic group. But a strong state can, and too frequently does, prevent the articulation of any interests except those of a tiny ruling elite. In a similar way, the development of the modern state has been facilitated historically by the emergence of capitalism (Dunn 1992). But it is also capitalism itself – especially as a powerful international force – which is seen by some as an essential component of democracy (Fukuyama 1992) and by others as a threat to democracy (Shaw et al., 1992). Thus, suggests Chapter 5, any arguments for democratization based solely or principally upon the effects of the market are inconclusive and unsatisfactory: the function of democracy cannot rest too heavily upon an armature of private property rights.

Chapter 6 then examines the most recent reaction to market-oriented discussions of democratization: the claim that a robust democracy depends upon our ability to 'strengthen civil society'. But is a focus upon 'civil society' the best strategy for addressing the daunting and pervasive power of both 'the state' and 'international capital'? A recent wave of development literature points hopefully toward the proliferation of grassroots organizations, each one facilitating the participation of individuals at a local level and enhancing the sense of civic responsibility of all (e.g., Sandbrook and Halfani, 1993; Edwards and Hulme, 1992; and Clark, 1991). There are two major weaknesses with this account. The first is the question of viability: can the 'grassroots' strategy achieve these aims? This issue echoes the discussion surrounding the need for 'participatory democracy' which has become more pronounced as the complexity and enormity of modern societies increase. Within the field of democratic theory the clearest debate is between 'protective' and 'participatory' models of democracy (Held, 1987). Protective models, which view democracy primarily as a system for protecting a sphere of liberties for citizens, have been criticized for promoting too constrained a theory of representation (and for fostering elite representation: e.g., Schumpeter, 1942); for failing to promote the degree of widespread participation upon which democracy depends for its continued existence (Pateman, 1970); and for permitting unsavoury (if not illegal) activities by citizens within these spheres of liberties (such as pornography: e.g., Mackinnon, 1987). But the contrasting 'participatory' model is not without its own flaws: it can be inefficient; it can be oppressive in its loss of anonymous decision-making (Mansbridge, 1977); and it can result in catastrophic and 'irrational' collective decisions on economic issues (Mitchell, 1983). The second weakness of the 'grassroots movement' model is that it fails to present a sound and persuasive theory of accountability. To whom are people within each organization ultimately accountable? To whom are the 'facilitating organizations' (especially internationally-based NGOs, which tend to be more influential both politically and financially) themselves accountable? And what is the basis of legitimacy underlying each organization: self-rule, or the fact that such organizations can be more effective than either the market or the state in providing for citizens' needs?

Chapter 7 situates the debate over democracy and development more closely by examining the political context surrounding the inflation of democratic meaning. Are conceptions of democracy congruent between interlocutors in the debate over democratization, or is the apparent concurrence regarding democracy as the legitimizing norm of politics held together only by the merest filament of agreement based upon a notoriously vague connotation of the word 'democracy'? And if the latter is a more appropriate interpretation of the globalization of democracy, can it remain more than a political fad into the twenty-first century? One means of considering the problem of interpretation is to examine the recent positions taken on this issue by supranational agencies (such as the World Bank, International Monetary Fund (IMF), and the new World Trade Organization (WTO)) which, because of their economic roles, act as effective mediators between developed states' conceptions of political legitimacy, and the client states' rendering of the same. Despite the rather awkward formal declaration of most of these bodies not to interfere with the politics of client states, these agencies have paid no little attention to the contentious issue of 'governance' in the current reevaluation of their roles, goals, and strategies. Developing states are increasingly pressuring for less conditionality and more autonomy in governing their affairs, arguing that local cultures as well as unique domestic political and economic circumstances ought to be given special consideration. There are, however, conditions (especially concerning political representation and human rights) which liberal states often refuse to concede on normative grounds. Chapter 7 concludes by re-examining what the functions of 'democracy' in our current political environment ought to be, and argues that the only viable way of balancing the cultural claims of nations with the individual integrity of the individuals living within them is to insist upon a very basic conception of 'democratic neutrality' which preserves the ability of democracy to prevent the concentration of power based upon political or economic influence, or even upon the *prima facie* ability of cultural elites to preserve their own sources of power.

In sum, then, this book examines the consequences of the globalization of democratic norms. It is almost a truism to say that the legitimacy of contemporary states is judged according to the standard of democracy. But this, in turn, has roused a number of voices to protest that, insofar as *nonwestern* states are judged according to manifestly *western* criteria, an obvious and egregious injustice is occuring; and it is merely the overwhelming power of the industrialized democracies which permits them to assert the ostensible neutrality of the norms which they impose upon others. To correct this injustice, they continue, it is essential to modify the definition of democracy so that it reflects cultural and political qualities unique to specific societies. This book argues that such an approach is wrong. Rather than continually and uncritically expanding and modifying the term, we must insist upon a very clear and limited understanding of democracy. This is *not* to argue, in an equally obtuse manner, that all western forms of democracy (for liberal democracy, as Chapter 2 illustrates, is itself far from a monolithic concept) are superior to all modifications thereupon. They are not. A particularly condescending but ubiquitous account that declares private property rights to be prior to and more important than democratic norms, for example, is one 'western' interpretation of democracy that shall be addressed in subsequent chapters.

Yet the debate of the 1970s and 1980s (e.g., between (neo-)liberals and (neo-)marxists) which disputed the extent to which political decision-making precedes the private property rights of individuals has been increasingly superseded by debates about whether group identity ought to take precedence over individual autonomy, whether the opposite is true, or whether the two positions can be effectively reconciled. To what extent is this shift in focus regarding the proper substance of democracy itself related to issues of 'globalization' (e.g., the increasing inability of contemporary states to effect a redistribution of resources between individuals due to the constraints of international trade)? It is evident that where the gap between citizen expectations and material distribution widens, the perception of individuals that their state is responsive to them weakens. It is conceivable that the identity-oriented demands of specific groups (e.g., for specific language or religious rights) serve a *political* function, allowing governments to uphold the claim that 'the government remains accountable to the people' especially where states have become increasingly unable to meet the material demands of their citizenry. But the political explanations for shifting interpretations of democracy are complex and perhaps limitless; and many will doubtless have to remain within the realm of speculation. Deliberate or unintentional, however, the increasing focus upon identity over redistribution as the preeminent concern of democracy exacerbates both economic and social divisiveness within as well as between states, and threatens the fragile fraternity upon which modern democracy is grounded. Early theorists of democracy, including Rousseau and Tocqueville, were quite attentive to the need to mitigate divisions between groups in order to secure the cooperation needed to base political obligation upon consent rather than coercion: sanctioning segregation and factionalism, whether economic or social, in the name of democracy may be the most dangerous threat of all to the future of democracy.

These existing theoretical tensions within democracy have been exacerbated by the trend to globalization. This has occured in two preeminent ways: first, the dependence of states upon international trade has imposed a series of constraints upon what a polity may collectively do without jeopardizing the level of material comfort to which it is accustomed, or to which it aspires. How to accommodate the domestic redistribution of wealth, whether to do so at all, and how to address the resentment of those who grow ever poorer in increasingly wealthy societies are some of the most troublesome questions confronting a 'globalized' economy. Second, the awareness that there exist an indefinite number of ways to make life comprehensible, and that people cling to their own familiar customs and values with some tenacity, has underscored the increasing role that 'cultural identity' plays within the moral language of democratic theory. Generally, the two trends are emphatically dissociated: political economists study the former, and political philosophers concern themselves with the latter. But both issues are central to any robust and mature understanding of democracy, for democracy is, most fundamentally, about how to secure the inclusion of all members of a community in such a way that does not permit an overwhelming concentration of power (and to do so in a way that provides a stable political environment). Despite the rhetorical support for democracy articulated in an increasing number of languages, the worry for many is that the effects of globalization seem more often than not to obstruct rather than to facilitate both economic and cultural inclusion.

Contemporary economists tell us, reasonably, that democracies will not work in the absence of a healthy economy; yet early democrats such as Rousseau presented equally sensible arguments that democracy could not work where economic inequality became too extreme. The point where economic viability must be balanced with a sense of inclusion is amongst the most importunate of political issues in developed as well as developing countries; and the electoral rebuke given to the savage (though effective) neoliberal administrations in most western states frequently was impelled by some articulation of the need to balance market efficiency with economic inclusion (such as 'stakeholder capitalism', which was never much more than a fuzzy concept but which recognized the need to rethink the way in which the economy selectively offered its rewards).

But even as the organized left has increasingly accepted that the market is a twitchy beast which cannot be commanded too imperiously, and that demands for economic inclusion must be tempered judiciously due to international constraints beyond the effective control of any state, demands for inclusion of a different type (*not* subject to the constraints of international forces) is presented with increasing vigour. Inclusion, on this account, requires the participation of individuals within a context of traditions, customs, and values which they can instinctively understand through long familiarity. That 'democracy' developed within an unmitigatedly western context, of course, lies uncomfortably with the claim that 'a cultural background is crucial' in circumstances where the cultural context in question is unapologetically undemocratic. But if the point of democracy is that it permits people to live their lives as they see fit, then must the western trappings of democracy be imposed upon all peoples? And if democracy can be such a fluid concept, then at what point in these cultural transformations does it simply stop being democratic?

The conviction that the definition of 'democracy' can ever be conclusively set and, more naively, the belief that such an accepted understanding could solve entrenched political conflicts are expectations that have been effectively refuted by the challenges mounted against positivism from the mid-twentieth century on. Nonetheless, the uncritical acceptance of countless versions of 'democracy' claimed by numerous political elites threatens to undermine the very value of the institution which these same interests claim to be the basis of modern political relations. Notwithstanding the very real constraints of modern politics, in which principles are tempered by compromise and obscurity facilitates agreement, a clear sense of what the moral ground rules consist of, and why, is essential to avoid rule by force cloaked in the rhetoric of autonomy and freedom. A deference to difference, to private property, or any prima facie value unalloyed with rules preventing the concentration of power jeopardize the very *raison d'etre* of democracy; and it is for this reason that the term deserves to be contested and dissected despite the political sensibilities which may be offended. I hope only that the discussion mitigates the offence.

1

Contextualizing the debate over democracy

> It is clear that the real world of democracy is changing.
> (C. B. Macpherson 1965: 2)

The role of democracy in development debates

From the exhilaration of revellers celebrating the obsolescence of the Berlin Wall to the horror of the Balkan wars, the modern experiment with self-government has been both gratifying and chastening. Regardless of the consequences, the emphasis upon political autonomy and self-government continues to define both the substance and direction of modern politics. 'Democracy' is one of the most commanding ideas influencing the character of contemporary political relations; yet it is also a term that is very difficult to define precisely or satisfactorily. Democracy is seen to exert a globalizing force upon the international community; yet its most enthusiastic proponents argue that it must be a localised, grassroots phenomenon to be of any value. Democracy is an abstract, imprecise idea with very specific historical roots, yet it has had a tangible and forceful impact upon every state in the world. It is, moreover, too often viewed as an indisputably alluring ideal. This ideal, simply stated, is that democracy can both facilitate and protect individuals' command over the way in which their life is to be lived. It is quite possibly this 'diffuse and urgent hope' that human life 'may come to be more a matter of committed personal choice and less a matter of enforced compliance with impersonal and external (and unwelcome) demands' (Dunn 1992: 256) which accounts for the compelling and persistent appeal of modern democracy. But the interpretation of what it means to 'take control over one's own life' has widened dizzyingly beyond the nineteenth-century liberal belief in the sufficiency of political liberties, accountable government, and a good education to provide autonomy for individuals.

Beyond recent philosophical disputes regarding what is meant by 'individual autonomy' and 'meaningfully lived lives' (see, e.g., Kymlicka 1989 and 1995; Taylor, 1992; and Tully, 1995), there are also powerful political reasons to broaden, and even to obscure, what is meant by democracy. As a system of governing the modern nation-state, 'democracy' has almost become (despite its ambiguity) an uncontested good. This is obviously a positive development to the extent that regimes which routinely harm and distress their citizens are now called to account for these actions; actions which violate the expectations of rights, due process, and accountability established by liberal democratic norms. These regimes are obliged to do so, for the most part, simply because such norms now form the moral parameters of much modern discourse. But by making democracy the only standard of legitimacy, states which do not enjoy the levels of economic development, the historical legacy of stability, or the political culture of individualism must either distort the meaning of 'democracy' to make it achievable, or risk being penalised and censured for failing to embrace the democratic movement. Yet the more widely the term is used, the less precision it has; and the more indistinct the term becomes, the less utility it has regardless of the ideological context within which it is used.

Some supranational bodies and aid agencies have attempted to resolve this dilemma by increasingly avoiding the use of the word 'democracy' (with its liberal connotations) as a moral standard of political legitimacy and replacing it with the more amorphous term 'good governance' (e.g., World Bank 1989, 1992, and 1994; OECD 1995; Commission on Global Governance, 1994). The rationale for this strategy is that it permits these agencies to operate within developing states without being seen as imposing specific western norms on the recipient states, on the one hand, yet not clearly accepting (and thus legitimizing) practices which to western sensibilities would likely be unacceptable, on the other hand. Large governmental organizations such as the UN, IMF, World Bank and WTO, as well as the innumerable non-governmental aid agencies, require the financial support of the more economically sturdy liberal democracies; and they cannot be seen to depart too widely from common western perceptions regarding what is ethically tolerable. At the same time, certain developing states may simply decide that this economic support is worth less to them than the ability to ignore the moral requirements which accompany such funds. By utilizing a more opaque term such as 'governance' (which implies some degree of public responsiveness, efficiency, and dispersion of power without specifying either the degree to which they must obtain, or the institutions required to achieve them), according to proponents of this approach, both dangers can be averted.

This is the wrong strategy to take. The ambiguous approach, in practice, simply requires that a state attempts to be responsive to some of its citizens' needs in some manner. What is objectionable is not, of course, that a state should attempt to do so, but rather that the 'governance' approach (unlike liberal democracy) offers no clear criteria for evaluation. (What constitutes a 'need'? Is free speech, for example, a necessity or a threat? Which citizens' needs are the ones a state ought to address: the business class? the poorest people? the political elites? And who ought to be the arbiter of such questions: the educated elites? those who interpret religious doctrine? the demos as a whole?) Yet if the two preeminent obstacles to democratization are that the nature of the goal is obscure and the route to its achievement even more uncertain, a third political hurdle is that it has become politically contentious even to demand that states must specify the criteria by which they themselves would choose to be evaluated. This is because the very assertion that the West ought to be able to evaluate the norms of 'the rest' is deemed by many to be distastefully redolent of imperialist behaviour. Not only does the dichotomization of 'evaluator' and 'evaluated' seem to characterize and perpetuate an unfair relation of power, but the mere criterion of clarity has itself been labelled oppressive. This, according to at least one strand of discourse, is because the stipulation of clarity obliges the less powerful to account for their actions and their beliefs in terms set by the more powerful, thereby undermining and delegitimizing any account that the more influential cannot (or choose not to) comprehend. But such a claim can only serve to fragment and polarize an already shaky political discourse. The request that political actors explain the schema of values (and beliefs about what is politically possible) which informs their political activity neither has to insult nor disadvantage the subject of the request. To be accountable, one has first to be comprehensible. Thus, rather than attempting to use a more obscure form of democracy ('governance') that is acceptable to all simply because of its vagueness, we must identify clearly what we mean by democracy, which aspects of it we find appealing (and why), and whether or not the objectives we seek through democracy can perhaps be achieved through other means. We have to be more rigid and clear in our account of what 'democracy' is, and why we value it; and we must be able to explain why this procedural system does not necessarily contain ulterior moral or political agenda.

To insist upon a clear definition of 'democracy' does not devalue or oppress nonwestern cultures and polities; nor must it eliminate the development of distinct social and political systems. The basic principles of democracy – that all people have an equal opportunity on an ongoing basis to determine the structure and direction of their society; and that minorities not be treated 'unjustly' – are open-ended enough to permit a broad spectrum of social organizations. Beyond these criteria, polities can and ought to be evaluated on the specific manifestations of these principles. Yet one contentious aspect of this, as noted above, is that any process of evaluation occurs at all. Is it acceptable that any state, and especially an economically vulnerable one, be obliged to account for its political values before it can apply for economic assistance from, or form trade links with, its more fortunate counterparts? A number of normative arguments have been presented for and against such a claim, and will be discussed within this book; but they should be considered within the context of certain observations. The first is that, if western societies themselves support the principle that political institutions must be both accountable and transparent, then citizens of those nations have both a right and a duty to know on what grounds international governmental organizations (of which their states are members) interact with non-liberal states. This may, of course, mean that individuals in liberal-democratic states are less likely to continue to support the programmes undertaken by these institutions (or even the institutions themselves). But the question of whether these individuals are justified in taking such a position is an issue separate from whether or not they should have a clear idea of what their state is doing internationally on their behalf.

The second observation is that the pursuit of a strict inter-pretation of democracy may at times lead to disagreeable con-sequences, both in developed and in developing states. A majority of individuals within a country may decide, given the nature of the international economy, to concentrate resources and distribute resources predominantly to those who can most efficiently invest and increase them. This consideration may, arguably, account for the widening gap in wealth between rich and poor in capitalist democracies such as the United States and the United Kingdom. It is a moot point whether the eco-nomic disparity within these countries occurs because of an insufficiently democratic process, or because democracy is too responsive to the desires of a large middle class increasingly willing to disregard the muted voices of economically marginalized groups within its own borders (e.g., Schrag, 1994). But the procedural requirements of democracy alone cannot prevent all distressing conditions from occurring. As eastern European states are belatedly and painfully recognizing, democracy is not a panacea. It is merely a strategy for dealing with frequently intractable issues. It is a political process that protects what is considered to be most important for the widest number of people; but it is (as Tocqueville resignedly observed) not without its own costs.

The explosion in development literature focusing upon democratization began in earnest after the obvious disintegra-tion of Soviet power not only within the USSR but also within the community of developing states (see, e.g., Wiseman, 1993). The disarray of formerly communist states meant that authoritarian regimes legitimizing themselves upon marxist principles (at least rhetorically, if not always in practice) could depend no longer upon either the economic support of the Soviet Union, or the claim that communism was just another form of democratic representation that met the fundamental needs of people more thoroughly than capitalist regimes could hope to do. The collapse of the Soviet empire also meant that the excuse of creeping communist totalitarianism could not be used by western governments (and especially the United States) to support equally vicious and authoritarian regimes whose only source of political credibility rested in their condemnation of the same marxist ideas.

Coterminous with the more overt redistribution of military influence has been the subtler globalization of international trade, the increase of intercontinental travel, and the development of powerfully penetrative networks of communication. At the very least, those with access to television have a better idea of what it is like to live within other countries; and these images, regardless of their veracity, can serve to belie the official rhetoric more effectively than ever before. Another trend that has become apparent is the inability of the vast majority of economic aid programmes clearly and permanently to improve the well-being of the programmes' recipients. Sub-Saharan Africa, especially, has become a playground for new theories of development, few of which remain demonstrably effective over time. The most prominent theme characterizing most 'democracy and development' literature has thus been simply to account for the phenomenon of democratization globally; or to explain, more selectively, why certain states or regions have or have not participated in this experience. The type of democracy to be sought, or even the reasons why democracy ought to be pursued at all, have been more infrequently at issue (although cf., e.g., Dunn, 1978; Chabal *et al.*, 1986; and Jung and Shapiro, 1995). Most discussions concerning the viability of democratization now rest upon various theories of political economy and political culture; most frequently, they focus upon the specific causal nature of the relationship between capitalism ('economic liberalization') and democracy ('political liberalization'); or between social forces ('civil society') and political ones ('the state').

Within this context, the most common debate focuses upon the identification of the agents of democratic transformation. Within the current wave of theorization about democratization, much discussion has been 'deeply rooted in the intellectual spirit of critical theory', in contrast to positivist approaches which informed many of the earlier analyses (Shin 1994: 141). The implication of this is that theorists generally have a more nuanced and flexible understanding of the nature of power, and they attempt to identify a wide range of variables responsible for the move towards democratic transformation. Power, in this broader interpretation, can be understood not merely as control of instruments of immediate coercion (the military and police forces) but also as the ability to develop and sustain an ideology which legitimizes current distributions of power, or which encourages people to identify their own interests with the health of their regime (Lukes, 1974).

Widening the conceptualization of power has resulted most significantly in the attention given to the role of 'civil society' in 'opening up' the political structures of developing states (O'Donnell and Schmitter, 1986). If power is to be understood as lying in 'the cultural and social patterns that shape and reshape the basic character of political life', then democratization must be comprehended within a much more detailed and subtle context (Robinson 1994). This interpretation of power also means that strategies for democratization can focus not only upon the choices and behaviour of elite groups, but also upon the perceptions and decisions of amorphous groups outside of the formal structures of power. The drawback to this approach is that the introduction of limitless variables considerably reduces the analytical rigour of the resulting theories. In a survey of literature on democratization, for example, Huntington (1991: 38) distills a number of general propositions:

1 No single factor is sufficient to explain the development of democracy in all countries or in a single country.
2 No single factor is necessary to the development of democracy in all countries.
3 Democratization in each country is the result of a combination of causes.
4 The combination of causes producing democracy varies from country to country.
5 The combination of causes generally responsible for one wave of democratization differs from that responsible for other waves.
6 The causes responsible for the initial regime changes in a democratization wave are likely to differ from those responsible for later regime changes in that wave.

Given these observations it is difficult to see how a 'theory' of democratization can be postulated at all. As in many accounts of social explanation, explanatory accuracy here has been gained largely at the expense of predictive utility.

This is, of course, not necessarily a bad thing. But problems may arise in conflating normative and empirical observations concerning democratic transformation. Many eager young scholars are focusing upon the possibility that non-state organizations may be the most efficient and equitable vehicles for democratic transformation. This position is only partly derived from the observation, noted above, that 'power' is something more than control over the apparatus of coercive political instruments. It is also derived from the view that democracy ought rightly to be about the participation of even the most marginalized individuals within a society. Thus the current focus of much democratization literature upon 'civil society' is perhaps more a normative statement regarding how strategies of democratization ought ideally to occur (through small but interconnected groups of empowered individuals uniting for the common objectives of peace, security, and freedom for all) rather than a sober consideration of how democratic institutions have in most cases been formalised (through pacts negotiated by elite groups). The long-standing debate in international relations theory between 'realists' and 'idealists' is now filtering into the debate over democratic transformation, and the complexity of the debate is compounded insofar as the objective now commonly accepted by most participants (democratic government) is itself a manifestly normative construct.

This complicates the discussion regarding the best strategy for achieving democratization: if one holds democratic values strongly, for example, how should one approach the possibility that democratic institutions may best be facilitated through elite negotiation? Or that the 'empowerment' of marginalized groups might best be facilitated with the assistance of non-governmental agencies which may be blatantly unaccountable in their own organization? The question is still open whether the contemporary fixation upon 'civil society' is a measured analytical judgement that non-state agents have the capacity to effect democratization, or whether this merely reflects the normative judgement that any other approach is less ethically acceptable.

What is striking in all this is the unwillingness of many engaged in the democracy-and-development debate to address the reasons why they see democracy as such a compelling objective. Again, the ultimate goals perceived to be important (such as individual autonomy) cannot always be articulated directly because they are essentially liberal values, and thus apparently culturally specific. One is left with the call for democracy disconnected from all its liberal baggage; and this can result in an activist's worst nightmare: a regime choosing through democratic mechanisms to pursue policies with egregious consequences for certain individuals or groups (e.g., contemporary Algeria). But if the democratic process is the measure of legitimacy, and the imposition of western liberal values is unacceptable, then there is no theoretical space left within which to disapprove of such an uncomfortable outcome.

What is it that we desire from a 'democratic' system? Within liberal democratic theory, for example, one axis of legitimation runs along the spectrum of 'individual freedom' to 'personal development'. While the two ideas are not necessarily mutually exclusive, the value of democracy for those espousing the former lies in the ability of such a system to protect an individual from any form of coercion beyond the requirement that one respect an equal amount of liberty for all. The latter, in contrast, sees the value of democracy in its emphasis upon the participation of each individual in the civic relations of the society as a whole. The resonance of John Stuart Mill's writings lies not in their ability to show us which of these routes is most important, but in their recognition that two such compelling ideas can probably never be happily resolved in any system of government. Underlying these legitimizing models of democracy rest two corollary conceptions of human nature: the former depicts the individual as an autonomous agent who has the capacity to make choices, and to be held responsible for them; and the latter fixes upon the image of the individual as an essentially social creature whose fulfillment rests in her relations with others. Again, these conceptions are not clearly exclusive.

It is therefore important to evaluate the appeal of modern democracy in order to identify what aspects of this superficially monolithic idea are valued by which political actors, and for what reasons. The romanticization of democracy, especially by newly-democratic states, is particularly dangerous because of the vast disparities in the objectives of different interests. Misunderstanding what various groups wish to achieve through a process of democratization can lead to the deadlock of political agenda or the exploitation of misplaced trust; both can result, in turn, in a dangerous level of disillusionment or a pathological distrust that severely undermines the political viability of a newly democratic state. The most formidable challenge to achieving a practicable system of self- government may thus not be the idea of self-government itself, but rather the need to coordinate the enthusiastic expectations of those embracing such a system.

International relations and the role of globalization

While the phenomenon of 'democratization' is becoming increasingly predominant within the field of international relations in general terms, the question of why, and how, democratization arises is frequently subsumed in this area under broader discussions concerning the nature of 'globalization'. Within this particular debate, the issue is what effects the globalization of human interaction (cultural, political, and economic) will have upon the tendency for more states to attempt to achieve and maintain democratic regimes; and the positions on this issue vary greatly indeed.

One position holds that the development of global communication and transportation networks, as well as the degree of international travel and migration by individuals have contributed to a series of demonstration effects that have shown not only that democratization can be achieved, but have also illustrated how it can be accomplished: 'people in the follow-on society learned from and attempted to imitate the techniques and the methods used to bring about the earlier democratizations' (Huntington 1991: 101). This perspective views globalization with optimism, and assumes that the snowballing effect will broaden and solidify the forays into democratic governance by smaller developing states. While some theorists holding this position seem almost deterministic in their belief regarding the inevitability of democratic development (Fukuyama 1992), the more cautious optimists hold that a flourishing of democratic states can arise given the establishment of a 'democratic global order' acting as an armature for the development of a larger number of national democracies (e.g., Held 1995).

But the contrary position argues that it is precisely the trend towards 'globalization' which undermines the likelihood of democratization in developing countries. Democracy appeared originally within the context of a sovereign state system and, on this account, it requires state autonomy in order to preserve democratic institutions (e.g., Guéhenno, 1995). The global pessimists argue that, to the extent that democracy is an expression of the 'national will', a weak state which cannot execute the 'people's will' due to international constraints will suffer a crisis of legitimacy. Numerous authors, for example, cite the increasing polarization of wealth in open, 'liberal' states, and claim that this disparity is due to the unwillingness of national administrations to tax highly mobile corporations able to seek the most generous tax environments in which to locate (e.g., Walker 1995: 53). Democracy can only work where 'the people' can control their own polity without undue influence from outside interests. This claim, of course, is what has so often linked the support for 'democracy' with demands for cultural self-determination (e.g., Kymlicka 1995). This pessimism is neither the exclusive preserve of the right nor the left. The neoliberals, observe Hirst and Thompson (1996: 176), exhibit a gleeful *schadenfreude* in their conclusion that the international economy is incapable of productive regulation and must therefore, like domestic economies, be left unhindered by regulation; the radical left, in turn, express a gloomy smugness in their ability to have predicted the totalizing destructiveness of international capital.

A third position, however, asserts that the phenomenon of globalization is, for better or for worse, simply overstated. Krasner, for example, argues that the assumption that 'greater interdependence' means 'greater dependence' is often quite wrong:

> The historical record is far more mixed than would be suggested by the conventional notion that interdependence is threatening effective State control. The basic long-term trend has been one in which States have become less dependent on the external environment. This has occurred primarily because political and economic development has made it generally easier for States to finance their activities, including those related to security, from internal sources, rather than international borrowing. (1993: 314)

While the poorer nonindustrialised states might well fit the pattern of interdependence-as-dependence, those states with sophisticated economies and effective bureaucracies are better able now to resist international pressures than they were historically.

Hirst and Thompson (1996) offer an even more sceptical account of the extent of globalization. While they do not deny that an 'enhanced internationalization' has occurred since the 1970s, they argue that this must be distinguished from the term 'globalization' with its far more extreme connotations. An 'inter-national' economy, they assert, 'is one in which the principal entities are national economies', where growing interconnections between states nonetheless are still characterized by 'the continued relative separation of the domestic and the international frameworks for policy-making and the management of economic affairs' (Hirst and Thompson 1996: 8). A truly 'globalized' model, on the other hand, is exemplified by the subsumation and rearticulation of national economies into the global system by international processes and transactions (*ibid.*: 10). They conclude that, on the evidence considered (the character of the world financial markets, the pattern of world trade and foreign direct investment, the number and role of multinational corporations, and the prospects for growth in the developing world), 'there is no strong tendency toward a globalized economy' (*ibid.*: 186). But this argument seems too easy, and too dependent upon semantics. Very few, if any, serious scholars do hold that nation states are in the process of becoming totally obsolete, or that globalization means that all the rewards of trade must be delivered with relatively equality. Despite their useful and interesting collection of evidence, Hirst and Thompson nonetheless have created a very pliant paper tiger to savage. They cite no examples of scholarship holding the extreme model of globalization to be conceivable, let alone taken seriously. International relations theorists are understandably concerned with the implications of the undermining of state authority, but do not assume its elimination. What Hirst and Thompson have accomplished, however, is the illustration of how discussions of globalization have dominated international relations theory to the exclusion of more careful and focused issues.

The assumption that democracy is increasingly taking root throughout the world due to globalization simply begs the question of why democracy itself seems to be, *pace* the radical left, such a major component of globalization. What the much-touted communications networks are broadcasting is a very complex picture of what democracies are. This picture is frequently a heady and desirable combination of prosperity, domestic stability, and interstate peace. (Seymour Martin Lipset's famous observation of the link between wealth and democracy (1959: 45–76) served as an early catalyst for ongoing debates concerning the causal links between capitalism and democracy.) Were these democratic states generally less prosperous, it is doubtful that they could excite as much anticipation or support. Likewise, long-standing democracies do tend to offer more stable and predictable environments for their citizens than authoritarian states over the long term by virtue of their rule-based processes and institutions.

But the current fascination of international relations theorists in the spread of democratic regimes seems to be more intensely fixed upon the relationship between democracy and peace than upon democracy and wealth. Why is it that democratic states are so reluctant to wage war on each other? Russett (1993) argues that 'the culture, perceptions, and practices that permit compromise and the peaceful resolution of conflicts without the threat of violence within countries come to apply across national boundaries toward other democratic countries' (Russet 1993: 31). While structural and institutional constraints (such as the need to secure broad popular support) play a significant role in this phenomenon, it is, he argues, primarily the existence of democratic norms and practices which determine the pacific conduct between democratic states. This phenomenon, while difficult to explain or identify precisely, is nonetheless widely accepted. Boutros Boutros-Ghali, in his 1992 report *An Agenda for Peace*, underscored the link between peace and democracy by stating that '[r]espect for democratic principles at all levels of social existence is crucial' for both domestic and international stability (Boutros-Ghali 1992: 10). See also Doyle 1983, parts I and II; although cf. James and Wolfson, n.d.)

The rhetoric of democratization has in this way even percolated into the sphere of foreign defence policy. Opposing the practice of ensuring domestic security through military capability, a number of political interests and academic voices have been pressing for an alternative form of domestic security referred to as 'common' or 'cooperative' security. The logic of this account is that, by stabilizing less developed states through the transfer of economic resources, democratic practices, and 'capacity building' expertise, industrialised democracies would have less to fear from the more volatile states, and could consequently reduce their military expenditure earmarked for security. Yet, despite the purely empirical question of whether such a counterfactual claim is true or not, there nonetheless remains to be resolved a critical normative issue: to what extent is the role of the state to serve the needs of its own citizens, *vis-à-vis* the needs of humanity at large? Does there exist a trust between state and citizen such that the state cannot use its citizens' resources for those outside the boundaries of the state? And if the rules of democracy according to which these states function stipulate that its citizens must consent to such a reallocation, how ought one to judge whether the state has in fact secured the consent of its citizens (and especially those citizens most in need of economic support themselves) to this practice?

Such a critique of 'cooperative security' does admittedly assume the primacy of state sovereignty as a moral and political imperative. Yet established democracies have operated on this principle for centuries, and the onus ought reasonably to rest upon committed internationalists to make their anti-sovereignty argument more clearly. Two further theoretical problems would seem, however, to arise from such a position: first, the principle of a more severely limited state sovereignty generally seems to fit ill with a great number of developing countries, which see the state as the primary instrument through which to protect the interests of their own citizens. And second, if state sovereignty is in fact strongly restricted, how is accountability between governors and governed maintained? To the extent that the political leaders of any nation can shrug off responsibility for deleterious outcomes by pointing to the influence of supranational forces, it would seem that the citizens of such states remain even less 'empowered' *vis-à-vis* their political masters than ever before.

The observations to be drawn from discussions of democratization in international relations literature are frustratingly similar to those which we can conclude from debates in comparative development: that the causal links involved in ascertaining why democracies do (or do not) arise cannot be stated with ease or simplicity; and that the normative issues underlying such debates too frequently remain invisible and undiscussed. It may very well be that the most intelligent discussions of democratization are simply descriptive accounts of the development and practice of self-government (or the failure to achieve it) within various contexts. The problem is that such inconclusive narratives are generally considered to be bad political science. The focus of political science (excepting political philosophy) is precisely the determination (or disproving) of political causality; that is the standard by which the discipline demands itself to be judged. The effect of this has been for current generations of political scientists to theorize all political phenomenon; and this has led to some excellent and useful material on the nature of political life. But it has also led to a fetishization of theorization *per se*. Concepts and phenomena cannot be introduced without having to be 'theorised'; thus we are inundated with 'theories' of democratization, or globalization, or civil society. Not all can be theorized equally satisfactorily. This is not to make a postmodernist statement regarding the inherently political nature of 'scientific' knowledge. It is simply to note, as did David Hume, that we must be willing at a certain point to acknowledge the limitations to the certainty of human comprehension (Hume 1955 [1748]: 72–89).

Political science, as a discipline, must be willing to set and to defend rigorous standards of accuracy and intellectual vigour. But it must also recognize when the attempt to theorize certain phenomena narrows the parameters within which the issue can usefully be understood. 'Democracy' is not merely the result of open economic relations, or of certain cultural norms, or of particular institutions or processes. The attempt to account for all the relevant variables may well be impossible regardless of how accurately we come to understand why one instance of democracy occured at a particular time within a particular geopolitical context. To insist that we be able to understand all instances of democratization at all times may well be to exhibit an intellectual insolence that undermines the limited achievements that the discipline can offer.

But there is another disservice perpetuated by the discipline that may ultimately prove more harmful still. This is the increasing unwillingness to challenge normative claims made in the political arena, especially within disparate cultural contexts. This phenomenon has grown out of the vigorous position held by many current scholars that the 'rightness' of certain values has been, and remains, closely connected to the political power of those articulating these positions. There is certainly much historical evidence in support of this claim. But the conclusion seemingly drawn by many is that it is wrong to challenge normative statements, especially of politically marginalized interests, because that is an unacceptable exercise of political force. This position has unintentionally been bolstered by forceful philosophical accounts which argue the import of cultural norms and values to the development of confident and independent individuals and societies. The more dubious claim now commonly asserted is that, as values are an inherent aspect of culture, and respect for cultures is an integral part of individual or group autonomy, it is politically unacceptable to confront or dismiss unfamiliar or unpalatable value claims. The irony, of course, is that concepts such as autonomy are themselves unrepentantly normative. 'Progressive' political activists are painfully divided between those who focus upon the epistemological uncertainty that does not permit them to make judgements on competing value claims, and those who hold that certain moral constructs – such as human rights – must be defended and fought for regardless of any indisputable proof of its being the correct set of values to hold. These debates will be presented more fully in the following section.

In the end, one of the few statements we can perhaps make with any certainty is that 'democracy' seems to have a greater appeal to more interests now than it has at any time previously. What we must do is to evaluate just what it is about this term that appeals to whom, simply because the very ambiguity of the term may well be its greatest weakness. If people support democracy due to perceptions that are empirically unsustainable, or because they view democracy as morally valuable for palpably different reasons, then we may have little reason indeed to believe that the global drive for democracy will last as long or remain as robust as we may hope.

I

Interpreting democracy: philosophical debates

2

The ambiguity of democracy

> . . . until about a hundred years ago democracy was a bad thing . . .
> in the next fifty years it became a good thing, and . . . in the last fifty
> years it has become an ambiguous thing.
> (C. B. Macpherson 1965: 4)

Can democracy be defined?

The overarching theme of this book, noted in the previous
chapter, addresses the current theoretical and epistemological
challenges to the practice of democracy: given that 'democracy'
is a reasonably-accepted standard of political legitimacy in the
modern world, whose account of what democracy is *counts*?
Does the attempt to 'respect cultural values' mean an inability
to challenge or discount certain interpretations of democracy?
Before turning to these issues, it is helpful to begin by clarifying
what is commonly meant by the standard or 'orthodox' understanding of democracy. This chapter then discusses current con-
troversies within the field of democratic theory: one axis rotates
upon the issue of negative versus positive rights – or, more
specifically, upon the question of whether democracy is more
properly about the protection of liberties (including the right to
private property) or the involvement of citizens in the decision-
making process. This is a fairly hoary debate within democratic
theory, but one which takes an especial importance when
national democracies become firmly engaged in global economic networks.

The second axis is built upon a distinct, and more modern,
issue: is democracy more fundamentally about the protection of
individual autonomy, or the coherence of cultural groups? And

if the two are not mutually exclusive, then how ought their competing concerns to be balanced? This debate is the subject of Chapter 3, which presents some of the more powerful and persuasive objections to 'liberal democracy' broadly stated. Chapter 4 is a response to some of the more forceful of these arguments, but it ought not to be considered a 'defence of liberalism' as much as an argument that any useful understanding of democracy must retain at its core a conception of neutrality that cannot accommodate many of the claims made by those championing the importance of identity, culture, and community. The reason I focus at length on this particular argument is because these debates – over the role of identity and culture – are the ones currently transforming the landscape of democratic theory. Yet the issue of property rights versus participation as the proper sphere of democracy is no less relevant for being an older debate, and especially so given the increasingly globalized context within which the issue is situated. The current chapter, in sum, serves as an introduction to these specific debates, which will be addressed in much greater detail in the ensuing chapters.

Why has a term which seems to have such a concrete manifestation in so many states become subject to countless interpretations by so many actors throughout the world since the late 1980s? Part of the explanation is that democracy is as much a political strategy as a philosophical position, and must therefore be molded to suit particular political interests and circumstances. Another part of the explanation is that democracy is, and has always been, an ambiguous concept philosophically; and it is only the habitual exercise of certain practices by given states which has made the term seem comfortably familiar and unequivocally distinct.

To grasp why it is that so many disparate interests can have such divergent conceptions of what 'democracy' entails, it is useful to look more closely at some of its (highly ambiguous) component parts. As a political objective, democracy is a diabolically indeterminate concept to capture because of its shifting and amorphous parameters. There is no undisputed minimum requirement of elements that must be present for democracy to be said to exist; it seems rather like a set of features which hold family resemblances to each other without a core essence. To the extent that there is agreement about the definition of democracy, it is generally seen as a combination of institutions (free elections, political rights, independent judiciary), political values (accountability, toleration, participation), and a propitious political context (a wide availability of alternative sources of information, an ability to meet the basic needs of individuals, an educated population) (e.g., Dahl 1971, 1989; Diamond, Lipset, Linz 1989, preface; Braybrooke 1968). In discussions of whether developing states are or are not 'democratic', two principal questions are generally posed: first, are the governors accountable to the governed? And second, are human rights respected by those in power? Ostensibly simple questions, both of these concepts are highly indeterminate and contentious theoretical foundation-stones, and palpable difficulties are encountered both in determining the existence of these concepts, and in justifying them.

Accountability

If democracy is about just rule, it is even more manifestly about power. Its Athenian origins, as far as we know, were unrepentantly grounded in the attempt to enlarge a factional power base rather than in the desire to promote the development of human autonomy for its own sake (Dunn 1992). Its subsequent political materializations, likewise, seem to have been more about challenging the sovereignty of a specific group of power-holders than about emancipating the human spirit. As Lonsdale (1986) has written, the idea of 'accountability' is neither particularly modern, nor limited to liberal societies. Accountability is an integral aspect of most power struggles to the extent that those who aspire to power can gain a potent source of support by declaring themselves to be more responsive than their opponents to the needs of the governed (Lonsdale 1986: 130–1). Liberal societies have analysed and systematized the institutions of accountability more rigorously than most traditional regimes; but the concept itself is a crucial component in most accounts of political legitimacy. Nonetheless, given that societies are now structured upon a system of state sovereignty, and engage in modern strategies of wealth production, the question is whether, and to what extent, traditional patterns of accountability remain effective.

'Democracy', as a description of the institutions and processes required for an appropriate degree of accountability to be maintained over time, has been successful largely because of its ability to accommodate a wide range of interests within a relatively stable political environment. But proof that accountability exists is more difficult to gauge; and it rests both in the active ability of some to choose by whom they wish to be governed, and in the tacit consent of the rest to accept the rule of those they have not explicitly chosen. But the idea of 'tacit consent' is, as Pitkin (1967) has noted, a troublesome concept because it grants a great deal of interpretive power to those who are to decide what ultimately constitutes such 'tacit' consent. A more coherent, albeit unsatisfying, rendering of 'accountability' is that which is built upon the idea of competing elites, each able to constrain the untrammeled exercise of power by the other (e.g., Schumpeter, 1945). This, however, undermines the liberal democratic account of political obligation which is, at its most persuasive, based upon the binding nature of an individual's active and ongoing consent. It is the ambiguous nature of accountability, even in the most stable of liberal states, which underlies much of the difficulty in presenting a clear definition of democracy.

Even non-democratic states generally attempt to offer some evidence of their accountability to 'the people'. This may be a pyramidal, one-party electoral system, the 'free' election of an administration that will be ultimately controlled by the military, a rigorous redistribution of social resources throughout the society, and so on. What determines a specifically 'democratic' accountability? 'Elections, open, free, and fair', writes Huntington (1991: 9), 'are the essence of democracy, the inescapable sine qua non.' The slippery terms, of course, are 'open, free, and fair': generally, this implies a spectrum of distinct candidates competing for at least a plurality of votes won within a context of universal suffrage. In practice it is rare that agreement exists over the nature of an 'open, free, and fair' election. Even in the industrial democracies electoral candidates' ability to stand for nomination in important positions is in part determined by their access to large funds and influential people. Moreover, as political parties increasingly battle for the disproportionate number of 'mid-spectrum' voters, candidates' policies lose much of their distinctiveness and political contests are fought on issues of personality. It remains far easier to identify which regimes are manifestly unaccountable to their denizens than to define satisfactory what accountability ultimately is.

Human rights

While most inhabitants of liberal democracies accept the idea of human rights as incontestable, and the legal manifestation of rights as a measure of civilization (e.g., Dworkin's 'moral progress': see *Freedom's Law*, 1996), it is doubtful that many would readily accept the idea of 'natural law' from which the concept of human rights grew. Traceable to its classical Greek origins, natural law has been an integral component of much western political thought. It can be crudely defined as an objective moral truth, evident to any rational human being; and it has generally functioned as the theoretical baseline of most western political theories, from those grounded primarily upon theological principles to those which presented social contract theories as a basis for political obligation. For the seventeenth-century theorist Thomas Hobbes, for example, the dictates of reason and human nature bade man 'to endeavour Peace, as farre as he has hope of obtaining it' (Hobbes 1968 [1651]: 190); while for his successor John Locke, natural law dictated that 'no one ought to harm another in his Life, Health, Liberty, or Possession' (Locke 1960 [1689]: 311).

It was Locke, too, who argued that humans naturally possessed rights to security and property. The rights to security of person derived from the natural law to maintain peace; while the inherent right to property was established both in man's natural possession of himself and his faculties, and in God's ultimate possession of all men. This laboured formulation was forceful in its argument for why the sovereign had no absolute or arbitrary power over either subjects or their property; and we tend today to accept many of Locke's conclusions without digging too deeply into their historical roots or logical persuasiveness. Notwithstanding David Hume's sceptical critique of natural law, Jean-Jacques Rousseau's sneering repudiation of property rights, and Jeremy Bentham's dismissal of rights as 'nonsense on stilts', however, rights discourse plays an integral and singularly powerful role in modern liberal democratic polities. But as Richard Tuck (1979) has shown, the modern account of 'human rights' is firmly grounded in a narrower base of *property* rights. The protection of human dignity and autonomy was, historically, of far less legal import than the protection of property. The ministration of the human soul could be left to the Church, but the preservation of property required the active intervention of civil laws.

Property rights are an essential element of contemporary economic relations of power, which depend heavily upon a normative account of why some people are entitled to exclude others from the ownership or control of resources. Whether current accounts of private property rights exist merely to justify the present distribution of economic power is, of course, a philosophical issue that is deemed less important than issues of efficient production, or fairer redistribution. Yet it is not in the ownership of goods but rather in the symbolic depiction of human dignity as a fundamental touchstone of social life (as Thomas Paine asserted), and well as in the acknowledgement that the mutual recognition of human rights is conducive to political maturity (as G. W. F. Hegel argued), that the modern import of human rights rests.

In early modern political theory rights can be broadly classified as 'natural', or 'civil', or both. Civil rights are legal constructions created and espoused by a society; natural rights are said to exist (due to the precepts of natural law) regardless of whether they are recognized legally or not. But while the existence of legal rights was easily discernable, justifying the existence of 'natural' rights not (yet) codified in law was more difficult. In practice the acceptance of rights as 'inherent' has generally depended upon the willingness of a majority of individuals to acknowledge this fact; but the irony is that the very point of having a 'right' is to protect the rights-holders from the whims of a fickle majority. Thus, to a large extent, rights are the symbolic articulation of the legitimacy of beliefs that already exist rather than declarations of what ought to exist. By the time groups are able to assert with public support that they do have rights, they frequently have enough influence to be heeded regardless of whether the discourse of rights is used at all. To that extent, rights are the rhetorical reflection of the actual balance of power rather than a logically coherent account justifying a distinct political status for a group or subgroup of individuals.

But natural rights are so attractive politically despite their ambiguities precisely because they offer an incontestable (if truistic) account of why they must be accepted: rights must be acknowledged because they are *rights*. They are claims of entitlement that ought to be respected because the rules of justice entail that we respect valid entitlement claims. Having a right means not having to account for one's actions and, in the same way, using rights discourse to establish moral (and political) claims means that there is less obligation to explain clearly why it is that specific demands are being made (beyond the fact those making such claims have *rights*). Thus aboriginal self-determination, for example, is often claimed on the grounds that aboriginal people have an inherent right to it; to ask why this right exists is to demand a justification of something that simply *is*. The problem, of course, is that such a method of establishing moral claims sharply reduces the dialogue that could oblige some parties to set out more clearly and coherently why it is that a certain political status is being requested; and it would similarly oblige the rest to articulate equally intelligibly why such requests are seen as reasonable or not. But if this objection seems too simple, the responses to it are not.

There are two replies to the suggestion that rights claims ought to be formulated in detail without recourse to the word 'right'. In the first place is the concern that making a case for a particular political status on grounds other than 'inherent rights' is too much like supplication: having a right means that one should not be expected to beg for what one rightfully deserves. Rights are, as Feinberg states, 'especially sturdy objects to "stand upon", a most useful sort of moral furniture' (Feinberg 1979: 87). And, in the second place, one could argue (with no little historical evidence) that those in a position to acknowledge such rights also have sufficient power to ignore even well-considered and closely-reasoned rights claims. (Or, as postmodernists might argue, power holders have the ability to use language in such a way as to make such requests sound either nonsensical or unreasonable.) Both replies raise important concerns. Nonetheless, to assert a right merely on the grounds that it is both inherent and self-evident is little more than a contestation of power that is thinly veiled in moral discourse. Living in a moral world means that moral agents at the very least attempt to communicate their reasons for acting as they do. It is difficult to deny that those in a position to define morality to their own benefit have used this ability to disadvantage those who appear to undermine their power base. But the unrepentant utterance of 'right' alone, combined with a show of violent force, is little more than a raw play for power. Thus while the symbolic utility of rights is quite significant, an overreliance upon rights discourse in establishing political claims can lead to an untenable proliferation of non-negotiable political demands that may ultimately undermine the resonance of basic rights claims (see, e.g., Glendon 1991; Young 1978).

Essential tensions

What people generally view as the most attractive aspect of democracy is that, ideally, it gives them the ability effectively to pursue what they want within a relatively stable political order. Yet the pursuit of happiness is not, whatever its manifestation, necessarily conducive to political stability. The unprecedented flexibility of liberalism as an emergent political doctrine rested in its apparent neutrality in accepting the values which individuals held most dearly, with the caveat that no one obstructs any other individual's exercise of their own set of values. Liberalism can, as political theorists occasionally remind us, remain independent of 'democracy' insofar as the former merely stresses a sphere of individual agency and autonomy within any given political system. Democracy may well be the best means of protecting this sphere of autonomy; but it is in this instance more a procedural mechanism than a statement of political beliefs. That many people view democracy more as a set of norms and values than as a system of stable decision-making is a testament to its historical roots within liberalism; and whether 'democracy' may itself exist independently of 'liberalism', with the latter's geohistorical trappings, is increasingly at issue and will be addressed more fully in subsequent chapters. But it is useful at this point to examine why it is that the 'pursuit of wants' accommodated by liberal democracy is increasingly difficult to reconcile with the achievement and maintenance of a stable political environment.

Political rights v. social entitlements

The most common political objective of liberals in the recent past has been the maintenance of a set of established rights, protected through the due process of transparent laws. The nature of a mature liberal democracy, wrote T. M. Marshall almost half a century ago, was that it would gradually expand its account of citizenship over time to include previously marginalized groups. Thus political rights (to due process, freedom of speech, an equal voice in government) would grow to include social rights (welfare, education, health care) and would, he argued, soon accommodate a very civilised set of economic rights (including the ability of workers to govern themselves in their place of work). Marshall may be forgiven for not predicting the way in which economic forces served to limit, rather than expand, the generosity of the state in providing for its citizens. What Marshall could have pondered without the gift of foresight, however, was whether the expansion of such rights would not have led to more fractious disputes between individuals or groups when the increasing number of rights began to collide.

The limited set of negative freedoms, and most especially private property rights, which served as the basis for nineteenth-century liberalism did not accommodate as much as confront the growing number of social entitlements created within most industrial democracies after the two World Wars. The negative liberties which provided a legal buffer for citizens from the government importantly included the protection of property ownership from arbitrary seizure by the state. But as these industrial states grew in material wealth, citizenship began to involve dividends in this increasing prosperity. Throughout the middle of the nineteenth century, T. H. Green lectured his students on the need for a liberalism that spoke of the material rights due to members of the polity by virtue of membership (Green, 1986); while L. T. Hobhouse made a similar case in his volume on liberalism published a few decades later (Hobhouse 1964 [1911]). Like the various strains of socialist thought of that era, the new breed of liberals recognized that the worth of negative rights was limited where individuals had not the material circumstances to exercise them.

While the normative basis for a radically redistributive form of liberalism had been presented early in the twentieth century, the political means as well as the political will to execute this redistribution did not exist until after the Second World War. Most industrialized democracies which weathered the First World War had realized that a wartime administration had the political support to enact far-reaching social legislation, and a number of early programs were established during this period. But it was the experience of the destructive effects of waves of unemployed demobilized soldiers following the First World War, along with the emergent Keynesian economic theories outlining constructive state involvement in the economy, which spurred the establishment of the array of social legislation which became cumulatively to form the framework of the modern 'welfare state'.

Thus the legal protection of the pursuit of economic reward in the eighteenth and nineteenth centuries was inherently destabilizing to the extent that these rewards were distributed very inequitably. The expansion of suffrage in the nineteenth century, and the development of social welfare in the twentieth, were attempts to stabilize the free pursuit of material happiness that was the cornerstone of much early liberalism. The confusion in the modern meaning of 'liberalism', which denotes both the *containment* of state activity in the economy and the *active involvement* of the state to redistribute economic wealth, is one preeminent legacy of this historical balancing act. Contemporary liberal democracy is thus expected to perform two uncomfortably antagonistic political tasks: to protect the private property of economic actors in order to facilitate their ability to reproduce their wealth, on the one hand; and, on the other hand, to protect other individuals from this very exercise by providing 'social safety nets' built by the state with the resources of those whose private property it has sworn to protect. This paradox was noted quite clearly by a number of (generally neo-marxist) theorists in the 1970s and 1980s, who predicted with varying levels of apprehension that this conflict of purpose would lead to a destructive 'crisis of legitimacy' in which both sides would express a high degree of cynicism about the ability of the state to perform its expected function effectively (see, e.g., Offe 1984; O'Connor 1973).

Universality v. difference

If the first essential tension of modern democracy is that between political rights and social entitlements, the second is between those who deeply value 'universality' and those who believe that a strong account of universality reinforces a status quo which serves to exacerbate the marginalization of those who do not enjoy a reasonable share of the benefits of their society. Very briefly stated, this controversy stems from two claims. The first is that the putatively 'neutral' processes and freedoms promoted by liberalism are biased towards those groups who effectively hold the political power. For instance, because 'beauty' is a private matter, it is a subject left to the discretion of individuals. Yet if the group of individuals with the most social influence is able to define beauty according to physical characteristics that happen to be more common to them than to others (e.g., white, thin, blonde, narrow-nosed), then other groups will be marginalized to the extent that beauty is valued in society and they, according to the current aesthetic standards, are simply not 'beautiful'. In the same way, feminists have argued that women have for a long period of time been defined in terms of their passivity, nurturing qualities, youth, and fecundity. To succeed politically or economically, however, women frequently have to be more assertive and self-oriented, to sacrifice childbearing, and to expect to attain the most power when their youthful appearance is lost. They may, in other words, only participate successfully publicly if they are willing to sacrifice their social identity as 'womanly' women. The characteristics that allow one to engage in public life success-fully as an 'autonomous agent', on this account, have diametri-cally opposed those qualities which define femininity; thus male identity is reinforced through political leadership, while female identity is lost. This, it is argued, is why the percentage of women holding public office at a national level is rarely over twenty per cent at best in most liberal democracies.

The second claim is that not only are many of the character-istics of liberalism not neutral, but that no truly just society can exist when neutrality and atomism are featured as the dominant qualities. We should, in other words, not aim for greater neutral-ity; we should simply be clear that we value it less. This is the basis of what has become known as 'identity politics': that what is most important to each individual is not simply her autonomy or freedom (qualities that are valued universally throughout the society), but also her membership in a vital and respected group with its own norms, values, and traditions. A sterile freedom is simply not valuable unless we have the strength of character to take advantage of it; and we cannot develop an ability to become 'autonomous agents' unless we are raised within a context which allows us to develop a sense of confidence and individual worth. To insist upon a 'universal' application of equal rights and freedoms where all individuals are manifestly unequal econom-ically and socially is thus to perpetuate grievous inequities. Those who dispute this position affirm that universalism is a crucial component of any viable liberal democracy; and that removing the blindfold of Justice will simply make a society more ungovernable. Despite the obvious imperfection of such a system, universal rules applied to all individuals equally are essential in maintaining a stable society. The more that certain groups of citizens are given special rights denied to others, the more acrimonious the battle for special consideration between ever more fragmented groups. These debates will be examined in more detail in the following two chapters.

But if liberal democracy is comprised of such glaringly contradictory ideas, then why has this fact been such a recent concern? It is likely that such a notable increase is due largely to the very success of liberal democratic ideas within the global political arena. Liberal democracy now has very few coherent and desirable political models against which to define and evaluate itself: where once liberalism was pitted against socialism or fascism, there is now (except for the more abstract or epistemological objections of the postmodernists) simply an internal debate about the nature of liberal democracy itself. This debate is no less fierce than its recent predecessors; it is, if anything, more painful in the realization that some problems (such as the marginalization of certain groups within liberal democratic polities) are as intractable as ever, and in the frustration of being unable convincingly and conclusively to ground fundamental principles of liberal thought. The more some liberal ideas are prodded and dissected, the more it may become uncomfortably apparent that sometimes their effectiveness depends upon a less critical acceptance of them. If postmodernism has a profound thought to offer to democratic theorists, it is the Nietzschean insight that a too-rigorous 'rational' analysis of liberal principles may destroy the very utility of the rational institutions upon which we depend so heavily (see, e.g., Žižek 1991).

The proper sphere of democracy

The desirability of democracy rests to a very large extent upon its instrumental qualities. Democracy is a system widely admired because of the freedom it permits for citizens to pursue the objectives they most deeply value within a relatively stable and predictable political environment. As societies become larger, more heterogeneous, and less bound by rigid moral codes, however, the demands placed upon a state obliged to referee between groups with increasingly disparate interests become onerous. The problem, it would seem, is that the stability cherished by democracies may well require a fairly uncompromising underlying consensus on the norms and objectives which serve as the moral framework of the polity. Theorists across the political spectrum have agreed on this point: Hayek (1960), for example, has argued that '[i]t is doubtful whether democracy can work in the long run if the great majority do not have in common at least a general conception of the type of society desired'; while Jon Elster (1986) has noted, too, that democratic politics can be deeply satisfactory only to the extent that fairly clear normative standards are accepted by the participants at the outset, just as overarching rules are required to enjoy playing games. The need to find an underlying – or at least overlapping – consensus has been increasingly debated in contemporary political philosophy (Rawls 1985); and the globalization of democracy has exacerbated debate over the extent to which democracy ought only to be a set of processes applied *within* a circumscribed set of aims and values, or rather a decision-making process that can be used to *change* these norms and objectives.

The question of what, precisely, comprises the proper sphere of democracy is one of the most intransigent issues to be found even within the most stable and longstanding democratic states. The keystone of democracy is accountability, and the process by which accountability is to be determined is the principle that the majority (or plurality) of voices wins the right to formulate public policy. But this alone does not say very much about *which* issues can be placed on the agenda for public discussion; nor does it explain what to do when the proper practice of democratic procedures nonetheless produces undesirable outcomes.

Participation and redistribution

The one point upon which most donor states and major multilateral aid institutions agree is that private property rights are an essential foundation for non-western countries' development agenda. 'Efficient institutions emerge when there are built-in incentives to create and enforce property rights', declares the World Bank (1992: 7). Private property rights provide both the motivation to save and to invest judiciously, and the ability to resist the political transgressions of corrupt governments. Private property can serve as a fairly significant sphere of power; this is a point emphatically acknowledged even by those *opposed* to the establishment of strong private property rights in developing states. As Chapter 5 will explain in greater detail, the debate surrounding economic liberalization revolves primarily between those who believe that autonomous spheres of economic influence in authoritarian states can undermine the untrammelled exercise of political power (and thus serve to encourage democratization); and those who fear that, regardless of whether such autonomous spheres of economic influence undermine the exercise of authoritarian power or not, the most marginalized groups are just as effectively disenfranchised if they face untrammeled economic power in the private sector as they would confronting unchecked political power by the state. Powerful economic elites may be an even more potent enemy, according to this account, because they may exercise their power in an atmosphere of political legitimacy secured by neo-liberal economic theory. If marginalized groups fail to flourish within an environment of economic and political liberalization, then the blame must rest not with the system or with the successful parties but with those who fail to succeed.

Notwithstanding such objections, however, private property rights remain a major component of the global development agenda. To receive substantial funding from the World Bank, or to participate in export trade under the auspices of the World Trade Organization, for example, a state must agree to recognize and protect private property rights as a key institution. The promotion of private property no doubt achieves many of the objectives noted by its proponents. But the problem with the reification of private property rights is that it limits the extent to which those who are not property-holders have an opportunity to influence many of the forces which directly or indirectly affect them.

One point that many proponents of private property rights fail to acknowledge is that there exists no coherent and uncontroversial philosophical basis for private property rights. As Waldron (1994: 90) succinctly notes, '[t]he history of property theory indicates that there is no consensus on legitimate acquisition.' Recall that the modern western conception of rights had its genesis quite firmly within an account of *property* rights rather than what we would today call 'human' rights, or rights that spoke to the protection of human dignity and individual autonomy. This account of property rights, in turn, had its roots in a fourteenth-century theological debate between the papacy and the Franciscan order (Tuck 1979: 3–31). Even the defence of private property rights with which we are most familiar – that of John Locke – was grounded upon an interpretation of what God desired for human beings in his creation of the world. Specifically, Locke's account confronted the justifications of absolutism of his day, and argued that each individual had 'a *Property* in his own *Person*' that could not arbitrarily be violated by the sovereign. Modern libertarians have built emphatic accounts of political freedoms upon this foundation; but Locke's own starting point was the ultimate ownership of individuals by God, 'whose workmanship they are', and who are given a fiduciary trust to look after the flora and fauna of God's world – including, pointedly, themselves, their children, and each other (see Ryan 1994: 243; Simmons 1992; Waldron 1988; and Tully 1980).

What modern proponents of private property rights so frequently fail to recognize is that they depend very heavily upon a profoundly deracinated justification of the right to private property. Those who do look beyond the declaration that private property rights are simply owed to individuals who gain property through 'fair principles of entitlement' such as hard work, thrift, or entrepreneurship (e.g., Nozick 1974) tend to proffer consequentialist justifications for private property. The eighteenth-century philosopher David Hume, who constructed a detailed articulation of private property rights not based upon the assumption of self-ownership, argued that such rights could nonetheless be justified through an appeal to the consequences of a private-property system. Wealth could more effectively be created within such a system, and the predictability and transparency of a private property rights regime enhanced the stability of the polity (Hume 1948 [1739]).

The logical flaws of this account have been well-documented (e.g., Waldron 1994). But they have not prevented such influential bodies as the World Bank, IMF, and WTO from wreathing their endorsements of private property rights in glowing terms of the economic efficiency and political stability expected to arise from them. Again, much evidence has been mustered to bolster the claim of efficiency growing from the establishment of such institutions (a recent World Bank document (1992: 7), for example, uses the divergent economic paths of seventeenth-century England and Spain as an example of the felicity of private property). But regardless of the variety of justifications offered, private property rights are held as effective solutions to the most severe problems of developing states. The consequences of such enthusiasm for private property rights, however, includes an increase in the uncritical acceptance of such rights as 'trumps' in the political arena. While this may well have the advantages noted by its proponents, it has a cost too: and that is the closing-off of certain areas from popular decision-making. If various public policies (such as industrial development, the protection of indigenous cultural or religious institutions, environmental regulation, and so on) are seen to infringe upon citizens' private property rights, they are removed from the public agenda and must be resolved within the marketplace. The objection voiced by many here is, consequently, that the only individuals who can influence the policies that may ultimately affect everyone are those who have the economic ability to do so. To the extent that accountability to 'the people' in these areas becomes accountability to consumers, one of the key principles of democracy – the equal voice of all in matters which concern everyone – is neglected.

The objection to this, in turn, is that to the extent that popular participation in political decision-making imposes a drain on social resources and increases taxation, participatory democracy is costly indeed. For when individuals are permitted to make decisions without accepting direct financial liability for the resulting costs, there is little motivation to contain such costs: 'The voter is free of a "reality test" in the sense that (a) he has little incentive to be informed, and (b) he need not consider the fiscal consistency of his choices' (Mitchell 1983). The obvious solution to the problem of such collective economic irrationality, as Mrs Thatcher well knew, was to stress the sanctity of private property and limit the spheres in which popular input had influence over the public purse. But it is instructive to remember that, in most of the industrialized democracies, the narrowing of the 'proper spheres of democracy' have not simply been achieved through governmental fiat: even Mrs Thatcher was elected. And well before the British Conservative Party determined to make all elected bodies directly answerable for their spending, Californians had themselves by 1976 voted on a referendum to limit the ability of the state to raise taxes for social spending (see, e.g., Schrag 1994: 52). It is precisely this split between 'tax payer' and 'tax user' which characterises the political programme of the 'new' right. But to what extent is it democratic *not* to allow citizens of a polity to demand costly public policies which may well place onerous demands upon those who contribute a larger proportion of the tax base? The argument can be made in the industrialized democracies that such constraints upon democratic participation have been chosen by a plurality of voters. The response, however, is a challenge to the principle that a plurality of votes can legitimately bar others from political involvement in a given area (such as the provision of educational or health services). If these (or other) public policies have a direct effect upon *all* voters, then why should a plurality of citizens determine that private property rights have 'trumps' over the voices of their fellow citizens?

The debate pitting private property rights against popular accountability is even more pronounced in the developing world, where external bodies rather than electoral blocs determine the scope of popular accountability. The development strategies of the IMF and World Bank have for a long period of time rested upon the orthodox economic principles of debt reduction, severely limited public spending, and privatization. More recently, the restructuring of the international trade order raised similar issues concerning the extent to which each individual state ought to be able to shape its economic development. Most developing states are quite cognisant that they must maintain and expand their share of export trade, as most of them depend heavily upon export trade for a large portion of their foreign exchange. But export trade is governed by rules established by the WTO, and participation in this trading system requires that private property rights (including intellectual property rights) be respected. Amongst others, the South Commission has noted that such protection for private property rights may interfere with other developmental goals of southern states. The unmitigated and unregulated exercise of the market may well raise the country's GNP, but it may also damage more fragile social or political objectives. 'Development', notes the Commission,

> is a process of self-reliant growth, achieved through the participation of the people acting in their own interests as they see them, and under their own control. Its first objective must be to end poverty, provide productive employment, and satisfy the basic needs of all the people, any surplus being fairly shared (1990: 13).

Amongst the most contentious points of the liberal trade strategy is the WTO's position on trade-related investment measures (TRIMs). This position holds that participating states cannot impose performance requirements upon foreign corporations (such as mandatory technology transfer, the purchase of local materials, environmental protection, and so on). But, argues the South Commission, '[t]here are very sound economic reasons why developing countries need to regulate the inflow of private foreign investment and to subject these investments to conditions and performance requirements based on their developmental needs and priorities' (1990: 251).

Nonetheless, the WTO insists that liberalization must remain the top priority, 'even though it may often involve significant transitional social costs' (WTO 1995: 17). And, because the WTO maintains strong links with the IMF and World Bank, client states must comply with the agenda set for them by these institutions. The problem for critics is not merely that states increasingly adopt market-oriented agendas, but also that they have not chosen them for themselves. The entrenchment of unconditional corporate property rights may potentially exact high social costs: Ian Robinson, for example, argues that '[i]nternational economic integration under neoliberal rules will tend to concentrate power and wealth in the hands of those who already have it, eroding the quality of democratic politics, and with it, the legitimacy of democratic political institutions' (1995: 377).

The ability of states to achieve a reasonable level of economic development may quite conceivably depend upon a strictly constrained sphere of democracy in which the state is not overburdened by demands it cannot honour. But it is unclear whether a political system in which citizens cannot themselves make crucial political decisions – choices regarding the nature and costs of economic growth – can be considered 'democratic' in any but a very limited sense.

The politics of identity

A second locus of disagreement regarding the proper parameters of democratic activity concerns the extent to which the protection and nurturing of identity should be considered a public good to which all citizens ought to have access. 'Identity politics', which addresses the relative status of groups distinct from, but surrounded by, a 'mainstream' population, frequently involves discussion regarding the distribution of material resources, and does have some similarities to the debate noted above. However, to the extent that the relative penury of a group may be stressed, it is generally used as a symbol of a more profound disenfranchisement. Moreover, while economic debates use 'groups' or 'classes' for analytical purposes, the normative objective is to integrate the individuals in these units more tightly into the larger whole. In identity politics, in contrast, the goal is to preserve the distinctiveness of the subgroup and to prevent greater integration of its members into the mainstream community. Identity politics can be viewed both as an out-growth of liberal thought, and as a critical response to it. To the extent that groups use the rhetoric of rights and human dignity and charge that their groups are treated *unequally* in compari-son to some perceived mean or standard denominator, they rely very palpably upon liberal principles and sentiments. But to the extent that proponents of identity politics hold that it is pre-cisely the specious account of neutrality assumed within liberal systems which perpetuates and exacerbates their marginaliza-tion, this account is a vigorous critique of the very universal-izing forces that liberals are said to value.

The glory of liberalism was seen by many to rest in its toler-ance for the diversity nurtured through a wide-ranging network of rights and liberties. By strictly limiting government interven-tion in policy-making to instances where a manifest 'harm' can be seen to occur, all citizens of a liberal polity were assumed to have the amount of space necessary to live their lives as they saw fit (Mill, 1972). Nonetheless, twentieth-century writers were increasingly sceptical about the worth of the negative lib-erties granted to citizens within an atmosphere of very pro-nounced economic and social inequalities. If tolerance for the unpalatable views of a sizable majority (or powerful minority) were strenuously protected against the objections of a much smaller or weaker group, speculated Robert Paul Wolff, then would not the much-touted value of 'toleration' itself serve to reinforce an already unequal balance of power? (Wolff, 1965).

To the observation that various sources of social and economic influence undermine formal political equalities were added more abstract theories concerning the nature of meaning and power. These strands of argument had a very firm basis in eighteenth- and nineteenth-century tracts written as objections to the growth of Enlightenment thought, which stressed rational means of dis-cerning knowledge and which rejected the authority of ideas not based upon a scientific epistemological framework. At the same time that scientific reasoning developed as the preeminent stan-dard of knowledge, however, articulate and unapologetic objec-tions to it were expressed frequently and forcefully. Early challenges to excessive or inappropriate rationalism can be found, for example, in the eighteenth-century writings of

Edmund Burke, who argued passionately that the consequences of Enlightenment thought would erode the fabric of social life, based as it was upon longstanding and idiosyncratic traditions. It was, he insisted, precisely those unexamined sets of values and rituals that served as a silent language between individuals and allowed them to comprehend each other's actions. To disparage such customs, however superstitious and irrational, was to undermine those institutions which most firmly held together members of a community. A more obscure eighteenth-century figure, Joseph de Maistre, maintained quite similar views. The lack of faith was seen by de Maistre as the cause of the eighteenth century being 'one of the most shameful and unhappy periods of human history'. Maistre, according to Holmes (1993: 21) held that 'man cannot live without some opinions adopted prior to examination and rational justification: "there is nothing more important for him than prejudices". To behave properly, individuals need beliefs, not perplexities.' These sentiments were restated later by various critics of rationalism such as Nietzsche and, in the twentieth century, by Heidegger and Strauss. Contemporary echoes of these ideas are found in two broad schools of thought: communitarians and postmodernists. While much overlap exists between these two approaches, the former stress the need for a historical and traditional grounding for human society in the face of an alienating and atomizing individualism (e.g., MacIntyre 1988), while the latter generally put greater emphasis on the epistemological critique of rationalism and the possibility of knowing 'truth' (see, e.g., Lyotard 1984).

From the observations and arguments contained within these accounts has arisen a much more politicized movement that focuses upon the social well-being of distinct groups within liberal societies (or distinct societies within a liberal world). This account argues that the 'liberal freedoms' guaranteed to all are detrimental to individuals not clearly part of the dominant social grouping because they permit the norms, values, and traditions of the dominant group to serve as the invisible common language that allows individuals to perceive events the same way (and thus to serve as a common frame of reference). To the extent that groups with distinct cultures operate outside of this 'common language' by virtue of a dissimilar set of norms and traditions, generally including a distinct language and religion, such groups function with a very clear disadvantage. They must work harder at understanding the invisible language that others can take for granted, and they are expected to find meaning in foreign and alienating customs and concepts (e.g., Kymlicka 1989).

Moreover, when 'individualism' or 'autonomy' or 'competitiveness' are seen as neutral values that allow citizens to flourish in their own individual spheres, groups which place value instead on mutual support and dependence are penalized for not operating within the 'rules of the game' which liberal theory holds to be both neutral and fair. Aesthetic characteristics, moral values, and consumer preferences which are said to be in the private sphere and thus not subject to state intervention are nonetheless detrimental to weaker groups when an informal hierarchy of value is established by a dominant group. What results is the hegemony of value in the private sphere set by the mainstream population that makes the specific invisible language of language and custom held by more marginalized groups undervalued or irrelevant. If individuals in these groups wish to remain within a context which has meaning to them, they are marginalized as a group; if they attempt to absorb mainstream values they face a personal crisis of identity in their inability to comprehend all facets of the dominant invisible language.

What, then, ought a democratic society to do in order to alleviate the marginalization of those who are different, if universal rights are unable constructively to integrate them? The responses are quite distinct: on the one hand are those who say we must simply try harder with the liberal tools we have (an education which sensitizes us to those who are different, the use of affirmative action policies, and so on). On the other hand, however, are those who hold that, as liberal principles *by their very nature* are responsible for the social disenfrachisement of those who are different, we cannot depend upon this route to ameliorate such problems. We must emphasize not those qualities which we all have in common, but those which make us distinct (Young 1990).

What this means, politically, is that the state must intercede and protect those qualities which define disadvantaged groups in order to fortify the 'context of choice' available to them. This may involve a number of things: self-governing powers or veto rights over certain decisions (Kymlicka 1995: 126), for example, or the punishment of individuals who exhibit even 'unconscious and unintended behavior, actions, or attitudes that contribute to oppression' (Young 1990: 151). The 'proper sphere of democracy' here has expanded by expecting state involvement in areas formerly understood to be part of the private sphere. The active reinforcement of cultural traditions or a 'positive group identity', the monitoring of insensitive behaviour on the part of dominant groups, and the granting of differential rights to certain groups are all aspects of contemporary pressures for a more nuanced and enriched form of democracy. No longer is the state viewed as an impartial referee, treating all participants according to the same rules. Because not all participants *are* equally able to promote their interests, and because some of their most valued resources (i.e., language and culture) cannot be protected except with assistance external to the group, the state is morally required actively to intercede on behalf of these groups.

Yet this articulation of democracy conflicts sharply with the way in which democracy is more traditionally conceived. Both equality of treatment and personal freedoms are seen as fundamental characteristics of democracy, and any attempt to modify or limit these principles is often viewed with great suspicion and hostility. Responding to calls for a more enhanced democracy, opponents argue that differential treatment is both unfair and destabilizing; and that curbs on individual behaviour undermine what is most valuable about democracy. Democracy works, they claim, precisely because of neutral institutions and the lack of blatant political favouritism of groups, and because wide-ranging freedoms contribute to a dynamic political culture.

The role of democracy in the modern world

Democracy has been articulated as a desirable system of governance for states globally not only for moral reasons ('it treats people better') but also because it is seen to contribute to stability. It is perhaps worth recalling that early opponents of democracy strenuously decried it precisely because it was seen to be so manifestly destabilizing. 'Democracy' was, for many, merely a synonym for 'mob rule', and allowing individuals to govern the country when they could not effectively govern their own behaviour was seen as a clear route to disaster. Much is currently made of democratic attitudes (including a predisposition to 'regulated political competition, compromise solutions to political conflicts, and peaceful transfer of power') that reinforce the pacific behaviour of democratic states (Russett 1993: 33). Much has been written, too, of the ability of democratic structures to accommodate and regulate political discord which, again, contributes to the long-term stability of democratic states. But do we overstate the potential for democratic systems to enhance stability? We know that both long-term economic growth and cultural homogeneity were instrumental in the historical development of the emergent modern democracies; but the extent to which it was 'democracy' *per se* rather than prosperity or a similarity of values which contributed to political stability over time is less clear. Commentators on the early democratic systems were frequently ambivalent in their prognosis for these states: Tocqueville's approbation of nineteenth-century America, for example, was tempered by his recognition that it nonetheless contained the potential to elicit patently unpalatable outcomes (Tocqueville 1945 [1862]). Despite the advantages which have arisen through the sustained exercise of liberal democracy, the claim of political inclusiveness which proponents of democracy assert is frequently belied in the dissatisfaction and despair exhibited by so many members of democratic polities. And, while the political tribulations of some countries arise because democratic institutions do not function sufficiently well, those in other countries occur despite the fact that democratic institutions are running precisely as they are expected to. A further ambiguity of democracy, then, concerns the extent to which these undesirable outcomes ought to be addressed and mitigated (thereby modifying the nature of the democratic institutions and processes which systematically created and perpetuated them) or tolerated and accepted (because they are the outcome of legitimate democratic institutions and processes).

As democracy increasingly becomes the political (and moral) standard by which regimes are judged, it becomes more essential to understand what this standard entails. The function of democracy is, fundamentally, to ensure the diffusion of power by stipulating that each citizen has the ability to influence the outcome of political decision-making. One of the most perplexing difficulties to arise from this account, however, is how to address the concerns of those who are, as Guinier writes, the 'systematic losers in the political marketplace' (1989: 429). Guinier's position, like that of Rousseau, is that merely possessing the *opportunity* to vote is irrelevant in cases where individuals' votes are consistently 'wasted' within the minority of a winner-takes-all system. Votes cannot be said to be counted 'equally' unless the policies resulting from electoral competitions also reflect the 'lost' voices in some way: the right to vote, to have any bite, must on this account be thought of as 'the right to cast an equally powerful vote' (Guinier 1993: 1614).

It is this concern which has focused attention upon the rights of groups: by conceptualizing individuals as members of groups, and giving these groups specific rights *vis-à-vis* the mainstream population, their voices as individuals will thus have more force. Yet this approach assumes much, and must be considered with a great deal of caution. To the extent that 'democracy' is increasingly the standard of legitimacy because unequal dynamics of power between individuals are addressed, a legitimate group identity could only be determined in a 'democratic' way – i.e., through each individual in the group consenting in a formal and anonymous manner. The paradox is clearer stated another way: individualistic procedures are the only legitimate means of protecting traditional identity, even though traditional identity may well be very vehemently non-individualist. To the extent that a non-individualistic identity is given as the reason not to accept the standard of liberal democracy, it is simply not legitimate because it is never clear (without 'liberal democratic' procedures) that all members of a specific group accept these criteria.

Even more confusingly, if a group argues that it accepts the procedural requirements of liberal democracy, and chooses to use them to protect some aspect of its traditional culture, it is unclear why some groups can claim this process while other groups cannot. The answer commonly given is that some group traits, though not others, result in an economic and social marginalization (and thus deserve group rights) while others do not. This marginalization thesis lacks a strong causal argument (is it the case that some groups are economically marginalized because of their culture, or are they culturally marginalized because they do not have the economic resources to protect their lifestyle in the way other groups do?), and fails persuasively to explain why temporary measures (e.g., affirmative action policies) are more useful than group rights which permanently segregate communities. The attempt to ground individual 'empowerment' upon group identity is, I shall argue in Chapter 4, simply too ambiguous convincingly to act as the basis of a coherent public policy (or political philosophy). Once we begin to accept the argument that the role of democracy is to protect cultural or group identity, we confront a number of conditions which ultimately undermine the original intent of democracy as the attempt to diffuse power between individuals.

3

Expanding democracy

The metaphysical problem of our age is not in fact to reveal the universal in the inequality of social conditions, but to found differentiation in the limitless standardization of the networks.
(J. M. Guéhenno 1995: 96)

Impartiality and meaningfulness

Proponents of globalization have observed, no doubt with some satisfaction, that there is an increasing consensus across (and within) states that democracy is the correct standard upon which to judge the political legitimacy of states. But this contentment must, upon reflection, be considerably lessened by the realization that the consensus on what, precisely, is entailed by democracy has concurrently diminished a great deal. There are fairly clear political reasons why this has occured; and some of these political explanations will be more closely examined in Chapter 7. But rarely (especially in putatively democratic societies) are political actions taken without an attempt to give a sound moral justification for them: and moral legitimacy, in its simplest form, generally involves an attempt to act 'in ways that are capable of being defended impartially' (Barry 1989: 363).

Underlying the uneven global consensus regarding the moral appropriateness of democratic legitimacy, however, is an unsettling dichotomy between staunch proponents of liberal rights (both positive and negative) and those who insist that such absolutes are at best unjustifiable and, at worst, oppressive and imperialistic. In addition to the more familiar tensions within democratic theory revolving around issues of property rights and entitlement are more contemporary strains based upon epistemological debates, still grounded quite firmly upon questions of power. The interlocutors in this debate involve those who believe that 'democracy' is most fundamentally about structuring a political society according to 'neutral' and 'impartial' principles, on the one hand; and those who believe that, because such objectivity is manifestly impossible, democracy ought rightly to be about the self-determination of groups, whatever the principles upon which they choose to structure their societies. In this chapter and the next I examine this debate, and argue that any account of democracy must ultimately rest upon some account of impartiality. To hold that cultural self-determination is justified through reference to the meaningfulness of culture is both misguided and unsupportable. This is, I must emphasize, not to say that polities cannot be governed according to cultural traditions or beliefs: it is to say that such cultural institutions must be chosen, in Brian Barry's terms, according to principles of 'justice as impartiality', rather than defended on the grounds that 'cultural identity' is inherently a good thing and must therefore wield a great deal of normative power.

'Identity politics' are the greatest challenge to traditional liberal democratic principles within the contemporary political sphere. But identity politics are, as noted in the previous chapter, both an extension to liberal democracy, and a rejection of it. Insofar as people within identifiable groups perceive that they are not treated with equal respect *vis-à-vis* other groups or individuals, their objections are premised upon the unmitigatedly liberal values of equality and dignity. But to the extent that critics of liberalism argue that the methods by which equality and dignity are maintained lead to a 'meaningless' existence for them, the premise of neutrality underpinning a liberal democratic system of government is dismissed as either specious or irrelevant. The question of how to reconcile an 'impartially just' democracy with one that preserves a 'meaningful identity' for the individuals within it is thus one of the most pressing, and vexing, political issues for contemporary politics. This issue has been made even more importunate as the forces of globalization become more pronounced. The proliferation of political, economic, and social ties between nations mean greater pressure to operate according to similar rules. The economic relations of trade and of aid between states mean that some states do have an ability to pressure others to conform to certain forms of political governance. But ought they to do so? Or should the principle of state sovereignty be respected regardless of what such sovereignty entails?

The principle of state sovereignty is generally traced back to two legal antecedents. The 1555 Peace of Augsburg 'not only accepted the fact of religious disunity in Germany, but of political disunity as well' (Cowie 1977: 168), and permitted the princes to determine whether their states were to be Roman Catholic or Lutheran (but, pointedly, not Calvinist). This doctrine, which became known as *cuius regio, eius religio* ('whose territory, his religion'), required all subjects to accept their ruler's choice of religion, although dissidents were generally allowed to move to a more hospitable state 'after disposing of their property at a reasonable price' (Cowie 1977: 167). The religious peace of Augsburg lasted for sixty-three years, but was then succeeded by the Thirty Years' War. This conflict was, in turn, settled by the Treaty of Westphalia, which recognized not only rulers' entitlement to impose their religious convictions on their subjects, but also the princes' legal right to conduct foreign policy (including the declaration of war and the signing of treaties) independently of empire or emperor to whom they formally paid allegiance. Together, the documents of Augsburg and Westphalia formed the basis of the modern doctrine of autonomous state sovereignty, in which each state has the right to determine moral and political rules independently of any external authority.

Though it is arguable whether the concept of state sovereignty is itself a 'liberal' one, it is increasingly used by non-liberal states as a reply to external actors who charge that such states are responsible for human right violations. The moral right to self-determination that is increasingly articulated by distinct groups within liberal democratic polities also has its roots within the (relatively modern) doctrine of autonomous state sovereignty, even though (as I argue in Chapter 4) many political actors (and political theorists) increasingly articulate their scepticism of this legal construct. The task here is, however, not to evaluate the philosophical strength of the idea of state sovereignty, but to ask rather whether a broader, 'globalized' form of democracy makes any sense at all given its very specific historical roots. If 'democracy' is to be globalized, then what status is the doctrine of state sovereignty to have? Ought we only to recognize the autonomy of states if they are democratic? Do democratic states thus have the moral ability – or even obligation – to do all in their power to ensure that other self-governing states become democratic? Or are the liberal requirements of democracy simply too culturally specific for it be a 'meaningful' concept for many of those expected to conform to it?

These questions are not assisted by the loose meanings ascribed to most of the key terms of the debate. The previous chapter discussed some of the theoretical debates surrounding the idea of democracy; 'liberalism' is, if anything, more ambiguous still in its meaning. The rest of this chapter will look more closely at the 'liberal' nature of democracy. Beginning with a brief overview of the historical development of liberalism and liberal democracy, and their contemporary manifestations, the bulk of the chapter will examine current philosophical challenges to liberal democracy. These criticisms can roughly be classified into two approaches: those accounts that argue that liberalism's claim of objectively is false (and that this window-dressing of neutrality is used to cloak the attempts of those holding power to maintain it); and – somewhat paradoxically – those accounts that argue that liberalism is far too neutral in its construction of the polity (leading to a morally-directionless and spiritually-empty citizenry). Chapter 4, in turn, responds to the objections raised by critics of liberal democracy, and argues that any account of democracy grounded upon cultural identity rather than impartiality cannot present a satisfactory account of the containment and diffusion of political power which grounds the moral attractiveness of democracy in the modern global context.

Liberal democracy

Liberalism developed concurrently with much scientific and social progress, but it also had its roots quite firmly in the political turmoil of the seventeenth century. The first prototypical 'liberal' theorist, Thomas Hobbes, wrote his master work during Cromwell's interregnum of 1649–60, and had felt very keenly the years of civil war which preceded it. The Restoration of monarchical authority in 1660 and the Glorious Revolution of 1689–90 similarly set the backdrop to Locke's political writings; and both authors knew quite well the insecurity of arbitrary authority, political disfavour, and exile. The political conflicts swirling around Hobbes and his compatriots in the 1640s were primarily, though not solely, religious and economic. The Church of England faced strong challenges to the claim of religious authority from Roman Catholicism and Puritanism, as well as from the smaller groups of Calvinists, Anabaptists, and Presbyterians. Old agricultural wealth had quite different interests than the new industrial wealth; and the aristocracy were facing an increasingly defiant coalition of yeomen and artisans. But political divisions were not based solely on religious or class interests: the Parliamentarians who challenged the power of the Royalists, for example, were not always Puritans or industrialists (Hill 1964). Those who defended the privileges of the wealthy, both old and new, were confronted by the Diggers, the Levellers, and the Agitators. And underlying all of this was the increasing legitimacy of scientific thought, which challenged the mystery and superstition upon which both royal and religious authority rested.

The task which Hobbes set for himself was thus to construct an impartial account which could convince such fundamentally disparate interests to cooperate in the establishment of a stable political system. His impartiality was based upon individuals' capacity for reason and their fear of violent death rather than upon any partisan account of political authority; and his argument rested upon the demonstration that the consequences of disobedience were, in almost all cases, more onerous than those of obedience: 'expediency, not morality' was for Hobbes the basis for political obligation (Hill 1964: 277). Hobbes' account provided an early basis for liberalism in a number of ways: authority was to be based upon reason rather than superstition; it was to be grounded ultimately upon individual consent rather than upon tradition; and it was impartial in its account of justice. Though Hobbes was in no respect a democrat, it was his recognition of the need to get disputing parties to recognize each other as 'equal' that helped to undermine the common assumption that some individuals' interests were simply more worthy of consideration than others. Even if 'equality' were nothing more than a political fiction, 'yet because men that think themselves equall, will not enter into conditions of Peace, but upon Equall termes, such equalitie must be admitted' (Hobbes 1968 [1651]: 211).

It is, in essence, this Hobbesian account of politics which forms the basis of the modern relations between states. A formal equality exists between manifestly unequal states; and peaceful coexistence is usually sought not on any specific moral authority, but on the basis that life would, in general, be the worse under a regime of continual political conflict. Peaceful coexistence is bought with the currency of impartiality. But the problem with this account, according to some recent theorists, is that peace is achieved only by linking 'justice' too closely with 'power'. It is this relationship between liberalism and impartiality which forms the nub of the disputes regarding the current globalization of democracy; and it is discussed in more detail below.

Three underlying themes in Hobbes (individualism, rationalism, and economic progress) and one arguably non-Hobbesian notion – tolerance – form the basis of modern liberalism, and can be traced in their development from seventeenth-century thought to the present. The following account is a very brief synopsis of how these ideas took root and blossomed in the past three and a half centuries; and, while unavoidably superficial, it is useful to have a grasp of how (and why) such ideas developed in order better to evaluate many of the contemporary criticisms made of liberal democratic systems.

Individualism

To underscore the fact that the governments of the day were the product of deliberate human creation, rather than of organic growth or divine providence, a number of early modern theorists (including both Hobbes and Locke) postulated the existence of a state of nature in which, to varying degrees, individuals existed outside of a social community. It was the act of contracting with each other that formed the basis of a stable political regime; and such an act would in due course be undertaken by individuals who perceived that life in a stable political environment was simply more rational than anarchy.

Like many aspects of what became known as 'liberal' thought, the premise of individuals abstracted from their social relationships had been influenced by Puritan ideas. The most powerful element of the radical protestantism of Puritanism was its challenge to the hierarchy of ecclesiastical authority: in defiance of the established doctrine of the Church of England, as well as of the Roman Catholic church, Puritanism held that religious authority began at the local level and radiated outward in a loose federation of parishes. Clergy were responsible, in turn, to parishioner; for it was, after all, in the heart of each believer that religious truth was to be found, rather than in the law and tradition of the Church (Hill 1966: 488). And, while formal Puritan ideals held religious authority to rest with the (male) head of the household, 'the logic of radical Protestantism led to an egalitarian individualism' to the extent that the demand for religious toleration undermined patriarchal as well as priestly authority *(ibid.*: 477, 495).

Puritanism also incorporated an ideology of human dignity and responsibility; and it is no coincidence that one of the most emphatic voices for the establishment of universal human rights – that of Thomas Paine – was of good Quaker stock. A moderate equality between individuals in matters political and spiritual did not interfere with the ownership of property; the modern conception of Puritans as ascetic and unconcerned with material wealth obscures the historical reality that a great number of the rising artisan and merchant class were in fact Puritan. It was the reluctance of this economic class to contribute high taxes to the King for 'Ship Monies' to finance the Royal Navy which partly explained why so many Parliamentarians, and so few Royalists, were Puritans. It was also the Puritans who were known as 'the industrious sort of people' whose work ethic advocating the spiritual propriety of regular systematic work was essential in establishing the ideological framework for the Industrial Revolution. While condoning neither greed nor materialism, radical Protestantism did require hard work as evidence of moral rectitude: 'the Puritan instructed Christians to serve God by being good men of business; the Anglican instructed business men to serve themselves by being godly' (R. B. Schlatter, quoted in Hill 1980: 69. See also Hill 1966: 449–50).

Rationalism

Puritanism contributed, too, to the growth of rationality in its condemnation of the theistic religions of the day which emphasized the magic and superstitious ritual of Catholicism and high Anglicanism. The deistic emphasis upon 'the study of God's works in nature' rather than upon the acceptance of miracles and saints also fit well with the self-appointed task of the Royal Society of the established scientists of the seventeenth and eighteenth centuries to understand God better through the use of scientific principles. Deism was not always a popular approach to religion, however: Thomas Paine's defence of deism in the face of superstitious ritual, published later in his life, caused him to be branded unfairly as an atheist and to be shunned as an outcast not for his radical political views, but for his relatively moderate religious ones.

It was Thomas Hobbes who is best known for his attempts to base politics upon purely rational principles; and it was Edmund Burke who, a century and a half later, roared like Canute in his attempt to show why rationalism was very much the wrong principle upon which to structure social and political relations. For Hobbes, emphatic disagreements over beliefs could only be resolved if conflicting parties reasoned carefully about how their primary interests could best be preserved. To argue why a polity ought to be structured in one way rather than in another one consulted no authority but one's own reason; one's reason, in turn, would tell one to seek peace and stability above all else.

But it was Burke who best articulated the critique of the attempt to ground politics upon reason that would be unconsciously echoed by critics of liberalism two hundred years later. It was the arrogance of reason without an appreciation of tradition which, he argued, had led to the bloodshed and tyranny of the French Revolution. That which holds a society together, he argued, is not reason but sentiment: 'We know, and what is better we feel inwardly, that religion is the basis of civil society, and the source of all good and of all comfort' (1968 [1790]: 186). It was precisely the rituals and traditions, the language and the religion, which provided the ineffable content which gave meaning to lives of citizens. Accepting the authority of their own reason, individuals would destroy the whole original fabric of society and the links between generations: 'Men would become little better than the flies of summer' (ibid.: 192–3).

But evidence of the fruits of scientific rationality quickly undermined the force of tradition for tradition's sake; and 'reason', as a combination of syllogistic method and empirical evidence, became essential in arbitrating between conflicting accounts. The authority of neutrality was thus given an unprecedented value, along with a greater esteem for scepticism in matters that could not be resolved through scientific reasoning. Men might cast scorn upon the sentiment of tradition indeed, but the power unleashed by science over nature gave them little concern for Burke's warning that, divorced from their unique traditions and customs, they were little more than insects in the heat of the summer sun.

Economic progress

The Puritan Revolution had been couched in the terms of religious debate. Yet what emerged from the twenty years of strife caused by this dispute, writes Hill, 'was not the kingdom of God but a world safe for business men to make profits in, ensured not only by the overthrow of the old régime but also by the defeat of the radical revolutionaries, divided as they were among themselves' (1980: 34). The importance of liberty in the seventeenth and eighteenth centuries was primarily the liberty to own property without the fear of arbitrary seizure or onerous taxation by the Crown. David Hume spoke approvingly of the utilities to be gained by a system of private property rights; the economic progress to be gained thereby was justification enough. In more empirical terms his colleague Adam Smith explained the utility of repealing the Corn Laws which gave the Crown the power arbitrarily to set grain prices low enough in times of scarcity that the poor might afford to buy enough not to starve. The brilliance of Smith's logic, taken as commonplace today, was that the establishment of private property rights would motivate economic investment and prevent scarcity over the long term (Hont and Ignatieff 1983: 1–44).

But the fervour accompanying the rhetoric of progress was not to be limited to the spheres of science or economics. The idea of 'moral' or 'political' progress gained its own resonance, and throughout the nineteenth century much discussion focused upon the proper relationship between state and individual which would permit the development of a truly enlightened political society. John Stuart Mill's defence of individual liberty is the most coherent articulation of this perspective (Mill 1972 [1859]), but the Victorian emphasis upon the need to educate a citizenry spoke to the popular faith in the transformative power of knowledge. It was a widespread education in the liberal values which, by the middle of the nineteenth century, persuaded the nervous middle class that Britain had become safe for universal male suffrage. Yet it is, somewhat ironically, this same emphasis upon economic progress which currently plays such a large role in the attempt to make democracy a global phenomenon. Mill was himself sceptical about the degree to which individuals who had not benefitted from a rigorous liberal education could govern themselves effectively; but contemporary theorists seem much more willing to place their faith in the materialist spur to the development of responsible self-government. A focus upon the economic rewards of stable democracies avoids the Victorian insistence that democracy could only survive within the environment of gentlemanly virtues and civilized values that had to be firmly inculcated by a rigorous education. By stressing the reciprocal relationship between sound economy and democratic governance one can avoid the need to incorporate the political bias of specifically 'liberal' values: if, that is, any form of liberalism must incorporate 'biased values' at all.

Tolerance

Liberalism depends implicitly upon a high degree of toleration between competing conceptions of the good which, argues Nancy Rosenblum, 'is why Hobbes is not the father of liberalism' (Rosenblum 1989: 24). Tolerance has its roots, again, very firmly in the religious turmoil of seventeenth-century England. Well before the concept of the 'right' of religious worship became commonly articulated, the practice of religious tolerance was gradually established throughout the middle to late 1600s. Under the Puritan Cromwell in 1650 compulsory church attendance ended, while the Toleration Act of 1689 'finally deprived the Church of England of its monopoly position' (Hill 1972: 357). And, while the development of religious tolerance had its political causes, its ideological roots also can be seen in the Puritan acknowledgement that 'faith cannot be enforced': for religious affiliation to mean anything at all, it had to be adhered to willingly and actively.

It is a common mistake to assume that it was only the nascent liberal state which exhibited any disposition towards religious toleration. But as Kymlicka (1995) has written, the millet system of the Islamic Ottoman empire permitted enclaves of Christian and Jewish communities to practice their religions freely, given some limited constraints (such as enjoinders against proselytizing). Nonetheless, it was the development of liberalism in the eighteenth and nineteenth centuries which increasingly required forbearance as a mark of good citizenship. It can be argued that Britain's role as an imperialist power exposed its citizens to a wide array of strange customs and beliefs, and that its position of strength prevented much of the fear upon which intolerance is often grounded. But it was also as part of the quest for epistemological progress and intellectual growth that dissenting opinions and beliefs were increasingly permitted. Best articulated in the nineteenth-century writings of John Stuart Mill, the freedom to express odd or unpalatable ideas was essential in order to piece together the 'whole truth' from various fragments and half-truths: 'though the silenced opinion be an error, it may, and very commonly does, contain a portion of truth; and since the general or prevailing opinion on any subject is rarely or never the whole truth, it is only by the collision of adverse opinions that the remainder of the truth has any chance of being supplied' (Mill 1972 [1859]: 111).

Yet the recognition of a dark side to toleration was always present throughout the development of liberalism as a political doctrine. McCarthyism was an example of limits to which a stable democracy was willing to permit too overt a criticism of its fundamental beliefs; while those on the left, were beginning to note the drawbacks of too insistent a demand for tolerance. Robert Paul Woolf, writing in 1965, foreshadowed later criticisms of the principle of toleration. The logic of liberal tolerance, he argued, completely disregarded differences in relative influence between groups: a small minority could, for instance, be enjoined to exhibit 'tolerance' toward the influential opinions of a larger, more powerful group, thereby allowing its views to be overpowered by the sheer number of opposing voices (1965: 43).

What, then, is the modern manifestation of 'liberalism'? There are, as Brian Barry has written, at least three distinct conceptualizations of liberalism: one incorporating 'an atomistic sociology and an associated theory of natural, presocial rights'; one equated with 'a certain distinctive conception of the good'; and one tied to 'the idea that a theory of justice should be neutral between different conceptions of the good' (1995: 124). The first includes the concept of inviolable and free-standing private property rights, criticisms of which were noted in the previous chapter. The second will be the subject of the following two sections; and the third will be defended in the following chapter.

Democracy, in contrast to liberalism, is a procedural system constructed to recognize formally the principle that political legitimacy was grounded upon the consent of each citizen. Much has been made of the observation that liberal democracy was an ideology that evolved in order to accommodate the nascent capitalist system (see e.g., Macpherson 1962): capitalism requires all individuals equally to be responsible for their actions and to have inviolable rights to their property. The contractual negotiation for goods and labour entails that the individuals entering into the contracts do so of their own free will; and it requires the further assumption that such transactions voluntarily entered into are morally binding. And, for goods and labour to be freely traded, it is necessary to suppose that one holds full and unqualified title to one's possessions and to one's labour.

But the egalitarian focus inherent in the development of liberalism – the claim that all individuals are fundamentally equal due to their faculty of reason (Kant), their essential dignity (Paine), or their facility for self-development (Mill) – could not be completely reconciled with the emphasis on creative self-determinism or 'authenticity' that changed the modern meaning of individualism to connote 'distinctiveness', as opposed to a simple, uniform atomism. The normative confusion that arose from this juxtaposition was grounded upon the issue of whether people were to be valued because of their essential sameness, or because of their potential uniqueness. The contemporary critique of liberalism articulated by proponents of identity and identity rights is derived from this concern over authenticity. It argues that the uniform treatment of individuals upon which the liberal democratic conception of 'fairness' is based paradoxically harms people by denying them what they value most: their particularity. Rather than protecting and nurturing self-determining beings, as Mill expected, the homogenizing force of liberalism permits them only a narrow band of opportunity in which to develop their 'authentic' selves. There are two distinct but interrelated claims in this critique of liberalism: first, that liberalism is not 'neutral', as its exponents assert, but in fact promotes specific values that are foreign or unattainable to certain people; and, second, that liberalism as a system of universal rights and obligations distorts or stunts the identity of some people, thereby limiting what they may achieve individually or socially in their lifetime. The following two sections address these concerns in turn.

Specious neutrality

The idea of liberal democracy as a system of political organization that is neutral between competing claims has been dismissed as caustically by self-styled 'progressive' forces as it has by more conservative ones. Indeed, marxism and liberalism have commonly been linked by these critics in the dependence of the two schools upon assumptions of rationality, neutrality, and inexorable scientific progress. The more recent political disputes over the adequacy of liberal democracy have focused less upon the power inherent in the ownership of property and more upon the possibility of political impartiality, even though the consequences of this putative impossibility of objectivity are drawn quite differently by the respective critics. Many of these critics have been collectively labeled 'communitarian', even though some of the most virulent criticism of liberal democracy is articulated by the radically sceptical postmodernists who have been influenced by Nietzschean thought (evident in the claim that *all* moral codes between individuals are essentially a manifestation of power). Such a stance could not be further removed from the more Burkean conservatives who hold that, while moral codes cannot be usefully understood nor justified with reference to the criteria of rationalism, they are nonetheless the most valuable facet of human relationships.

It is perhaps useful at this point to distinguish liberal epistemology from liberalism *per se*. The former incorporates the assumption that rationality is a neutral evaluative construct, and that the normative objective of any political community must be to use the tools of rationality to construct a system of impartial justice. It may well be that 'liberalism' is the closest political manifestation of what these principles require; but it is the philosophical principles established by rational discourse which justifies liberal institutions, rather than liberal norms which use rationalism and assumptions of neutrality to legitimate liberal political institutions and processes.

Critics of liberalism and liberal epistemology, of course, argue precisely the opposite: that 'rational', 'objective' accounts of justice are constructed using the norms and traditions of liberalism in order to legitimize liberal political systems. The evolution of the discourse between John Rawls and his critics is perhaps the best example of how this debate has developed since the 1970s. In 1971, Rawls published *A Theory of Justice*, a more detailed and complex account of a paper originally published in 1958. His argument, very simply, was an attempt to show how principles of justice upon which all could agree might be formulated. Rawls begins from an 'original position', in which actors are hidden by a 'veil of ignorance' from knowledge of their particular talents, advantages, and weaknesses. Given that they cannot in this way design rules that would benefit only their own particular circumstances, they thus decide which broad political principles can serve as a fair framework for all. The outcome of this negotiation, as Rawls argues at length, would be agreement on securing the greatest amount of liberty for all, and the stipulation that relative inequalities are justifiable to the extent that they benefit the worst off in absolute terms.

Commentary on Rawls' work has been a growth industry for over a quarter of a century, and the force of such criticism has been extremely diverse. But one of the most unrepentant lines of criticism has been the claim that Rawls' account of the original position is overly abstract, and that the hypothetical individuals in this original position seem to exhibit curiously liberal qualities. As Thomas Nagel stated, '[t]he original position seems to presuppose not just a neutral theory of the good, but a liberal, individualistic conception according to which the best that can be wished for someone is the unimpeded pursuit of his own path, provided it does not interfere with the rights of others' (1973: 10). Thus Rawls emphasizes what, to liberals, is most important about individuals – their autonomy – and disregards other values which may be still more important to other individuals. This observation has been the basis of much of the recent criticism against Rawls by those concerned with 'identity politics'; and has led Rawls himself to modify his own position, correctly or incorrectly, in light of these criticisms (Rawls 1993b). But before examining the argument based upon the nature and value of 'identity', it is worthwhile to look more closely at the arguments levied against the way in which 'neutrality' is used in contemporary theories of justice.

Moral conservatism

The contemporary use of the term 'conservative' within much political discourse is increasingly, and erroneously, applied to those concerned with maintaining an economy relatively free of impediments imposed upon it by state regulation. The proper use of the term refers rather to those concerned with the preservation of a rich and nuanced environment of specific and familiar traditions. (And this concern, in turn, may well require the active involvement by the state to protect and nurture these traditions.) It was Edmund Burke who, as noted above, was jolted by his contemporaries' approval of the French revolution into articulating a condemnation of unmitigated change and a defence of the careful preservation of established habit, belief, and ritual. But Burke was not alone in his passionate concern for the preservation of a distinctive cultural fabric: the history of modern western thought from Burke to the present is replete with careful thinkers who have vigorously defended a stream of thought we may call 'moral conservatism'. A previous generation of political theorists, for example, could cite the writing of Michael Oakeshott as representative of this school; while the writer who currently is viewed as one of the most articulate and influential of the moral conservatives may well be Alasdair MacIntyre.

MacIntyre's most recent book is a detailed and provocative argument against the assumption that liberalism is a superior political system based upon 'objective' and 'rational' forms of thought that prevent the untoward biases or prejudices arising out of traditional distributions of power. Rather, he argues, liberalism is itself a tradition emerging out of, and competing with, other philosophical traditions. A 'tradition-independent moral standpoint', in his words, is simply impossible: liberalism is as dependent upon a core of assumptions and beliefs as its predecessors. Why is this? In the first place, argues MacIntyre, such assumptions of objectivity require

> some feature or features of a human moral stance which hold of human beings independently of and apart from those characteristics which belong to them as members of any particular social or cultural tradition. It is to some kind of universality, which can be conceived of as specifying and furnishing a tradition-independent moral standpoint, that resort must be had. (MacIntyre 1988: 334)

The German philosopher Kant famously attempted to base this universality upon the human capacity for reason; while other theorists, such as Thomas Paine (in his unapologetic response to Burke), have posited such universal qualities as resting upon the notion of a universal human dignity. A contemporary writer, Richard Rorty, has attempted in like manner to construct an account based upon the argument that a common denominator can be found in all individuals' fear of being treated cruelly. These observations about what makes us truly human, in turn, justifies what, in effect, are a system of liberal rights and freedoms.

But the problem with this type of argument, states MacIntyre, 'is that those conceptions of universality and impersonality which survive this kind of abstraction from the concreteness of traditional or nontraditional conventional modes of moral thought and action are far too thin and meagre to supply what is needed' to construct a neutral and impartial system of political justice. The type of individual who has been abstracted out of all cultural and social contexts is a completely unrecognizable individual, one who may not possess a respect for human dignity, an appreciation of the force of logic, or a desire to be seen to act justly. Moreover, he continues, it is a myth to conceptualize liberalism as a system of neutrality and objectivity holding fast against the unreflective and superstitious claims of various traditions. Liberalism, he maintains, actively promotes its own conception of 'the good' against rival accounts. The liberal account of 'the good' holds various values and assumptions – such as the equal value of human life, the import of liberty, and priority of individual over community – that are simply not open for debate. They are moral first principles, not up for dispute. Finally, liberal society must preach tolerance in the attitudes and behaviour of its citizens. If rival conceptions of 'the good' do not exhibit the same level of tolerance, then they are not permitted. And this, argues MacIntyre, means no less than that 'liberal individualism does indeed have its own broad conception of the good, which it is engaged in imposing politically, legally, socially, and culturally whenever it has the power to do so' (*ibid.*: 336).

Contemporary liberal philosophers equate 'the human self' with their particular conception of 'the liberal self'. Thus individuals are compartmentalized into spheres (productive, domestic, artistic, etc); and '[t]he claims of any one sphere to attention or to resources are once again to be determined by the summing of individual preferences and by bargaining' (*ibid.*: 337). This means that not only is the idea of a unified and coherent 'self' dismissed, but also that individual preferences themselves count as good reasons for actions and for demands, rather than merely as points to begin debate over conceptions of public good (*ibid.*: 338). Bargaining replaces discussion; thus 'rationality', according to a modern liberal, consists,

> [f]irst of all in the ordering of his or her preferences by each individual, so that those preferences may be ordinally ranked by their presentation in the public realm; second, in the soundness of the

arguments whereby preferences are translated into decisions and actions; and third, in the ability to act so as to maximize the satisfaction of those preferences in accordance with their ordering (ibid.: 342).

But this account of 'practical rationality' offered by liberalism is not, MacIntyre maintains, the only conception of practical rationality. Indeed, logic and argumentation are under this account actually limited, as people with different preferences are not required to engage in a philosophical enquiry to determine who has sounder views; rather, within a liberal system, 'rival appeals to accounts of the human good or of justice necessarily assume a rhetorical form' of assertion and counterassertion, simply because 'no overall theory of the human good is to be regarded as justice' (ibid.: 343).

Thus, concludes MacIntyre, liberalism has its own internal standards of rational justification, its own set of authoritative texts (and disputes over their interpretation), and it 'expresses itself socially through a particular kind of hierarchy': just as other intellectual traditions do (ibid.: 345). And, to the extent that liberalism itself despite its claims cannot provide a neutral-independent ground for confronting the claims of various traditions, MacIntyre is doubtful that such neutrality can ever be established within any type of epistemological or political framework.

Feminism

The feminist critique of neutrality has at least three different components: the claim that the liberal *state* is not objective; the argument that neutral liberal political *norms and values* are in fact biased; and the position that the basic conception of *scientific rationality* which liberalism uses as an arbiter between conflicting views is itself imbued with patriarchal values.

The liberal state is commonly viewed as a disengaged referee arbitrating between competing interests. Yet, as most feminists agree, the fact that the liberal state is expected only to involve itself with the public sphere and to avoid regulating the personal means that established power relations within this private sphere (and especially within the family) are maintained and even protected (e.g., Okin 1989). Feminists concerned with the establishment of laws protecting women as well as children from domestic abuse were until recently continually frustrated by both legislators' and enforcers' reluctance to intercede in domestic disputes despite the high number of violent assaults that occured within the home. This unwillingness of state legislators to engage in 'personal' matters was often articulated quite clearly regardless of the observations that 'the liberal state has regulated and controlled the family, in innumerable ways, and in such ways as to reinforce patriarchy' (*ibid.*: 42). A common example of this phenomenon was the refusal of many liberal democracies to hire married women (and the wholesale firing of many married women) from public sector jobs in order to provide employment to the wave of men recently demobilized from military service.

A much more insidious form of perpetuated inequality, according to more recent feminist theory, rests in the political values and beliefs upon which the premises of universality and neutrality are based. Why, ask contemporary feminists, is it the case that women are so highly represented amongst the poor, the unemployed, and the underemployed even within states which pride themselves upon a lengthy history of political rights and responsiveness to voters? If democracy is based upon the principle of majority rule, then why do women – who almost always constitute a slim majority over men – hold less political power and fewer economic resources as a statistical grouping? The answer many feminists give is that the values upon which liberal political ideals are based are essentially male values, despite their claim to universality. The classical liberal construct of autonomy, Okin points out, rests upon 'the often unstated assumption of women's unpaid reproductive and domestic work, their dependence and subordination within the family, and their exclusion from most spheres of life' (*ibid.*: 41). The theories of individual autonomy are more persuasive, she notes, if you accept Hobbes' imagery of people popping out of the earth like mushrooms rather than living lives determined by the needs of dependent children.

The problem, argue many theorists, rests not with liberal democratic states as much as it does with liberal democratic theory: men and women have different experiences, conceptions, and values; and a theory based upon the false assumption of similarities and universalism will necessarily fail to address the needs or realities of every individual. 'What is needed', argues Mendus, is a way of conceptualizing difference which renders it compatible with equality, but also, and crucially, does not simply increase social differentiation. Yet more radically, what is needed is a recognition that in much traditional democratic theory the concepts of equality, difference, and disadvantage are themselves gender-based: they assume a standard of normality which is inherently male (1992: 215).

This emphasis upon 'difference' as a forceful challenge to the assumptions of universality also informs many of the objections to liberal democracy posed by cultural minorities and theorists from non-liberal states, and will be examined in more detail below. But a sharper focus upon the specific claims made by feminist theorists here are quite instructive: why is it that the theoretical assumptions underlying liberal democracy are, according to many feminists, necessarily biased (and, for feminists, inherently male)?

Young (1989) points to the historical development of the modern western state, and argues that the universal values and norms espoused by liberalism were 'derived from specifically masculine experience: militaristic norms of honour and homo-erotic camaraderie; respectful competition and bargaining among independent agents; discourse framed in unemotional tones of dispassionate reason' (Young 1989: 253). From the conception of the public sphere as a realm of 'manly virtue' and 'citizenship as independence, generality, and dispassionate reason', women were naturally seen as generally unfit to participate in this realm because of their immediate concerns with the private sphere, as well as because of their evident lack of 'the dispassionate rationality and independence required of good citizens' (ibid.: 254). But why is it that intelligent and educated liberals believed that it was women's nature, and not the institutions structuring it, which was responsible for the position of women vis-à-vis men in the liberal polity? The reply to this question can best be understood by examining the third component of the feminist critique of neutrality: the argument that knowledge itself is socially constructed, and thus vulnerable to whatever powerful political ideologies inform it.

One line of feminist argument asserts that 'true knowledge', (as Mary Daly, for example holds), 'is intuitive and/or female, and that rationality is a mere ideological weapon which men have used effectively against women' (Grant 1987, 100). The argument that women are, by nature, simply not as rational as men seems rather self-defeating for feminists but is, nonetheless, still prevalent. In such an account even the laws of logic are oppressive: Ginzberg (1989), for example, argues that the logical construction of *modus ponens* (if P, then Q; P; therefore Q) was a 'male patriarchal creation oppressive of women'. Nussbaum, in her discussion of Ginzberg, explains that '[t]he argument seemed to be that *modus ponens* is a male-invented way of defining who counts as a rational being, and that women very often (more often, it is suggested, than men) fail to recognize modus ponens as a valid form of inference' (1994: 59). But a much more powerful criticism of rationality has been made by those arguing that 'scientific rationality', as a criteria for distinguishing truth from falsity, is itself merely a social construction and thus susceptible to normative influence. The claim that science, commonly believed to be the best example of neutral and objective knowledge, is influenced very significantly by unsubstantiated beliefs and assumptions was articulated in a clear and forceful work by Thomas Kuhn in 1970. Building upon the central argument of Kuhn's book, feminist epistemologists began examining the ways in which scientific rationality, despite its reputation as an unbiased means of discovering truth, could nonetheless perpetuate assumptions that privileged men over women.

Again, at least two different claims are made here: first, that scientists as individuals are human beings and thus susceptible to deeply-entrenched and unexamined social norms; and second, that science, as a discipline, is 'social' insofar as 'the rules or norms of justification that distinguish knowledge (or justified hypothesis-acceptance) from opinion must operate at the level of social as opposed to individual cognitive processes' (Longino 1992: 201). There are, notes Longino, two distinct meanings of scientific objectivity: first, that '[s]cientific theories provide a veridical representation of the entities and processes to be found in the world and their relations with each other' (truth via correspondence with observation) and second, that '[s]cientific inquiry involves reliance on non-arbitrary and nonsubjective (or nonidiosyncratic) criteria for accepting and rejecting hypotheses' (truth via appropriate patterns of inference). Both forms of truth-finding are contextual: 'evidential relations', argues Longino, 'are not autonomous or external truths but are constituted by the context of background assumptions in which evidence is assessed . . . Background assumptions are the vehicles by which social values and ideology are expressed in inquiry and become subtly inscribed in theories, hypotheses, and models defining research programs' (*ibid.*: 204). The criteria for determining what constitutes truth in science depends at least partly upon human judgement and is thus fallible; and even observational evidence of truth is subject to human interpretation, as observational data 'do not consist in reports of any old observations, but in observation reports ordered and organized. This ordering rests on a consensus as to the centrality of certain categories, the boundaries of concepts and classes, the ontological and organizational commitments of a model or theory, etc' (*ibid.*: 206).

The observation that the practice of science is to an extent a social construction has led some feminists to more radical conclusions than others. Sandra Harding, for example, insists that because all of natural science 'is located inside social history', the natural sciences are therefore 'usefully conceptualized as a subfield of social research' (1992: 576, 575). Other feminists take a more measured view and dismiss the claim that sciences such as physics are inferior to fields of research such as sociology: Susan Haack, amongst others, objects that the argument that all sciences (and practices grounded in scientific legitimacy) are oppressive to women because examples can be provided where accounts of science (or practices based upon scientific legitimacy) have been used against women is to commit a particularly self-defeating kind of *non sequitur* (Haack 1996).

Debate remains intense between feminists who claim that 'science' or 'rationality' is inherently male, or implicitly socially-determined, and those who maintain that the methods employed by 'science' are indeed neutral regardless of the fact that the window-dressing of scientific discourse has been used for nefarious political purposes. Nonetheless feminist theory, and especially feminist epistemology, has overall been very successful (especially within the social sciences) in shaking the placid assumption that the 'scientific method' will necessarily provide a closer insight into 'the truth'. This debate surrounding the neutrality of both philosophical liberalism and scientific rationality has also been utilized increasingly within the debate over the role of cultural allegiances in a world in which liberal principles seem to have gained an unprecedented level of rhetorical force.

Postcolonialism and the concerns of cultural minorities

Like feminism, postcolonialism views the assumptions of neutrality (both political and epistemological) within liberalism as inherently biased. The claim of objectivity is used to enhance the influence of those already possessing the power in the relationship between colonizer and colonized; and it is the superiority of liberal 'enlightenment' and scientific rigour over tribal superstition that, according to postcolonial theorists, keeps the colonized in a position of inferiority even after the establishment of formal autonomous statehood.

Postcolonialism, as a distinct and self-conscious school of thought emerged in the 1980s and has been influenced very clearly by claims developed by feminist and postmodern thinkers. But the substance of postcolonialism – the claim that objectivity is a political strategy of oppression – is a great deal older than that. At the height of Algeria's fight for independence from France, Franz Fanon wrote passionately about the dark oppressiveness of western enlightenment: 'Colonialism', he declared,

> is not satisfied merely with holding a people in its grip and emptying the native's brain of all form and content. By a kind of perverted logic, it turns to the past of the oppressed people, and distorts, disfigures, and destroys it . . . the total result looked for by colonial domination was indeed to convince the natives that colonialism came to lighten their darkness. The effect consciously sought by colonialism was to drive into natives' heads the idea that if the settlers were to leave, they would at once fall back into barbarism, degradation, and bestiality. (1991: 210–11)

Thus liberation for colonized peoples was, for Fanon, to reject the 'tiresome reasoning', 'oppressive logic', 'stiffness' and 'scepticism' imparted by the colonial masters in favour of the 'lyricism', 'frankness', 'liveliness', and 'irresponsibility' of the 'poets of negritude' (ibid.: 213).

The objective of most contemporary postcolonial thought is generally more moderate. Its proponents seek not political liberation as much as an epistemological respect for a diverse array of understanding for what is real and what is valuable; they desire not always to be judged solely by the standards of rationality and logic but by their own criteria of comprehension. The goal of postcolonialism, writes Gyan Prakesh, is 'to force a radical re-thinking and re-formulation of forms of knowledge and social identities authored and authorized by colonialism and western domination' (1992: 8). But postcolonialism, even more so than feminism or postmodernism *per se*, has been received sceptically by many social scientists. '[T]he popularity that the term postcolonial has achieved in the last few years', argues Arif Dirlik, 'has less to do with its rigorousness as a concept or with the new vistas it has opened up for critical inquiry than it does with the increased visibility of academic intellectuals of Third World origin as pacesetters in cultural criticism' (1994: 329).

The claim that scientific objectivity and liberal neutrality are indeed far from unbiased has achieved its intellectual bite not through the school of postcolonial thought but rather from western theorists schooled within a tradition of liberal thought (and the postmodern reaction to it) who have become increasingly concerned with the condition of cultural minorities within liberal societies. This school, whose emphasis is upon 'the politics of difference', critiques the assumption of universality upon which, they assert, liberalism is grounded; and argues that such an emphasis upon universality rather than a particularity devalues and disadvantages groups whose characteristics (based upon race, gender, ability, language or religion) deviate from the norm upon which assumptions of universality are based.

The most thoughtful and articulate account of the way in which the universal ideals of liberal democracy can further marginalize disadvantaged groups is perhaps that which has been presented by Iris Marion Young. She argues that,

> where differences in capacities, culture, values, and behavioural styles exist among groups, but some of these groups are privileged, strict adherence to a principle of equal treatment tends to perpetuate oppression or disadvantage. The inclusion and participation of everyone in social and political institutions therefore sometimes requires the articulation of special rights that attend to group differences in order to undermine oppression and disadvantage. (Young 1989: 251)

Starting from Derrida's critique of the 'metaphysics of presence', Young argues that the ideal of impartiality upon which liberal justice is grounded produces a 'logic of identity that seeks to reduce differences to unity' (1990: 97). This homogenization of identity assumes an impartial point of view 'that any and all rational subjects can adopt, precisely by abstracting from the situational particularities that individualize them' (1990: 101). But, as other theorists have pointed out (e.g., Sandel 1982: 179), this ideal of impartiality divorced from any social context distorts what is important about an individual. By assuming that the values and traits of the dominant political and social group are universal and neutral, the myth of impartiality oppresses groups outside this charmed circle of privilege:

> The standpoint of the privileged, their particular experience and standards, is constructed as normal and neutral. If some groups' experience differs from the neutral experience, or they do not measure up to those standards, their difference is constructed as deviance and inferiority. Not only are the experience and values of the oppressed thereby ignored and silenced, but they become disadvantaged by their situated identities. (1990: 116)

While the blatant racial and gender biases of previous generations have to a large extent been addressed through laws that disallow discrimination due to such characteristics as race, gender, age, or disability, argues Young, marginalization continues at a more subtle level: 'Our society enacts the oppression of cultural imperialism to a large degree through feelings and reactions, and in that respect oppression is beyond the reach of law and policy to remedy' (1990: 124). Thus, in order to mitigate the perpetuation of 'conscious acceptance but unconscious aversion', a democratic polity must avoid assimilationist ideologies that allow different groups to participate in social structures only 'after the rules and standards have already been set', thereby requiring individuals within these groups to prove themselves according to specific rules and standards that may be foreign or uncomfortable to them (Young 1990: 164). Simply to expect that a liberal-rights regime will correct such disadvantages is naive and wrongheaded because, as legal theorist Martha Minow argues, 'to treat existing arrangements and assumptions as the baseline for rights is to consign persons to an often unfair and prejudicial status quo' (Minow 1990: 382).

The solution, according to Young, is not a strategy of assimilation but rather one that 'asserts the positivity of group difference. ' The politics of 'group assertion' allows such groups to 'discover and reinforce the positivity of their specific experience' (Young 1990: 166, 167), and requires institutional mechanisms that include the self-organization of group members, group analysis and generation of the public policy proposals and, most controversially, group veto power on policies that directly affect a group (Young 1990: 184).

Young addresses a clear political problem that continues to vex self-styled democratic and tolerant polities: the realization that, despite formal recognition of the 'equality' of all groups, many of them remain marginalized socially, politically, and economically. But it is less clear precisely how such marginalization occurs, and how membership in an identifiable group with exclusive political rights can ameliorate this political disenfranchisement. The clue that serves as a possible answer is Young's claim that 'attachment to specific traditions, practices, language, and other culturally specific forms is a crucial aspect of social existence' (Young 1990: 163). But much remains unsaid in the assertion of the word 'crucial'; an adjective which must serve as the moral linchpin for the normative demands of such groups that they be recognized by virtue of their specific identity. Is the claim a modern naturalistic fallacy in which the sociological reality of the 'is' somehow is transformed into a philosophical 'ought'? Or is there a convincing account of why it is that cultural identity possesses a commanding normative force in the establishment of non-universal political rights?

Identity as a primary good

The critique of 'neutrality' as a cornerstone of liberal democracy that has been articulated from many disparate sources is, as we have seen, actually a complex argument with several different layers or facets which are frequently undifferentiated from each other. There is, first, the epistemological argument that asserts that reality is a social construction, and that therefore no convincingly objective account of it can be presented. A second, and slightly different, objection to neutrality is that specific values and norms are, by virtue of being values and norms, inherently incapable of being neutral. Yet such values – the liberal norms – are often held to be neutral, and any deviation from such norms is deemed erroneous, unacceptable, or simply inferior. And, because certain groups often hold such 'inferior' values or standards because of tradition or physiology, the claim that mainstream values are neutral values is seen to be a way of keeping marginalized groups out of the political mainstream. This is the objection to neutrality based upon an account of political power. The third dimension of the critique of neutrality is the psychological argument which holds the liberal assumption that individuals are 'blank slates' who can arbitrarily choose their own values is both wrong and harmful. People require meaning in their lives; and this meaning is imparted to them through their cultural context well before they reach the age where they can think in a rigorously analytical manner. It is this third component of the critique of neutrality upon which the drive to expand the meaning of democracy is largely based; and it is, as I shall argue in the following chapter, also the weakest argument.

Culture and meaning: 'no man is an island'

The ubiquitous emphasis upon 'culture' in the drive to expand democracy is based, first, upon a quest for meaning within a liberal framework and, second, on the declaration that each citizen's framework of meaning ought to be granted an equal respect. One of the starkest accounts of the need for 'meaning' in human life was written by a Jewish concentration camp survivor, who observed that those most likely to survive the gruelling experience were those who felt themselves imbued with a clear purpose:

> any attempt to restore a man's inner strength in the camp had first to succeed in showing him some future goal . . . Whenever there was opportunity for it, one had to give them a why – an aim – for their lives, in order to strengthen them to bear the terrible how of their existence. Woe to him who saw no more sense in his life, no aim, no purpose, and therefore no point in carrying on. He was soon lost. (Frankl 1985 [1959]: 97–8).

It would be simple to argue, as many postmodernists do, that the contemporary focus upon culture in liberal societies is a reaction to Enlightenment thought, which stressed rationalism in political thought to the exclusion of tradition and culture. But this assertion would give a distorted picture of the development of liberal thought. Indeed, many of the arguments for the preservation of language, religion, and cultural heritage were articulated quite powerfully over two hundred years ago as part of the German Enlightenment: for, while political theorists sometimes fall into the habit of assuming that the English (and Scottish) Enlightenments are the sole source for modern political thought, various European regions developed their own responses to the growth of scientific thought and the development of commerce.

Johann Herder, a major figure of the German Enlightenment, is particularly intriguing in his attempt to reconcile a 'liberal' political reform with the preservation of particular language and cultural traditions. Herder, writing during the second half of the eighteenth century, focused his criticism upon 'the hereditary system of political rule, the nobility, the institution of serfdom, despotism and political censorship, and all forms of arbitrariness in the ordering of political life' (Barnard 1965: 139). Self-determination was the only form of political rule that respected the dignity of the human spirit; yet, he argued, political self-determination was not based upon pure rational calculation of self-interest, but on a respect for a culture's particular heritage. The protection of language, religion, and tradition were thus essentially political because they were the only means of achieving a stable form of political autonomy: like Rousseau, Herder argued that people's freedom was found in the voluntary and uncoerced observation of laws. Likewise, 'nations were only free when they were obeying laws that were inherent in their historical traditions'. When the legal entity of the state was one and the same as the ethnic community, coercive sanctions would be unnecessary 'because the laws would be an expression of a people's social consciousness' (ibid.: 143). In comparison to many modern proponents of 'culture', both liberal and communitarian, Herder was careful to articulate very clearly why it was that language was the key facet of culture that had to be both nourished and preserved. Language, Herder thought,

> is the medium through which man becomes conscious of his inner self, and at the same time it is the key to the understanding of his outer relationships. It unites him with, but it also differentiates him from, others. Imperceptibly it also links him with the past by revealing to him the thoughts, feelings and prejudices of his past generations, which then become deeply ingrained in his own consciousness. He, in turn, again by means of language, perpetuates and enriches these for the benefit of posterity. In this way language embodies the living manifestation of historical growth and the psychological matrix in which man's awareness of his distinctive social heritage is aroused and deepened. (ibid.: 57).

There are, of course, contemporary theorists who do conceive of human beings as being 'constituted by language': Jürgen Habermas, for example, places discussion between human agents at the centre of his Theory of Communicative Action (1983). Yet Habermas does so in an attempt to construct a 'rational' framework for consensus; issues of 'culture' as non-rational values and traditions do not play such a prominent role as they do in Herder's account.

Charles Taylor, in contrast, attempts to provide a much richer account of the way in which human identity is constituted through language and in the diverse array of social 'narratives' that are comprised of the interwoven threads of particular traditions and beliefs concerning what gives value to human existence. One is a 'self', writes Taylor, 'only among other selves. A self can never be described without reference to those who surround it' (Taylor 1989: 35). To be surrounded by a 'web of interlocution' which involves stories by those around one concerning what is important, and why it is so, is what defines one's identity: 'that is why we naturally tend to talk of our fundamental orientation in terms of who we are. To lose this orientation, or not to have found it, is not to know who one is. And this orientation, once attained, defines where you answer from, hence your identity' (ibid.: 29). Political systems which attempt to base moral systems solely upon self-referential structures of individualism simply cannot act as the basis of either meaning or identity; for, in such a system, 'nothing would count as fulfillment in a world in which literally nothing was important but self-fulfillment' (ibid.: 507).

Taylor's aim here is, ultimately, to argue against any over-simplification in determining the moral guidelines, or the lack of such moral codes, upon which any political society ought to ground itself. And, at this level, it is simply good sense to say that, on balance, it is perhaps best to have a deeper understanding of why it is that we hold what we do. But what political applications, beyond a Socratic appreciation of self-knowledge, can be distilled from his account? It is, as many others have argued, a recognition of the role that a rich, contextual account of identity plays in configuring a just theory of democracy. A detailed criticism of this argument – that cultural identity has a key role in such a theory of democracy – will be presented in the following chapter.

Identity as a political right

To the extent that individuals require a sense of meaning that is shaped by a participation that is not the product of personal choice within a cultural community, culture (as the fundamental component of identity) is seen as worthy of protection through the designation of a specific 'right'. Exponents of rights to the cultural contexts which inform individuals' identities argue that we cannot merely assume the existence of common bonds between people which act as a background armature upon which liberal processes and institutions can be built. We must explicitly recognize that cultural identities are essential in the development of relatively autonomous individuals who can act with confidence and direction in living their lives in a way which they find satisfying and coherent, because there are times and places where individuals are not able to enjoy the benefit of a strong cultural heritage. It is for this reason that specific groups embracing values and customs distinct from those of the mainstream ought, if they seem as a group to do poorly within a liberal framework, to be able to impose claims upon the larger group to rights (i.e., rights to the exclusion from certain laws to which all others are subject, or to resources needed to sustain the smaller communities in question) that will allow them to retain a vibrant form of the group's culture which embodies and determines the identity of the individuals within it.

Group rights, argues Kymlicka (1996: 24, 25), cannot simply be assumed to contradict individual rights: they can, in many case, supplement and strengthen them. Far from limiting basic civil and political rights, he writes, 'they help to protect the context within which those rights have their meaning and efficacy', especially in cases where minority members who have citizenship rights in the mainstream society are 'politically impotent and culturally marginalized'. Contrary to liberal thought commonly conceived, oppression can easily occur even when individuals are granted the full range of liberal rights and liberties: 'the identification of oppression', then, requires 'sensitivity to the specific context' of the relationship between liberal societies and minority groups.

The common understanding of contemporary democracy is, arguably, very much a liberal democracy. It is based on the premise that all individuals are to be respected equally, and that each person's account of 'the good' must be respected within the parameters of neutral processes and institutions. One of the most forceful calls for the expansion of democracy beyond this account is the argument that a system of differential, rather than universal, rights are required to protect the formative context within which individuals can find comprehension and meaning. Some have argued that such identity rights can properly be termed individual rights:

> It is individuals who profit or suffer from the group's image, and it is their personal suffering and the prospects of improving their individual well-being that motivate policies of affirmative action. Hence, policies granting representation to groups, or arguing that various groups should be proportionately represented in all public positions, are not motivated by concern for the welfare of the group, but by concern for its individual members. (Tamir 1993: 42–8)

But Tamir's efforts to reconcile the elements of liberal individualism with the resonance of meaning offered by identity groups lacks logical coherence: 'individuals should not be seen as encumbered by duties imposed upon them by their history and their fate', she argues, 'but as free to adhere to cultures and religions of their choice' (*ibid.*: 39). But if we were in fact all free to select meaningful affiliations at will, then one of the strongest arguments for group rights – that the social devaluation of marginal groups' traditions is devastating because individuals *cannot* choose their formative cultural contexts, and are therefore destined to remain forever trapped by a devalued context of meaning – is effectively undermined.

The argument for group rights is as powerful as it is because of the assumption that we are not in fact all free to choose at will the groups which may impart the most compelling aspects of our identity. Kymlicka argues very forcefully that special rights are due certain groups because they have no choice in determining whether they will belong to a popular, powerful cultural group or one whose culture has little or no social cachet:

> While these group-differentiated rights for national minorities may seem discriminatory at first glance, since they allocate rights and political powers differentially on the basis of group membership, they are in fact consistent with liberal principles of equality. They are indeed required by the view, defended by Rawls and Dworkin, that justice requires removing or compensating for undeserved or 'morally arbitrary' disadvantages, particularly if these are 'profound and pervasive and present from birth'. (Kymlicka 1995: 126)

The identity groups to which Tamir refers may, by the same token, not want all comers to claim membership in their group at will. Like an exclusive club, the very distinctiveness of a group may well depend upon its ability to restrict membership. The Kahnawake Mohawk band in Quebec, for example, chose to evict from the reserve 143 band members who did not have a lineage of pure blood going back several generations, in order to protect what it called the 'genetic quality' of the community (*Toronto Globe and Mail*, 17 March 1994, A1).

While the arguments in favour of expanding democracy to encompass differential rights as well as (and often prior to) universal rights are diverse and contain a number of different premises, there are a number of similarities between them. Both Kymlicka and Charles Taylor, for example, begin from the assumption that a sense of being part of a clearly defined, respected cultural grouping is required to have a strong feeling of personal identity, and that the cultural group to which one belongs is not usually a matter of choice. Taylor builds his argument for the recognition of people's particularities upon the principles of equality and dignity, both cornerstones of liberal thought. To be an equal member of any society, not only must we have equal rights, but our identities must be given equal value. And, as our ethnic background informs these identities, our cultural heritages cannot be ignored or scorned without damaging our sense of personal dignity:

> the demands of multiculturalism build on the already established principles of the politics of equal respect. If withholding the presumption is tantamount to a denial of equality, and if important consequences flow for people's identity from the absence of recognition, then a case can be made for insisting on the universalization of the presumption as a logical extension of the politics of dignity. Just as all must have equal civil rights, and equal voting rights, regardless of race or culture, so all should enjoy the presumption that their traditional culture has value. (Taylor 1992: 68)

Like Young, Taylor argues that identity is an important focus for liberals because severe inequalities can be perpetuated and reinforced even where universal political rights exist; this is because 'dominant groups tend to entrench their hegemony by inculcating an image of inferiority in the subjugated' (*ibid.*: 66). To address this almost invisible relationship of power it is necessary to acknowledge the equal worth of different cultures; and such recognition may well involve differential rights for different groups.

Will Kymlicka's argument is based upon the premise that 'it's only through having a rich and secure cultural structure that people can become aware, in a vivid way, of the options available to them, and intelligently examine their value': 'cultural membership is important in pursuing our essential interest in leading a good life, and so consideration of that membership is an important part of having equal consideration for the interests of each member of the community' (Kymlicka 1989: 165). Unlike Young, who holds that belonging to certain groups beyond those defined culturally (for example, gender identification) is an important aspect of personal identity, Kymlicka argues that 'membership in a culture is qualitatively different from membership in other associations, since our language and culture provide the context within which we make our choices' (Kymlicka 1994: 25). Community (group) rights are thus clearly distinct from affirmative action policies, as the latter attempt better to integrate individuals into mainstream culture, and exist only so long as integration is notably incomplete. The former, in contrast, attempt to preserve distinct spheres within which minority cultures can be protected and will not, unlike affirmative action rights, dissolve at some undetermined point in the future when they are required no longer. Such differential rights are justified because members of minority cultures are systematically disadvantaged within the 'cultural marketplace'. This form of disadvantage is especially pernicious precisely because loss of cultural membership 'is a profound harm that reduces one's very ability to make meaningful choices' (*ibid.*: 25).

Kymlicka carefully distinguishes the different groups and types of claims involved in discussions of 'collective rights': national minorities differ from ethnic groups, which differ again from social movements; and a group's claim to exercise 'internal restrictions' against its own members is quite distinct from the demand for 'external protections' against the larger community (Kymlicka 1995). By limiting collective rights (as claims for external protection) to national minorities, argues Kymlicka, the demands for differential rights for certain identifiable groups can be reconciled with liberal democratic principles because 'the liberal value of freedom of choice has certain cultural preconditions', and thus 'issues of cultural membership must be incorporated into liberal principles' (*ibid.*: 76).

The controversial claim in this attempt to expand democracy to include group rights based upon identity is that some individuals, by virtue of a particular group affiliation, have rights that others do not and cannot have. The justice of these differential rights depends upon more than one distinct argument: for example, as Kymlicka himself points out, the claim that special rights are a result of historical agreements is quite distinct from the argument that equality demands special recognition for, or protection of, minority cultures (Kymlicka 1994: 24–5). But it is the argument that identity is such a profound and vital quality that it trumps universal human rights which is the most forceful and popular account in much contemporary political thought, and it is the coherence and persuasiveness of this account which shall be the focus of the following chapter.

4

Can there be non-liberal democracy?

Cuius regio, eius religio [whose territory, their religion] was a rotten idea in 1555, compared with universal religious toleration; and its successor is no better.
(Brian Barry 1995: 4)

What is a 'non-liberal' democracy?

The globalization of democracy involves a particularly vexing paradox. The moral attractiveness of democracy has been recognized by either governing administrations or their opponents within every state; but there is much less widespread enthusiasm for the liberal principles of individualism and universal human rights that, in western states, underpins the practice of democracy. How, then, can democracy serve as the new global measure of political legitimacy if the liberal ideals upon which it is based are viewed as both foreign and oppressive to so many? The obvious answer is that democracy, as a principle of self-rule, can be expanded to include collective self-determination as a justificatory principle as well as that of individual autonomy.

Or can it? If it is to be accepted that democracy can say nothing about the way that individuals are treated within communities, as long as the communities themselves exercise collective autonomy, then what, if anything, distinguishes 'democracy' from 'national self-determination' *per se*? This chapter responds to the arguments presented in the previous chapter, and contends that democracy cannot be divorced from some of the putatively 'liberal' principles from which it grew. This, however, should not unduly alarm those concerned that the acceptance of such principles means that each unique and distinctive culture would either be sucked into an abyss of empty materialistic uniformity, or subject to the imperialist whims of large capitalist states. Many of the critics of liberal democracy have presented scathing accounts of liberalism based upon rather selective interpretations or even misleading presentations of what that term means. Liberalism, as some contemporary theorists have persuasively argued, is a concept of such wide interpretation that little is to be gained through debates over what liberalism 'really' is (see, e.g., Barry 1995). What is important for any account of democracy to keep, regardless of whether one wishes to label it 'liberal', is an account of relative neutrality between competing parties in order to mitigate the degree of power maintained by some interests over others. The exercise of cultural traditions, no less than the definition of a specific 'culture' itself, are potentially very potent manifestations of political power.

Over thirty years ago, C. B. Macpherson stated that 'democracy is not properly to be equated with our unique Western liberal-democracy' alone, and argued that 'the clearly non-liberal systems which prevail in the Soviet countries, and the somewhat different non-liberal systems of most of the underdeveloped countries of Asia and Africa, have a genuine historical claim to the title democracy' (1965: 3). Given that this argument was articulated at the height of the Cold War, Macpherson's assertion was not particularly well received. Yet much of what he said seems to have anticipated the contemporary debates regarding the true nature of democracy and, while his account of the 'communist variant' of democracy has been completely dismissed, his argument for the 'underdeveloped' conceptualization of democracy has become more powerful than ever. Why has this divergence occured?

When Marx used democracy to refer to the dictatorship of the proletariat, Macpherson suggests, he was in fact utilizing a fairly precise understanding of the term as the liberation of the working class from capitalist institutions through winning political power: 'Its rule would be democratic because it would ccomprise the great majority of the population, and because its purpose would be the humanitization of the whole people' (1965: 15). Even a 'vanguard' state run by an elite could be considered democratic insofar as the people, freed from an oppressive existence, 'will freely support the kind of society that the vanguard state has brought into being' (ibid.: 20). Thus a

communist form of government can be called democratic to the
extent that it is based upon an ideal of human equality, 'not just
equality of opportunity to climb a class ladder, but such an
equality as could only be fully realized in a society where no
class was able to dominate or live at the expense of others' (*ibid*.:
22). But this model of democracy is rightly given little, if any,
credibility by contemporary democratic theorists (e.g., Held
1987: 263); and the reason it is dismissed is because there is good
reason to believe those who hold a concentrated degree of power
within a state will do their best to redefine their society's interests (such as 'freedom from oppression') in order to retain their
power. How, then, does Macpherson's 'underdeveloped' model
differ substantively from his discredited 'communist' variant,
given that both reject individual rights and freedoms as the
fundamental starting-point for democracy?

As with current non-liberal claims to democracy, Macpherson's model begins with the observation that 'the soil in which
liberal ideas and the liberal state flourish' is 'not natural' to
non-western, non-industrialised societies; but 'something
imposed on them from outside and from above' (Macpherson
1965: 24):

> Their traditional culture was generally not attuned to competition.
> They generally saw no intrinsic value in wealth-getting and gave no
> respect to the motive of individual gain. Equality and community,
> equality within a community, were traditionally rated more highly
> than individual freedom (*ibid*.: 25).

Drawing on Rousseau's depiction of democracy not as an
amalgamation of individual interests but as the collective
determination of what was best for the society as a whole,
Macpherson argued that the claim of many non-liberal developing states for democratic credentials 'rests largely on the
proposition that there is in these countries a general will' which
would clearly be undermined by a political system based upon
the preeminence of individual interests (*ibid*.: 24). To call such
a non-liberal system democratic, he writes, 'is to make the
criterion of democracy the achievement of ends which the mass
of people share and which they put ahead of separate individual
ends' (*ibid*.: 29). The classic formulation of democracy, he adds,
was Rousseau's argument that political obligation can only be
incurred by those who author a law, and that such laws ought
to be articulated after considering the proper interests of the
society as a whole. The moral worth of every member of society

is respected, but it is respected according to the moral framework of that society rather than by the strictures of liberal individualism. And, as traditional non-liberal societies increasingly face the overwhelming influence of technologically advanced liberal states, they depend more than ever upon cultural solidarity to resist such a forceful but foreign set of norms and systems: what they require, argues Macpherson, is 'the dictatorship of a general will (or of a vanguard in the name of the general will) over an undifferentiated people' (*ibid.*: 31). The ideal of liberal-democracy, concluded Macpherson, 'is consumers' sovereignty – we buy what we want with our votes. ' To become an autonomous state, a traditional non-liberal society cannot adopt liberal-individualist norms without losing its distinctiveness as a society. To be democratic within this non-liberal context, then, means 'to be moving towards a firmly-held goal of an equal society in which everybody can be fully human' (*ibid.*: 33).

What distinguishes this account from the now-discredited communist variant? It is the assumption of the worth a culturally-distinct community. We now dismiss the assertion that those 'oppressed by capitalism' comprise an identifiable group who can rightfully join ranks to shake off the capitalist chains of their oppression. But there is currently much more sympathy for the view that, where 'class' does not serve as legitimate reason to oppose the individualizing force of liberal democracy, 'culture' does. The class-based account of democracy Macpherson presents is roundly condemned for offering an account of 'freedom' or 'dignity' or 'meaningfulness' which in practice justified quite reprehensible atrocities that, for liberal individualists, seemed morally atrocious and politically illegitimate. The argument in this chapter is that 'culture' and 'identity' are the concepts which prevent exponents of democracy from seeing the relevant similarities between the discredited communist version of democracy and the contemporary communitarian account of democracy. Cultural identity plays an enormous justificatory role in these accounts. But if non-liberal accounts of democracy based upon cultural identity cannot withstand vigorous theoretical examination, then what remains of non-liberal democracy is little different from what Macpherson attempted to justify as class-based accounts of non-liberal democracy. Can 'cultural identity' withstand these criticisms, and serve as the justificatory principle for a non-liberal democracy?

A non-liberal democracy, in essence, differs from a liberal democracy first in the assertion that the claims of neutrality, objectivity, and equality valued so deeply by liberal democrats are in practice means of marginalizing and devaluing non-dominant cultures. A non-liberal democracy, secondly, would recognize that the protection of individuals' interests is not always prior to those of the community and the traditions of the community. Even within liberal democracies this would mean, as Kymlicka writes, that 'the majority will sometimes be unable to prevent the violation of individual rights within the minority community. Liberals have to learn to live with this, just as they must live with illiberal laws in other countries' (1996: 28). And the reason that the minority non-liberal communities within liberal democracies, or the majority communities in non-liberal states, are right in doing so is to promote and protect the culture of the community. Without a clear culture to provide a context within which individuals can find meaning and self-value, individual rights are empty and pointless. Culture, according to this account, must therefore be prior to individual interests because it is culture which provides the environment that allows individuals to take advantage of such rights: 'The primary good of self respect requires that popular sovereignty is conceived as an intercultural dialogue. The various cultures of society need to be recognised in public institutions, histories and symbols in order to nourish mutual cultural awareness' (Tully 1995: 190).

The most thoughtful proponents of the 'cultural context' argument (Taylor, Young, Kymlicka, Tully) attempt to articulate various accounts of political relationships in which the dignity of individualism espoused by liberalism is preserved and nurtured within a political system that can 'mutually recognize and accommodate the cultures of all the citizens in an agreeable manner' (Tully 1995: 191). But this approach begs several very important questions: to what extent is the claim that culture is a prior good ultimately commensurable with the nurturance of 'free and fulfilled' individuals? Must democratic liberalism really lead, *tout court*, to an existence of stultifying uniformity and cultural imperialism (as Tully, amongst others, charges), or can a vision of diversity and respect of difference be achieved more convincingly within an unapologetically 'liberal' democracy? Is culture as important as such theorists claim, or is it merely a fashionable rhetorical assertion with little of substance to support the political force given to it by its proponents? And finally, does the reification of the value of culture into a set of inviolable political rights involve a political cost that its exponents are unwilling to recognize?

Rights to cultural identity

A nation, wrote Benedict Anderson, is an imagined political community. It is based upon collective understandings of a common past; tales of pride, victory, and compassion; laments of destruction and atrophy; and mutual anxiety concerning an uncertain future. These feelings are articulated through a common language; and it is through this language that 'pasts are restored, fellowships are imagined, and futures dreamed' (1983: 140). Cultural heritages are not static; they develop and change spontaneously and, as Anderson notes, they are occasionally crafted very deliberately by national elites for very specific political purposes. But it is, admittedly, remarkable that cultural attachments remain so tenacious in an era of ideologies which have claimed superiority based upon 'rational' or 'scientific' principles (see, e.g., Fukuyama 1992). How political scientists should understand this phenomenon, and the role that cultural attachments ought to play in modern political organizations, are amongst the most importunate of modern political debates. Yet 'cultural identity' is allowed to do too much normative work in much contemporary political thought: the claim that a stable and competent individual must be grounded in a 'secure cultural context' is, as it stands, too thin an argument upon which to ground very powerful political claims.

Defining culture

'Culture', writes Tully, 'is an irreducible and constitutive aspect of politics' (1995: 5); and it is such a fundamental component because it 'provides the context within which we make our choices' (Kymlicka 1994: 25). If culture plays such an enormous role, and must be seriously considered in the development of public policy, then it is reasonable that we should ask what, precisely, culture is. There is, as Haack has written, an increasingly wide subtext of meanings connected with the word 'culture'. It can refer to lifestyle choices (the 'high culture' of opera goers and merlot drinkers as opposed to the 'low culture' of beer drinking and football games); ethnic affiliation (Spanish culture or Slovak culture); or even the (generally unchosen) common traits of a small group (such as 'deaf culture' – see Sacks 1989). But it has also become a term used with specific political and epistemological connotations: of late, observes Haack, 'western culture' (which is anything related to the dominant grouping of contemporary North American society) is seen as being in an improper position of privilege *vis-à-vis* 'cultures of what are taken to be oppressed, marginalized, disadvantaged classes – classes identified in terms of color, sex, and sexual orientation'. The result of this is that 'the term "culture" has been extended far beyond anything its ordinary elasticity permits; for, so far from respecting the usual contrast of culture with nature, we are now to take "black" or "female" as designating cultures' (1995: 398).

Culture is commonly understood to be a shared set of collective values and customs which, as Herder argued, forms the basis of the way in which individuals communicate with each other. And, because destroying or devaluing the culture would destroy or devalue the individuals' sense of meaning and self worth (Taylor 1992), such cultures must be protected. But does such a claim regarding the role played by culture presuppose a degree of agreement and harmony that does not, in reality, exist? 'Two things', declares Brian Barry, 'can be said with confidence':

> One is that no contemporary society is really homogeneous. The other is that claims to derive conclusions from the allegedly shared values of one's society are always tendentious. It they were not, it would have to be regarded as a remarkable coincidence that the shared values a political philosopher says he has detected always happen to lead to conclusions that he already supports. (1995: 5)

There is, he concludes, 'no such thing as a set of underlying values waiting to be discovered'.

The definition of 'culture' as a meaningful context that must be preserved leads to its own philosophical difficulties, which I shall describe in the following section. But an equally intransigent political problem which arises in connection with the claim that any particular culture is defined by one set of norms and traditions rather than another is the question of who is to decide of which characteristics a given culture consists (or, more specifically, which aspects of that culture are so important that they ought to be protected politically). In modern Quebec, for example, laws which not only encourage the use of French but also prohibit the use of English (on signs, or in places of work) are justified because they are said to protect the French language, which forms the cultural context within which Quebeçois find meaning as individuals. Historically, however, the Catholic religion was as powerful as the French language in determining a distinct 'Quebec identity': separate educational institutions and social services were established in Quebec because they were directly run by the Church according to the Catholic faith in contrast to other areas of Canada, where such services were generally secular and state-run. Why, then, is the Catholic religion not protected as actively as the French language? If the preservation of the distinctive Quebeçois culture is important, then it is arguable that its citizens must be told to practice Catholicism as well as to speak French; and if the use of English can legally be limited, then why should the practice of non-Catholic religions not also be severely circumscribed? And if one argues that Quebeçois simply prefer to become increasingly secular, and thus religion should not be forced on them, then why penalize those in Quebec who simply prefer no longer to speak French? Again, if pervasive traditional customs must be preserved because they form the context of meaning for the individuals within these groups, then how is it that some essential traits – like religion – are consequently ignored while others – such as language – are actively enforced by the state?

Choices must be made regarding which traits are important, and which are not; and these political decisions are made by political agents. There is so often an assumption that certain culturally-distinct groups freely and equally agree as individuals on the specific aspects of their culture: Tully's argument, for example, depends very heavily upon the abstract and romanticized notion that the 'customs and ways of peoples are the manifestation of their free agreement' (1995: 125). But this account completely disregards the patterns of power within each of these communities. What justifies the assumption that a culture is the result of free and spontaneous interrelationships between each and every member of a community? The historian Eric Hobsbawm, in his survey of 'invented traditions' since the industrial revolution, notes that such revered customs were frequently constructed to establish or legitimize relations of status and authority; or to impose 'socialization, the inculcation of beliefs, value systems, and conventions of behaviour' (1983: 9).

Cultures can be modified, manipulated, and selectively enhanced by the more powerful interests in a society for very specific purposes; to assume that such relations of power do not exist is to exhibit a startling degree of disingenuity.

Ethnic culture and personal identity

This section examines the claim, presented in the previous chapter, and espoused most articulately by Will Kymlicka and Charles Taylor, that a 'secure cultural context' is a right necessary to protect and enhance the personal identity and sense of self-worth of cultural groups outside the dominant cultural context. But what is meant by a 'secure cultural context'? Culture, by its very nature, is (like a living language) continually fluctuating and metamorphizing; and except for a few potent symbols it rarely remains predictably constant over time. Cultures continually shift against and merge into each other. Given the ability of modern technology to collect and dissipate widely disparate ideas and practices, very few individuals within any cultural groups are clearly 'separate and distinct'; and few individuals within any cultural grouping are 'totally in' or 'totally outside' their cultural group. Modern linguistic minorities gradually adopt norms and practices and vocabularies both from the mainstream practices and from other minority groups. It is not clear when (or why) such changes make a cultural context 'insecure'. And, if security refers to a belief that cultural practices will remain constant and predictable over time then, as noted above, the very nature of a living culture, especially within a technologically advanced and socially heterogeneous society, has not been properly or realistically understood. And, by the same token, if culture is indeed an ineffable, overlapping, and shifting social phenomenon, then to what extent can concrete political rights to one certain aspect of that culture be defended?

Another objection to the political and philosophical currency given to culture as an essential aspect of individual identity is the way in which it is said to impart 'meaning'. A culture, writes Kymlicka, 'provides its members with meaningful ways of life across the full range of human activities' (1995: 76). Societal cultures define 'the range of socially meaningful options for their members' (ibid.: 79); it provides options and 'also makes them meaningful to us' (ibid.: 83), and such 'meaningful options depends on access to a social culture, and on understanding the history and language of that culture' (83). And so on. The reference to 'meaningfulness' occurs frequently and continually throughout Kymlicka's work (e.g., 1989: 172, 197; 1994: 25; 1995: 89, 90, 93, 101, 103, 105, 127; 1995: 89, 90, 93, 101, 103, 105, 127). 'Meaningfulness' plays a very fundamental role in his theory, and it is thus surprising that so little effort is made to unpack precisely how this term ought to be understood.

While one may be able to point to extreme cases and say that profound individual insecurity is endemic within a geographically identifiable group, one begs the questions of how one evaluates 'cultural insecurity' in less dramatic or politicised instances, and why the specific traits of cultural minorities ought to be enhanced in order to promote self-esteem. The latter concern is generally met with the argument that choices formed without the benefit of a 'secure' cultural context (however defined) are not 'meaningful' (however, again, defined). This answer, however, requires a clear explanation of what is meant by meaningful choices, and how they are to be distinguished from choices which are not meaningful. If a person decides, for example, to become a doctor simply because that is the family tradition (and, less nobly, in order to be able to purchase a wide selection of consumer goods), is this to be considered a 'meaningful' decision? What are the criteria of 'non-meaningful' choices? What if the individual making ostensibly superficial choices insists that these decisions are personally eminently meaningful? One might avoid these questions by replying that what is meaningful for different individuals simply varies from one situation to the next; but this makes the term too vague and subjective to do any real philosophical work. If one wishes to make the argument that a secure cultural context is essential for the formulation of meaningful choices, and that this condition justifies the establishment of rights granted to some but denied to others, then one must bear the onus of making the philosophical distinction between 'meaningful' and 'meaningless' personal choices.

The claim that culture imparts a fundamental sense of meaningfulness has become highly politicized and, in the process, has lost much of its philosophical coherence. For example, Kymlicka argues that membership in a minority culture, one which structures one's comprehension of one's value and choices, can be considered a 'morally arbitrary disadvantage' and, like other such arbitrary disadvantages which one must shoulder through no choice of one's own, this membership entitles the bearer to special rights or privileges (as, for example, handicapped individuals are seen to hold a just entitlement to special parking privileges denied to able-bodied individuals). But this argument cannot account for the repeated insistence by many others that the cultures of minority groups ought to be reconstituted where they have been irremediably erased. Menno Boldt, for example, amongst others argues strenuously that in cases where traditional Indian culture has been destroyed or absorbed into mainstream culture, it is important to 'revitalize, adapt, and develop their cultures for living and surviving in the modern world' (1993: xx). But if the argument for special cultural rights is that individuals are already contained within a moral horizon which they cannot replace without severe costs, then such differential rights cannot be granted to individuals who have never themselves lived within this cultural context (much as they might have liked to).

Politically, then, the argument that certain minority groups (such as aboriginal Indians in Canada) ought to have differential rights (such as access to traditional systems of justice) only makes sense in particular cases (within the isolated northern communities) where the fabric of traditional culture remains relatively intact. But this would mean that the similar ethnic groups (e.g., southern aboriginal communities) which have adopted mainstream customs and values could not claim equal treatment as the isolated communities by virtue of their ethnic identity. Where traditional languages are no longer widely spoken, and traditional values no longer widely held, the argument that individuals are disadvantaged by virtue of belonging to a minority culture is substantially weaker. An argument could well be made for special privileges – such as educational scholarships – due to, say, the egregiously cruel treatment that previous generations may have received and which is seen to affect the current generation. But this would only entitle the current generation to measures that would integrate them further into mainstream society; it would not self-evidently justify rights that would segregate them from the rest of the larger society.

Non-ethnic culture and personal identity

The issue of whether people do feel more secure within a clearly defined ethnic culture is separable from the issue of whether this phenomenon, if true, ought to impart certain rights for some (and corresponding obligations for others). Indeed (as I shall suggest in a following section) the tendency for people to feel more secure within a well-defined cultural context is as much a worrisome circumstance as a condition that ought to be protected.

Much of the political support for distinct cultures is based upon a philosophical trend that has increasingly focused upon 'personal identity'. But what is not being adequately discussed is the extent to which identities are frequently shaped by qualities and quirks that have nothing to do with an ethnic culture: why, then, ought these qualities to have any less normative force than ethnic traits? If, for example, one were born and raised in a collective of nonconformist anarchist poets, which sharply defined one's conception of who one was and what one's moral sensibilities were, why then ought not these values and characteristics to be as respected as racial or ethnic features? And what if, more vexingly, the values of this particular collective were somewhat socially obnoxious to others? To what extent ought they then to command respect? What group-rights advocates must show is that the cultural traits and values that one has by virtue of being born into a particular culture influence personal identity much more than would non-cultural characteristics (such as physical traits or sexuality) or group affiliations formed as a mature individual. This cannot simply be assumed.

I. M. Young attempts to address this criticism by arguing that the relevant norms and characteristics must be those of 'social groups, not interest groups or ideological groups' (1990: 186). But it is not clear that this differentiation can be sustained, as ideological values are often so closely connected to a social context in which a person develops and reinforces their identity: there may even be cases in which the only defining characteristic of a particular group is that their ideological values (such as anarchism) are clearly distinct. It is, moreover, not clear that our identities cease developing once we have reached adulthood. What if one, having reached a painful midlife crisis, decided to join the collective of socially maladept anarchist poets, whose social and moral belief systems give one a sense of moral order and give one's life a new meaning? If this social context now allows one to make decisions which one finds meaningful, then why should one not be able to demand that

individuals within the wider polity respect that group's ideological and social values by giving them specific general rights (to,
for example, 'group analysis and group generation of policy proposals in institutionalized contexts where decisionmakers are
obligated to show that their deliberations have taken group perspectives into consideration' (Young 1990: 184)?

If the normative force of cultural specificities rests in the fact
that they define a person's identity, then the same would be true
for the collective of anarchist poets into which one was born
and bred, or which one later joined to make one's life meaningful. If one is denied the value of one's formative context, then
one must be the victim of a social injustice. Kymlicka writes
that,

> cultural structure is crucial not just to the pursuit of our chosen
> ends, but also to the very sense that we are capable of pursuing them
> effectively . . . Cultural membership is not a means used in the
> pursuit of one's ends. It is rather the context within which we choose
> our ends, and come to see their value, and this is a precondition of
> self-respect, if the sense that one's ends are worth pursuing. And it
> affects our very sense of personal identity and capacity. (1989: 176,
> 192)

In what way is this argument not true for our middle-aged
member of the anarchist poets' collective? It would seem that if
one's social or formative context is important for the way in
which it makes sense of our world, then limiting groups with
special privileges to specific cultural groups is unjustifiably
arbitrary. Who ought to have the ability to determine which
traits or qualities define a person? Just as liberal theory assumes
that mature adults must always be the final arbiters of what is
in their best interest, so it must acknowledge that each individual is the best judge of which characteristics or schemas define
and shape their identities. To assert that one simply knows that
another person is defined predominantly by their culture or specific group traits rather than other factors seems as oppressive
as refusing to believe that cultural characteristics are important
at all.

Theorists such as Young, Taylor, Tully, and Kymlicka have in
their respective ways constructed forceful arguments for the
recognition of the crucial importance of cultural or group-spe-
cific contexts. The political implications of such arguments
have been the source of many painful debates about the relative
normative weight to be granted to individuals, *qua* individuals,

and to groups, *qua* specific cultural entities. (Some, for instance, might ask why a well-off person who belongs to a disadvantaged group ought to be given special privileges over a struggling individual who belongs to a traditionally advantaged group.) It is an indisputable virtue to be sensitive about the particularities that mark some individuals as different from others. This is the basis of the value that liberalism places upon tolerance and cosmopolitanism, something which is frequently forgotten in the current intellectual assertions that liberalism is a universalizing and homogenizing force. But the 'politics of difference' attempts to formalize this responsibility to be sensitive to others' differences. Young, for instance, writes that individuals are victims of 'oppression' if the qualities that define them (skin colour, language, gender, ability) are not valued, even if formal legal institutions exist which disallow discrimination on the basis of these attributes. What follows, argues Young, is that people and institutions 'can and should be held responsible for unconscious and unintended behaviour, actions, or attitudes that contribute to oppression' (1990: 151). But Young's definition of 'oppression' is too selective rather than, as some might argue, too encompassing. For if we have a right to protect these qualities which define our identities then, as I have suggested above, there are no good reasons to limit these traits to 'cultural' ones. And, given that it is almost impossible to be able to discern quickly which traits are particularly valuable to individuals as crucial elements of their identities, it seems unreasonable to put the onus of responsibility for recognizing such sensitivities upon 'people and institutions' writ large.

One person, for example, may be very sensitive about their thinness, and wistful comments by plump friends about their good fortune to be thin – comments meant with the most positive intentions – may be personally upsetting. Or a comment of 'my goodness, but your glasses are thick' that seems little more than a statement of empirical fact may be quite devastating to someone who is very sensitive about their failing eyesight. While sensitivity to people's feelings of self-identity is undeniably a desirable quality in such circumstances, it is difficult to expect people always to intuit which traits or characteristics are most fundamental to a person's identity, and even more formidable politically to institutionalize this responsibility to be sensitive. The very laudable objective of the 'politics of difference' is for the important differences that characterize individuals to be valued. But how is it always possible to emphasize the value of certain traits that emphatically define a person's identity? Can severe myopia, a characteristic that may shape what one can and cannot do, and how people view one, ever be presented as a valuable trait? Or is it more worthwhile to stress one's personal value despite this characteristic?

One may respond that specific characteristics ought only to act as the basis of special political recognition if such characteristics (such as race, gender, ability) are the reason for systematic political disadvantage and oppression. Let us assume that we have a number of very thin and exceptionally myopic individuals who are far less successful at finding good employment than perfectly sighted people of average weight. Statistically we find, too, that a thin, myopic person will be much less likely to have a good relationship, will earn less than the average national income, and so on. Moreover, such physical characteristics are the identity-traits of which most of these individuals are most conscious. Does this account of 'disadvantaged identity' then justify the establishment of permanent differential rights in place of standard universal rights or temporary affirmative action policies? The latter are useful tools for preventing discriminatory treatment or for promoting the status of a particular group. Why, then, are permanent identity-based group rights required?

The reply, again, would be that despite formal political equalities, certain characteristics held by a group are not sufficiently valued by those in positions of political, economic, or social influence. The former are 'disadvantaged' despite formal political equalities (or temporary affirmative action programmes) because the characteristics important to them are not equally valued by others. Because these characteristics are not valued, a sense of self-esteem is denied; and because a sense of self-esteem is denied an individual is placed at a disadvantage *vis-à-vis* more confident individuals. Rather than basing self-esteem upon characteristics of 'group difference', however, why not focus upon the disparate qualities that are distinct to each individual? Instead of deliberately constructing a new 'culture' that is to form the basis of a group identity, and thus self-esteem (as Menno Boldt argues), why not encourage and develop individuals' own particular abilities and talents and downplay the importance of cultural traits? Unless a clear and persuasive account of the formation of personal identity is presented to support the claim that cultural traits ought to be privileged over other sources of personal identity, the establishment of group rights based upon the need for a 'secure cultural context' cannot be philosophically justified.

The analogy with states

A very intriguing, and initially persuasive, argument that Kymlicka (and, to a certain extent, Tully) make in favour of the claim that group rights ought to be accepted as a reasonable aspect of contemporary democracy is what Kymlicka calls the 'analogy with states'. The existence of formal states, as well as the practice of officially regulating immigration into them raises, as he writes, 'a deep paradox for liberals':

> Most liberal theorists defend their theories in terms of 'equal respect for persons' and the 'equal rights of individuals'. This suggests that all 'persons' or 'individuals' have an equal right to enter a state, participate in its political life, and share in its natural resources. . . In fact, however, these rights are typically reserved for *citizens*. (Kymlicka 1995: 124)

If citizenship is indeed an 'inherently group-differentiated notion', then there is no way in which 'good liberals' could defend the existence of state boundaries and restrictions on immigration and at the same time deny the legitimacy of group rights based upon cultural identity.

This argument is rather ingenious but, when examined closely, loses its persuasiveness. In the first place, Kymlicka places much of the force of his overall argument on an 'if it exists, then it must be logically coherent' strategy: because we can find examples of sovereign states recognizing the autonomy of some cultural groups, liberalism can therefore theoretically accommodate group rights.

This, of course, is *prima facie* debatable: just because a practice is accepted does not in itself mean that it is logically congruent with stated principles. Slavery, for example, and the denial of political representation for women were practiced by 'liberal' states for centuries; yet it was the sustained argument that these practices did in fact constitute logical contradictions that led to their demise. To say then that 'group-differentiated rights have been a long-established part of the liberal tradition' and that 'such rights are *logically presupposed* by existing liberal practice' (*ibid.*: 124, emphasis added) may in fact simply mean that good liberals, being made aware of their existence, must put an end to them or risk being accused, as in the case of slavery, of hypocrisy.

But Kymlicka still has a better argument than this to make. 'What', he asks, 'can justify restricting the rights of citizenship to members of a particular group, rather than all persons who desire it?' The answer he supplies is that such restrictions are justified largely 'to protect people's cultural membership':

> Liberals implicitly assume that people are members of societal cultures, that these cultures provide the context for individual choice, and that one of the functions of having separate states is to recognize the fact that people belong to separate cultures (*ibid.*: 125).

But this line of reasoning is unsupportable. Many countries may well limit immigration to those 'who are like us' – and many liberal countries until relatively recently manifestly did – but this is a practice that will strike most liberals as grossly unfair. Except for a proficiency in the native language, which can be justified on the grounds of efficient accommodation (and on the grounds that anyone, with application, can learn to speak a different language), few contemporary liberals would accept the claim that their state ought to deny entrance to, say, blacks or orientals on the grounds that the 'cultural context' they wished to preserve was a white anglo-saxon culture. In fact, most liberals would no doubt reject such restrictions on the grounds that they are blatantly racist.

A business establishment such as a restaurant is quite justified in limiting the number of people who can enter its establishment at any one time (most fire regulations demand such regulations). What such establishments cannot do is to limit entrance to those of a certain race, and deny it to others. Likewise, social clubs are allowed to limit membership to a certain number, but they most certainly cannot limit membership on the basis of ethnicity by using the argument that 'their kind won't fit in' or that 'it will destroy our cultural homogeneity'. Liberal immigration policy works on a similar principle: while membership can justifiably be limited to prevent any and all individuals from claiming membership at will, it cannot rightfully limit membership on the basis of race. Kymlicka's argument that liberal theorists invariably limit citizenship 'to recognize and protect our membership in distinct cultures' is therefore clearly mistaken. Any self-professed liberal state which continues to limit immigration to certain ethnic groups and deny it to others could and ought to be accused of manifest racism in its immigration policy. Limiting numbers of potential immigrants of all nationalities and cultures is not at all evidence of attempting to protect a 'distinct culture'.

State sovereignty, in the modern sense, has existed for no more than four hundred years; and there is much current debate about the extent to which sovereignty still exits in any but a symbolic sense of the word. And, *pace* Kymlicka, just because it did exist in a strong sense for a period of time is no good philosophical justification for its continuation. Even such a 'good liberal' as John Rawls has recently written that state sovereignty is – and ought to be – restricted in its influence (1993a: 59).

The shape of global democracy, according to so many prominent theorists, is based upon the argument that group rights must take precedence over and form based upon principles of universality and neutrality. But to the extent that a key argument in support of this position is grounded upon the ideal of state sovereignty, it is an argument rooted in an eroding foundation.

Neutrality v. uniformity

'The long history of European-indigenous relations', writes Kymlicka, 'suggests that even if indigenous peoples have citizenship rights in the mainstream society, they tend to be politically impotent and culturally marginalized' (1996: 24). There is no lack of evidence on which to ground such a claim. But the question that this declaration begs is the rather important one of whether liberalism by its very nature must result in such an outcome and, if so, *why* that must be the case. What is the causal relationship that necessarily determines the oppression of marginalized groups under a system of putative neutrality?

As explained in the previous chapter, the argument that liberal democracy is not – and cannot *ever* be – neutral between competing demands is a principal claim which grounds the demand for non-liberal forms of democratic governance. Universal conditions for citizenship are oppressive because they are simply not neutral: they are based historically upon 'masculinist' notions of 'homoerotic camaraderie' (Young 1989) or upon specious assumptions that traits such as individualism and competition are valued by all cultures (Minow 1990):

To treat the candidates to admission [to citizenship] 'just like all the rest of us' is not to treat them justly at all. It is to treat them within the imperial conventions and institutions that have been constructed to exclude, dominate, assimilate or exterminate them, thereby ignoring the questions the politics of recognition raises concerning the universality of the guardians and the institutions they guard. (Tully 1995: 97)

This is a very provocative argument, and it has been quite passionately argued, as we have seen, by a number of contemporary theorists. But in addition to the objections to this noted above, there are two further quite fundamental problems with this account. The first is the assumption that, because minority groups have historically been badly treated by 'liberals' within a 'liberal' political system, they will always be treated badly by liberals within a liberal polity. The second problem, related to the first, is the selective account of liberalism that these theorists choose to adopt. Liberalism is, most philosophers agree, an extremely broad, occasionally contradictory, amalgamation of connotations and definitions: are they all, in every manifestation, an 'imposition of uniformity' that leads not to unity 'but to resistance, further repression and disunity'? (Tully 1995: 197)

The 'passes for' fallacy

The 'passes for' fallacy is a term used by philosopher Susan Haack in her critique of feminist epistemology: because racist and sexist claims have indeed 'passed for' objective scientific observations, according to this account, science itself – and all the standards upon which 'good science' is based – must therefore be irreclaimably biased. This argument, states Haack, is both fallacious and 'pragmatically self-defeating'. There is certainly much evidence that scientific claims to objectivity have been – and no doubt still are – used to serve the interests of those in established positions of power. But, notes Haack, 'the inference from the true premise that what has passed for known fact or objective evidence is no such thing, to the conclusion that the notions of knowledge, fact, evidence, etc., are ideological humbug, is manifestly invalid' (1995: 404).

A similar argument can be made regarding the way in which a neutral (or 'liberal') system is used by many contemporary theorists. For Tully, for example, the tradition of liberal constitutionalism, based as it is upon the principles of uniformity and universality, has resulted in 'disastrous and abhorrent failures'

(1995: 187). The only means of exorcizing the oppressive legacy of liberal imperialism is to recognize formally the diversity of culture. 'Legal, political, and cultural plurality', rather than the imposition of uniformity and regularity, is the only alternative to the continued exploitation and marginalization of minority groups: '[a]ccordingly, the language and institutions of modern constitutionalism should now take their democratic place among the multiplicity of constitutional languages and institutions of the world' (ibid.: 185).

Minority groups have suffered tremendously at the hands of imperial powers. But it is another thing completely to say that a system of universal human rights must *necessarily* lead to imperialism or the oppression of minorities or, in Tully's words, to an 'empire of uniformity'. Colonialists may well have attempted to justify the mistreatment of aboriginal peoples with reference to Locke's prototypical liberal theories, and certain elements of what is considered to be 'liberalism' – such as the imposition of private property rights – may well continue to disadvantage ethnic minorities around the globe here and now. But has the case really been made that 'liberalism' is not and can never be anything but a universalizing, totalizing, homogenizing force? Kymlicka writes that we should disregard 'the facile assumption that the demand for group rights is somehow a byproduct of current intellectual fashions, such as postmodernism' (1996: 22). Yet in a very important way the quest for group rights is precisely a byproduct of postmodernism; for it is postmodernism that has promoted the idea of 'liberalism' as a relentless process of uniformity and homogeneity that forces each and every characteristic of diversity into a monolithic mold of stultifying uniformity. This is an impression of liberalism that is increasingly taken for granted by those advocating group rights; but it is a very selective (and selectively negative) view of what liberalism must entail. Without this account of liberalism, however, it is difficult for group rights theorists to refute the argument that the shocking political treatment of minorities is due to too little respect for universal liberal rights rather than to an excess of it.

Are universality and neutrality nothing more than cultural biases?

From Sandel through MacIntyre, Walzer, Taylor, and other contemporary political philosophers, the principles of individualism upon which liberal democracy are grounded are dismissed for completely misrepresenting the nature of human development. Liberal doctrine, they say, requires that we assume that people are fully constituted as complex 'selves' prior to the formation of social relationships: but this is obviously false. We cannot assume that people can, as Hobbes wrote of the state of nature, pop into the world like mushrooms, fully formed and ready to begin interacting with others. But in the first place, as Stephen Holmes has argued, it is misleading to overemphasize the abstractness of individualism within liberal thought. Early modern liberals used the device of a state of nature not as an interpretation of anthropological history but rather to buttress the argument that 'human beings were not naturally divided into superiors and inferiors': they were equal enough that the consent of all ought to be attained before political authority could be considered legitimate. 'But liberals did not therefore conclude that the human self was factually "disencumbered" of ascriptive particularities', he adds; 'liberals, too, have eyes to see' (Holmes 1993: 194, 196). What abstractness means is not that we must all think alike, talk alike, and act alike. It means that 'if I am concerned solely about your rights, I will treat you like a generic person, not as the warm and colorful individual you are, caught up in a tightly knit web of social relations' (*ibid.*: 229). What, then, of the claim that equality and neutrality are themselves cultural values that may not be valued by non-liberal ethnic groups?

Equality is indeed a 'liberal' value, and a belief in the equal moral worth of individuals underscores the writings of early modern liberals such as Locke, Paine, and Wollstonecraft. But equality need not necessarily be rooted in the idea of equal moral worth. Assumptions of universal equality can also be made for purely instrumental reasons: viz., that they are 'the only ones capable of forming a basis of reasonable agreement' between people who must find some way of getting along with each other despite differing conceptions about how best to lead their lives. What contemporary peoples must determine is not only what the best set of moral doctrines may be, but also how we are to live together, 'given that we have different ideas about how to live' (Barry 1995: 6, 77). We cannot assume that people will in fact want to coexist with others. But if they do, it 'leads directly to a very strong presumption in favour of equality here, since it invites us to ask why anybody should freely consent to being treated less well' than anyone else (*ibid.*: 70). The search for a stable and peaceful coexistence is not an exclusively 'liberal' trait. And the 'equality' in question is not a declaration of moral substance but rather a parallel recognition between all participants in the quest for peaceful coexistence that they cannot insist that others adopt their own conception of 'the good' any more than others could insist upon imposing their beliefs upon all parties. But is this neutrality between competing accounts of 'the good' itself a part of the liberal value system?

Judith Shklar, for example, sees liberalism as a 'guide to practical politics' that 'must avoid any tendency to offer ethical instructions in general':

> Liberalism must restrict itself to politics and to proposals to restrain potential abusers of power in order to lift the burden of fear and favour from the shoulders of adult women and men, who can then conduct their lives in accordance with their own beliefs and preferences, as long as they do not prevent others from doing so as well. (in Rosenblum 1989: 31)

It is crucial here to make some distinctions between various connotations of liberalism. What self-pronounced non-liberals dislike is generally not that they cannot force their own beliefs on others, but that their own beliefs will be threatened or disallowed. And, under a system of 'liberalism as autonomy' that many theorists defend, this may be a real concern. But Shklar's account of liberalism is quite different and does not, as she explicitly states, require that all individuals think and act alike. Tully too, as we have seen, has a very distinct account of liberalism as a belief system that will not permit individuals to 'conduct their lives in accordance with their own beliefs and preferences'. Yet a system of neutrality, as Barry argues, does not at all involve destroying these beliefs and preferences.

The reason that neutrality is seen as a manifestly 'liberal' value is, according to Barry, because the critics of liberalism tend to conflate 'second-order' (or procedural) and 'first-order' (or substantive) conceptions of appropriate behaviour. However, he argues, 'second-order impartiality does not entail universal first-order impartiality' (1995: 12). In other words, one can exercise one's specific beliefs and values (which are not 'neutral') in one's day-to-day life; and yet also recognize that, in dealing with others who do *not* share these values, one must revert to 'justice as impartiality', which is a system of 'principles and rules that are capable of forming the basis of free agreement among people seeking agreement on reasonable terms' (*ibid.*: 11). The only way of establishing a fair system of cooperation between conflicting belief systems, according to Barry, is to begin with the acceptance by all concerned that disputes about the good are unresolvable and that all conceptions of the good should be treated on equal footing. This is what, for Barry, is meant by 'neutrality': it involves an acceptance that 'no conception of the good can justifiably be held with a degree of certainty that warrants its imposition on those who reject it' (*ibid.*: 169). But does this not then jeopardize the very belief systems that a system of neutrality was designed not to oppugn? Once one accepts the sense of scepticism needed for this account of neutrality, does it not pollute one's belief system (which may well depend upon a strong sense of faith for its existence)? Not at all, replies Barry. '[T]he impression that there are two positions – scepticism on one side and dogmatism on the other – is misleading' (*ibid.*: 171):

> What we really have is scepticism on one side and a host of conflicting dogmatisms on the other. These dogmatisms can be confronted with other people who are equally dogmatic but hold something quite different from him. He has to explain why they are all wrong to be certain about what he believes in. And the others have to do the same. . .
>
> There is nothing to prevent anybody from accepting that his conception of the good could reasonably be rejected by others and saying 'All the same, I'll pursue it as hard as I can'. More seriously, there is nothing to prevent a majority in a society who share a certain conception of the good from taking the same hard line and making it the basis of the society's institutions. It is only when modern scepticism is combined with a commitment to finding reasonable terms of agreement that it generates neutrality. (*ibid.*: 172)

Neutrality, in sum, is not a culturally-specific principle. Liberalism, in many of its incarnations, does admittedly hold that justice requires the state not to favour any conception of the good over any other. Yet, at the same time, the history of liberal thought exhibits a wide array of values (a defence of autonomy, tolerance, and individual development; a belief in the need to acquire knowledge; epistemological uncertainty; a firm belief in the rights of the individual; scepticism towards firm beliefs in *anything*, and so on) that belie such a facile claim to neutrality. Neutrality is, more fundamentally, a political strategy for any group of interests that wish to coexist rather than an ideological outgrowth of any particular culture. To the extent that democracy presupposes the desire for peaceful coexistence, a certain degree of neutrality between participants in a democracy is a fundamental prerequisite, not a cultural bias. And given the requirement that globalization increasingly imposes upon all of us to interact with each other, an account of 'impartial justice' would seem to be the most reasonable manner of dealing with the imperatives of globalization. To the extent that some argue that neutrality is impossible in *any* sense, we are left without a moderate and practicable *modus operandi* upon which to structure global relationships. And without such a global protocol, we are left with the realists' bottom line: that power is the ultimate tool of negotiation. It is ironic that those who refuse to acknowledge that even a second-order form of neutrality is possible are frequently amongst the ones most vulnerable to the political will of the most powerful.

Cultural identity and the politics of exclusion

Self-esteem is important. To establish a system of governance upon the principles of autonomy and authenticity and then to disparage individuals because of their inherent traits is brutally unfair. It is unfair because it undermines those very qualities upon which free agency, or the capacity to make decisions for which one claims responsibility, is based. It must be acknowledged that no modern democracies are guiltless of such practices; and it is undeniable that many identifiable groups within these polities are still much less well-off than others. But is the development of autonomy and authenticity best served by recognizing the principle that some groups can claim politics rights denied to others?

The claim that self-esteem is a trait that can be created through the political act of segregating cultural communities is too reliant upon a particularly passive account of identity as the basis of self-esteem. 'National identity is particularly suited to serving as the "primary foci of identification"', writes Kymlicka, 'because it is based on belonging, not accomplishment' (Kymlicka 1995: 89). And that is *precisely* what is wrong with it: people are valued for the circumstances of their birth rather than for what they choose to do. By basing self-esteem upon cultural identity, to what extent are we confining people to an identity that has been arbitrarily conferred upon them? The ideal of authenticity, as Taylor explains, penetrated deeply into European cultures in the late eighteenth century. Before this, 'no one thought that the differences between human beings had this kind of moral significance.' But now, in contrast, 'there is a certain way of being human that is my way. I am called upon to live my life in this way, and not in imitation of anyone else's life. But this gives a new importance to being true to myself. If I am not, I miss the point of my life, I miss what being human is for *me*' (Taylor 1992: 29; see also Rorty 1989: Chapter 5).

Yet it is not simply these differences that are important, but also the fact that they have been created and chosen by each person. That is why they create self-esteem. It may be true that such choices can only be made against the backdrop of a 'pre-existing horizon of significance', but what gives our identities such intense meaning is that we have created them through arduous work and difficult choices. The idea that we are responsible for the consequences of our actions underlines our belief that who we are is essentially reflected in what we do and in the choices that we make. If authenticity is to be considered an essential aspect of self-esteem, then each person grows not by clinging to arbitrarily imposed cultural characteristics, but by confronting and adapting to encounters that challenge their own sense of selfhood. Self-esteem is a dynamic process, not simply a static characteristic to be achieved by permanently identifying with powerful external forces.

Not only is cultural identity overvalued because it is a passive form of self-appreciation, but it is also potentially dangerous because it defines people according to their capacity to exclude others. This is not to say that group identity is irrelevant; history is rife with examples of how membership in certain groups has been the reason for marginalization, humiliation, and disenfranchisement. But it is to argue that the basis for membership in a political community should be more firmly grounded upon relevant similarities rather than upon noticeable differences.

To give individuals the confidence to use their formal democratic 'voices', it is important not to disparage the personal characteristics which make them what they are. But the insistence that such arbitrary characteristics merit special political rights can have troublesome and possibly pernicious consequences. The inviolability of the value placed upon cultural identity is politically dangerous, as it can be used to justify the insupportable treatment of individuals merely on the basis of difference. This is, paradoxically, exactly what the 'politics of difference' attempts to overcome. But if group identity is acknowledged as what is fundamental about a person, then the cultural particularities which bond individuals to each other can also be used to bar those who do not share such characteristics. The politics of inclusion become the politics of exclusion. Political systems based upon cultural identity are structured very clearly upon the vital importance of the distinction between 'us' and 'them'. When identities are formed and maintained by emphasizing the differences between groups (as opposed to the differences between individuals), prejudice and intolerance no longer have to be defended. Cultural identity as the basis for political rights means that an individual's value depends primarily upon belonging to a group; those who find themselves alone and adrift in a strange place thus have no inherent value unless they, too, can point to the tribe to which they 'belong'.

Too strong an emphasis upon cultural identity discourages identification with those who are clearly different from oneself; to stress the primacy of particular group bonds is to deter individuals from breaking free of these bonds and to experience the vulnerability of being unique in one's identity. Yet it is this very experience of vulnerability which develops and enhances people's sensitivity and tolerance of others. By formalizing groups' demands for exclusive rights, the paradoxical result may possibly be to make individuals within all groups less sensitive to the needs of others.

Is there a difference between democracy and self-determination?

As discussed above, group-rights exponents attempt to justify an account of democracy that excises certain fundamental liberal assumptions and institutions, while maintaining a claim to legitimate authority. Neutrality and universality, as well as the priority of individual rights, are strongly disputed; and the claim that cultural identification must be preserved and respected is made both by liberals supporting group rights

(Kymlicka) and by communitarians (Taylor). But to what extent is such an account still 'democratic'? And, if it is deemed democratic, then to what extent does this account differ from the self-determination of territorially-based groups, simply stated? Many group-rights theorists (most explicitly Kymlicka and Tully) argue for group rights on the basis of liberal acceptance of self-determination. Popular sovereignty, writes Tully, 'is the single most important condition of legitimacy in the contemporary world'. This itself is debatable. Many have made the same declaration about 'democracy'. But popular sovereignty refers simply to the ability of peoples 'to govern themselves by their own laws and ways free from external subordination' (1995: 194–5). Is there, then, any substantial difference between self-determination and democracy at all?

There is. 'Popular sovereignty' is a notoriously vague concept. One may glibly assert that the 'customs and ways of peoples are the manifestation of their free agreement' (Tully 1995: 125), but it is perhaps reasonable to ask by which standards one may evaluate whether, and to what extent, this 'free agreement' exists as the basis of custom. That people continue to practice their traditional customs and ways may perhaps be viewed as tacit consent; but tacit consent is a problematic concept and has been so at least since Locke's blithe employment of it three centuries ago (Pitkin 1967). Despite the numerous limitations and disadvantages of a liberal system of representative democracy, it does at least provide a means of determining the extent to which individuals support their political system. The argument that 'the practice of traditional customs are a manifestation of popular sovereignty' cannot stand alone; we must have an explanation of what the traditional customs are, and the way in which the rulers are accountable to the ruled in a way that is satisfactory to the latter. And, as importantly, we must know whether certain groups or individuals within the wider group of 'the ruled' themselves have a say in these customs *vis-à-vis* the more powerful social groups in such traditional cultures. One cannot credibly deny or ignore the fact that all communities, traditional and otherwise, have their own internal dynamics of power.

Accounts justifying the legitimacy of traditional customs on the basis of 'popular sovereignty' are unsatisfactory because they do not offer any means of determining which traditional customs have been the result of reflective acceptance, and which have been established due to internal power dynamics. Merely assuming that a group exhibits 'popular sovereignty' because it is not subject to external rules or mores is insufficient. But if popular sovereignty (as the self-rule of a group) is not, *pace* Tully, itself satisfying criteria for determining legitimate political authority, then what is? It is the determination of whether any individuals suffer from the exercise of undue power and influence by state or non-state actors. Democracy differs from national self-determination in that the former requires a systematic and transparent limitation on the exercise of power so that individuals are not disadvantaged or silenced against their will. But any system which insists that individuals must be respected and protected in this way is, by definition, a liberal one. There is no such thing as a 'non-liberal' democracy which is distinct from 'self-determination' *per se*, as any articulation of standards used to evaluate whether 'popular sovereignty' is indeed 'popular' at all brings in very manifestly 'liberal' principles (protection for individuals, a system of due process that favours no one by virtue of their position, and so on). Democracy, to be called democracy at all, must recognize a wide array of individual rights. But can such a system perhaps coexist with the recognition of group rights?

Most group-rights theorists have attempted to construct an account that meets the concerns of groups demanding self-determination while remaining palatable to liberal sensibilities. To a great extent, it seems that there would be little difference in practice between an account based upon individual rights which permitted wide freedoms for individuals to follow the customs with which they felt comfortable; and an account based upon group rights in which members felt a deep (albeit non-institutionalized) respect for fellow members. The former account assumes that groups will have sufficient freedom to 'flourish meaningfully' and that they will not suffer, as Tully argues, from a stultifying uniformity imposed upon them. The latter account assumes that ethnically-oriented political groups will not, contrary to alarmist liberals, mistreat individuals who do not have formal political rights as individuals against the group. Ideally, then, it would be irrelevant which of the two approaches we supported, as both individuals *qua* individuals and individuals *qua* group members would act reasonably and feel content. The reason we must choose between these accounts, however, is that too many cases arise in our far-from-ideal world where these best-case assumptions do not hold. Groups may indeed fail to flourish in a 'meaningful' way within communities respecting a wide array of individual rights. Or an individual within an ethnically-based political group may simply decide that she is being treated unfairly by the community. Then what?

If individual rights have any force, then they must protect the individual against the sentiments – and possibly against the perceived general good – of the wider community. And if group rights have any force, then they must, likewise, at some point protect cultural practices in a way to which individuals may very well object. The issue is where ultimate political authority lies, and this is what is at stake in the discussion of hard cases. The most thoughtful attempt at reconciling individual and group rights is perhaps that offered by Kymlicka; but even this account is obliged after some probing to support one side or the other. Kymlicka argues that we must distinguish between two types of group rights: internal restrictions, which are 'intended to protect the group from the destabilizing impact of internal dissent'; and external protections, which protect the group from the impact of any external decisions made by the larger community which may disadvantage the group. Liberals can and should, he writes, 'endorse certain external protections, where they promote fairness between groups, but should reject internal restrictions which limit the right of group members to question and revise traditional authorities and practices' (1995: 37). Yet at some point, as Kymlicka recognizes, the hard cases will surface. And in such cases the question remains: is 'the protection of meaningful cultural context' sufficient justification to override recognized liberal individual rights?

In order to protect themselves against the larger community, for example, a minority group within a liberal polity may ultimately refuse to be subject to the larger state's charter of rights. Should we then intervene and impose a liberal regime in such circumstances, especially if the smaller community is itself divided on such an issue? Kymlicka argues that we cannot; that, even if illiberal and unjust internal restrictions are imposed, the larger community ought not to coerce the community to recognize the individual rights which any individual outside the minority group can claim. We ought instead, he argues, 'to promote liberal values through persuasion and financial incentives' (1996: 27), just as we would with states lying outside our borders.

But why, exactly, is it that we do not coerce states outside our border to recognize liberal democratic rights? Kymlicka argues that it is because we acknowledge the prior right to self-determination and state sovereignty. But in doing so he begs the question of why state sovereignty is in fact prior: this is simply another example of the (faulty) 'analogy with states'. It is an empirical fact that most liberal democracies do not 'coerce' all states to recognize individual rights in cases where clear violations of rights exist. But this is largely because such an action, even if morally justifiable, would be imprudent: the costs (military and otherwise) of a coercive political action against a large state (such as China) are extremely high. It is not at all clear that such military forbearance is due to the assumption that state sovereignty is morally prior to individual rights, rather than due to the sheer force of expediency. The argument, again, is tautological: it uses for proof (i.e., the analogy with states) that which it has set out to establish (that ethnic groups within liberal states ought to be given the same respect as established states) by begging the question of why it is that established states' autonomy ought to be morally respected at all. The problem, as others have noted, is that 'Kymlicka has bought uncritically into what has been described as the romance of the nation-state and simply extended it to national minorities' (Barry 1996b: 155).

Is there such a thing as a non-liberal democracy? Can a form of self-government which does not recognize the primacy of individual rights be considered a democratic polity at all? The theorists who espouse the 'politics of identity' have argued that, because cultural identity is an essential component of individuals' capacity to understand their lives and to form stable relationships with others, group rights based upon cultural identity can and ought even in liberal states to be accepted as a basis of legitimate democratic authority. The objective of this approach is to hearten and encourage those who do not fit well into the mould of 'sameness' to which liberal values are ascribed. There is much to be commended in this approach: it aims to intensify people's awareness that they have an enormous capacity to hurt, to humiliate, and to incapacitate through the 'unconscious fears and aversions that continue to define some groups as despised and ugly bodies' (Young 1990: 124). Paradoxically, however, this approach can also discourage tolerance of those who do not share cultural or group similarities. In its attempt to explain precisely why group differences are important, this account places unquestioning value in belonging to a specific group; and, as such, it discourages the attempt to form self-identity as a unique and idiosyncratic manifestation, a vulnerability that forces all individuals to become aware of the experience of being different from everyone else. People are instead encouraged to find 'meaningfulness' by focusing upon the differences between groups, an unapologetically passive form of identification which builds upon their capacity to exclude others and disposes them to set themselves in opposition to others.

This is not to deny that the psychological ties we form by virtue of racial characteristics or belief systems are important to us: such a claim would be patently unsupportable. What can be questioned is the extent to which such traits or beliefs can be used to justify a set of exclusive and permanent political rights which others have a clear obligation to honour, and which can challenge and supersede individual rights. Yet, while it is understandable that people desire to be valued on the basis of the traits with which they identify most strongly, the argument for differential group rights based upon cultural identity must first perform three intellectual tasks before it can stand as a convincing challenge to the liberal-democratic conception of equal and universal human rights. First, it must define more clearly what is meant by 'secure' cultural contexts. Second, it must provide a persuasive account of why a strong sense of personal identity or self-esteem can only arise through membership in this 'secure' cultural context; and, third, it should be able to show how this process of group identification will accommodate greater political tolerance and mutual respect than a political organization based upon universal human rights. Moreover, the criticism of liberalism itself upon which the argument for group rights is based is persuasive only to the extent that it is misleading and focused upon an highly selective account of what 'liberalism' is said to be. Group rights based upon cultural identity, then, are an unsatisfactory foundation upon which to build an account of a 'non-liberal' democracy. To assume that a culturally-homogenous polity is 'democratic' merely because it is based upon traditions with which its members comply is to offer a shallow and distorted account of democracy indeed. Despite the fashionability of this approach, there is little coherence in its wider interpretation of democracy. Any account of why a non-liberal state may be said to be legitimate cannot rest upon an argument based upon *democratic* legitimacy.

II

Explaining democracy:
causal debates

5

The market

> The market is at once supportive and undermining of democracy, in a number of different respects, and the accurate characterization of their relationship is therefore one of ambivalence.
> (Beetham 1996: 25)

Why has the role of the market changed?

If the first and most fundamental issue regarding the globalization of democracy is what, precisely, democracy is, the second question is how democracy comes about. And, while a wide spectrum of methodological investigations have been employed by comparativists (e.g., structuralism, elite compromise theory, strategic choice and rational choice theory: see Remmer, 1995) in order to explain the last wave of democratization, two causal variables are generally viewed as preeminently important, although neither commands unqualified support. The first looks at the form of economic organization – specifically, the market – as the causal key to democratization; the second views a particular form of social organization – 'civil society' – as the preeminent causal factor. This chapter, along with the following one, offers the rather unstartling conclusion that neither account is particularly persuasive, nor completely coherent. Nonetheless, because the normative claims implicit in statements about what democracy *is* are frequently dependent upon arguments that 'democracy can only come about in a certain way' (i.e., through the market, or through civil society), one must examine these causal debates more rigorously in order to determine whether, and to what extent, they can serve as persuasive justifications for specific interpretations of democracy.

While the debate regarding the causal links between democracy and the market is not new, much of the discussion has in the recent past focused upon the way in which international capitalism inhibited rather than promoted democratic institutions. During the late 1960s and early 1970s, *dependencia* theorists suggested that the emergence of authoritarian regimes in many Latin American states resulted from the need to quell political and social disturbances that arose due to the imposition of capitalist industrialization strategies. Recurring inflation and balance-of-payments crises led to widespread social protest, which in turn jeopardized the political stability essential for capitalist investment: thus, the economic elite were presumed either passively to support or actively to engineer military coups against democratic regimes in order to provide an economic climate free of excessive political instability (e.g., O'Donnell, 1978). The popularity of the *dependencia* hypothesis, however, diminished with an increasing body of empirical evidence which argued that industrialization and capitalist investment in Latin America occurred 'before as well as after the establishment of authoritarian regimes and also in their total absence' (Hirschman 1981: 117).

While the precise direction of the causal connection between democracy and capitalism has been strongly disputed, one ought to keep in mind that democracy itself was, in its original formulation, a strictly political issue rarely discussed in conjunction with any system of economic organization. Democracy initially arose as a specifically political solution to a problem of political factionalization in the Athenian city-state two and a half millennia ago: a democratic system of government at that time 'could scarcely have been further, either in purpose or in content, from a plausible proposal for how to organize modern states in a capitalist world economy' (Dunn 1992: 240, 255–6). Nonetheless, the belief that there is a clear causal relationship between late twentieth-century capitalism and democracy has become increasingly popular. In this account, it is the desire for the material benefits of a capitalist system which inexorably propels a developing state to adopt democratic institutions. Historically, the link between the market and the development of modern democracy is well established. As the Crown in seventeenth-century England was able to tax with impunity the growing bourgeoisie (largely in order to finance wars of increasing magnitude), the frustration at being subject to arbitrary taxation led the emergent commercial elite to support the collapse of the old regime in favour of constitutional monarchy. One crucial outcome of this development was the entrenchment of the concept of 'natural' and inviolable private property rights; an idea that was articulated by seventeenth-century philosopher John Locke as a means of conserving and cultivating the resources given by God to 'mankind in common' (Locke 1960; Tully 1980; Horne 1990) and which culminated in the American Constitution's declaration of the sanctity of life, liberty and estate. By accepting that the fruits of one's labour were inviolable, the Crown was enjoined from seizing this wealth (through confiscation or taxation) except with the consent of the governed. This espousal of private property rights, divorced from its original Lockean justification, fostered the establishment of powerful economic elites that were able to challenge and counterbalance the political influence of those holding formal title to govern. Democratic rights and property ownership in England were thus closely linked; individuals without title or property were generally denied the right to participate politically. Only with the sizable expansion of the middle classes in the nineteenth and twentieth centuries did suffrage expand to include all adult citizens regardless of their title to property.

The dominant variable which distinguishes the genesis of democracy in early modern England from contemporary newly-industrialized countries (NICs) is that, in the latter, 'capitalism' has been an exogenous rather than an endogenous force. In order to 'catch up' with the success of capitalist states elsewhere, developing nations have commonly followed policies of state-led industrialization. This strategy, however, effectively centralizes economic and political power in the hands of a single dominant elite which has little motivation to disperse this power more widely within society. It is for this reason that development theorists of the 1960s and 1970s blamed the increasingly brutal authoritarian regimes upon the pervasive ideology of capitalism (e.g., Frank, 1975). Yet, two decades later, it is the force of international capitalism which is generally seen to provide the impetus for democratic reform. Why?

It was only due to the fragile quality of the indigenous capital-owning classes that the state bureaucracies within NICs were initially obliged to become involved in economic development after the dismantling of colonial regimes in the three decades following the Second World War. As these nations became more highly integrated into the international marketplace, however, the 'economic and social regulation and control provided by authoritarian regimes' became 'irrelevant and counterproductive' (Robison 1988: 56, 57). In states increasingly geared to export-oriented industrialization, excessive bureaucratic control and regulation severely impedes the ability of domestic industries to organize themselves and their distributional systems predictably, efficiently, and flexibly (Mardjana, 1993: 50). Import-export restrictions diminish the ability of firms to import required components or production materials and to ship finished products abroad. Bureaucratic corruption and overregulation dissuade foreign firms from bringing investment capital into the country; rampant nepotism and favouritism penalizes competitive firms in favour of well-connected ones, and so on. Thus, both host countries and transnational corporations have an interest in limiting government activity in the economy. The latter advocate 'some form of democracy as a way of "opening up" the markets of exclusionary authoritarian regimes to foreign goods and services' (Potter 1993: 364); and the former are driven to 'hand over economic responsibility to the private sector' due to their 'inability to handle the growing economic crises of the 1980s: debt, inflation, growing balance-of-payments deficits, fiscal crises, declining investment, and decaying infrastructure' (Robison 1988: 57).

The 'imaginative appeal of democracy', as the ability of individuals collectively to choose how they wish to organize their society, is by no means a recent development. What has changed since the reorganization of Athenian politics some two and a half millennia ago is that the development of relatively stable and well-regulated market systems has made the practical conditions of democracy more viable (Dunn 1992). Democracy and capitalism are no longer isolated concepts. But if democracy has only flourished within economic frameworks based upon some degree of free exchange, it does not logically follow that such conditions will necessarily lead to a democratic political reorganization. The market may arguably be a necessary variable, but it is quite patently not a sufficient one (cf. Beetham 1996).

A market system is conducive to democratic politics for two predominant reasons: first, a well-functioning market requires a certain scope for the free activity of individuals within a framework of stable and predictable laws. People who are subject to the arbitrary actions of rulers are understandably ill-inclined to invest their resources in an environment of unpredictability. Adam Smith, who made this observation quite compellingly in the eighteenth century, is thus frequently considered the quintessential proponent of liberal democracy even though his magnum opus, the *Wealth of Nations*, never directly espoused (or even discussed) representative democracy. Indeed, many early proponents of representative democracy – such as James Mill – qualified their enthusiasm for democracy with a strict condition of well-entrenched private property rights (Stimson and Milgate, 1993). Nonetheless, as C. B. Macpherson (1962) and others have argued, it was from this observation of the relationship between an efficient market and political freedoms that the modern conception of 'liberal rights' developed and came to play such a large part in modern political discourse.

The second way in which market systems enhance the conditions for democracy is by preventing political elites from 'capturing' the market for their own purposes. If a democratic political administration is considered to be jeopardizing the smooth functioning of a capitalist economy it is removed and replaced. The precise extent to which political leaders stand at arm's length from the economic elite constitutes a lively debate in any capitalist democracy: for while political elites in general seem to do rather well in economic terms, they are limited in the extent to which they can use the market for their own purposes once their interests and those of the market no longer coincide. The following two sections will examine these respective claims more closely.

Private property rights and the diffusion of power

The assertion that a strong market prevents the concentration of political power is hardly a novel observation; it was, for example, the theme throughout most of Friedrich Hayek's works. The point has become commonly accepted: state ownership and control of the means of production, writes Larry Diamond, 'is intrinsically incompatible with democracy, which requires some distribution of power resources so that political competition can be real and the state can be held accountable' (1992). But the more recent phenomenon of note has been the degree to which so many states – and not merely western industrial democracies – have become dependent upon export revenue (WTO, 1995: 10). The logical conclusion that is frequently extracted from this is that, as external forces (the pressures of competing effectively in the global marketplace) oblige state officials to loosen their control on the domestic market, a 'political space' arises in which domestic voices of protest and dissent can more easily make themselves heard. It is generally on this rather tenuous line of reasoning that many exceptionally optimistic visions of a democratic world system lie (e.g., Fukuyama, 1992).

Discussions of democracy throughout the twentieth century have been punctuated by the cautious recognition that market states can, and have often been, particularly brutal authoritarian states. It is the force of 'globalization', in the development of communications technology, the diffusion of ideology, the spread of international non-governmental organizations and, most pointedly, the rigour of the international market which is said to distinguish the contemporary dynamics of democracy from earlier variants. But what is less frequently asked is the direction in which, and the degree to which, this diffusion of power obtains. To whom, precisely, is power diffused?

In the first place, it is not immediately apparent that a state's quest for a stronger role in the international marketplace will necessarily require the government to remove itself from a close involvement with the business sector. It may be true that, where the political elite themselves have strong interests in industries which profit from protectionist policies (such as import-substitution industrialization), these political ties hamper the ability of businesses to compete effectively. Indonesia is one example of this: as falling oil revenues required the Indonesian state to turn to its other export industries, it became quite apparent that these were far too hobbled by protectionist policies to compete effectively. By 1985, the Indonesian government quietly initiated reductions in import tariffs and took the notable step of hiring a Swiss firm to reorganize customs, ports, and shipping organizations in a move to reduce the egregious level of corruption in these operations. The privatization of several state industries followed, as did internal reorganizations of other public enterprises aimed at improving economic efficiency. This, in turn, emboldened private businesses and the media to speak more critically of other aspects of government policy (see Robison, 1986; Fierlbeck, 1994).

But all countries do not share relevant similarities to Indonesia. Many other South East Asian states are able to form partnerships between state and industry, and are able to compete globally more effectively under a system of managed rather than laisser-faire capitalism. More significantly, this managed capitalism seems to work more effectively when democracy remains relatively restricted. There are good reasons for this: a strong popular influence

> will find it difficult to hold the line against unbalanced increases in consumption at the expense of investment, and difficult to direct government assistance to uses which can meet a national interest test rather than a clamorous importunity test. Conversely, where the executive is relatively strong, there is a better chance that policies will not careen from side to side because of frequent turnover in power. This makes for a more stable business environment, facilitating longer-term corporate investment. And it helps the bureaucracy to oversee the operation of the economy. (Wade 1990: 374)

Thus, even in an environment of rigorous international competition, an independent large-business sector is not always essential for a state to participate effectively in the global marketplace. But even to the extent that a competitive domestic market permits 'some distribution of power resources so that political competition can be real', there is no clear evidence that the 'power resources' will be diffused beyond the control of these large industries themselves.

This may, of course, be all that is necessary to facilitate a very basic understanding of 'democracy' as the competition between power elites. To the extent that any political competition exists at all, a diffusion of power may arise when political elites appeal to the wider population as a means of strengthening and solidifying their bases of power. This was, after all, arguably the way in which democracy evolved in the first place. But this account depends little upon the international marketplace itself as a causal variable; nor does it involve any conception of political accountability or a recognition of people *qua* citizens. A related argument concerning the role of the market deals not explicitly with the existence of competition *per se* but rather with the political potential of private property rights. One of the clearest accounts of this position is Mancur Olson's 1993 article which argued that 'the security of property and contract rights' were a primary component for the establishment of lasting democracy. This is, of course, a highly controversial position, not only for those who remain unenthusiastic about the prospect of democratization, but also for those who strongly *favour* it. To the extent that strict private property rights do establish a bulwark against the arbitrary activity of the state, it is understandable why a dominant political elite would evince a limited show of ardour for such an institution. Yet a great number of both theorists and activists are equally reluctant to endorse a strong system of private property because of the fear that an independent market, and especially one closely entwined in a system of international capital, would prove even less accountable to the citizenry as a political body than would an authoritarian government. This concern will be discussed more fully in the following section.

The hope that the establishment of rights to private property could protect people's growing wealth from arbitrary seizure and taxation was, of course, first clearly articulated in seventeenth-century Britain; and it is Britain's experience of the transition from a market society to a democracy which provides the historical model of causality upon which current assumptions of market-led democratization are grounded. But Olson attempts to provide a theoretical account of this transformation which does not depend upon this historically and culturally specific development. He begins his discussion with an observation drawn not from seventeenth-century Britain but from early twentieth-century China: why, he asks, did people prefer the warlord (or 'stationary bandit'), who continuously stole from the population, to the roving bandits who would soon depart after looting them? Olson argues that the stationary bandit had an interest in preserving the accumulative capability of his subjects, as this would increase the amount he could steal from them. His subjects, in turn, might 'expect to retain whatever capital they accumulate out of after-tax income and therefore also have an incentive to save and to invest, thereby increasing future income and tax receipts' (Olson 1993: 568). And the larger the stake which the stationary bandit had in the society, the greater an incentive he would have to provide public goods for the society – such as security – which would protect and enhance his own profits.

Nonetheless, continues Olson, the monopoly position enjoyed by the warlord means that he would be inclined to use this monopoly of coercive power 'to obtain the maximum take in taxes and other exactions' (*ibid.*: 569). This onerous level of taxation thus lowers the wealth produced by the society as incentives to produce are undermined, which will, in turn, diminish potential tax revenues. To maximize his own return, then, an autocrat will want to convince his subject that 'their assets will be permanently protected not only from theft by others, but also from expropriation by the autocrat himself':

> A stationary bandit will therefore reap the maximum harvest in taxes – and his subjects will get the largest gain from his encompassing interest in the productivity of his domain – only if he is taking an indefinitely long view and only if his subjects have a total confidence that their 'rights' to private property and to impartial contract enforcement will be permanently respected and that the coin or currency will retain its full value. (*ibid.*: 571)

But to be completely secure that they would be able to invest their resources to the highest degree possible, people will want an independent system that can guarantee both their possessions and the stability of the system of investment. The government, then, must both be strong enough to last, and be inhibited from violating individual rights to property and contract enforcement. And the conditions which, in turn, are necessary to protect these requirements (i.e., an independent judiciary, respect for law, and independent rights), concludes Olson, 'are exactly the same conditions that are needed to have a lasting democracy' (*ibid.*: 572).

Olson never does stipulate that an authoritarian government's focus on maximizing economic returns will ultimately or necessarily lead to a fully-fledged system of participatory democracy. What he does argue is that democracy bolsters economic growth by entrenching economic freedoms. This implies, in turn, that democracy is defined primarily by its economic freedoms; which conveniently neglects that aspect of democratic thought which argues that even private property rights ought to be subject to the decision-making authority of the populace. Such accounts generally assume the primacy of private property rights as 'natural' or preexisting or simply inviolable rights despite the lack of a coherent philosophical justification for such accounts (see, e.g., Waldron 1988). The question of rightful authority over the distribution of property has proven a concern for democratic theorists from James Mill onward; and it has been a source of criticism for the opponents of democracy from Aristotle to the present. It is notable that when states with a significant polarity of wealth agree to a system of universal suffrage – South Africa, most recently – the stipulation of firm private property rights is a clear precondition in order to protect the wealth of the minority from the 'rapacious majority'.

The causal link between the market and democratic government is relatively forceful, then, to the extent that 'democracy' is understood as the establishment and protection of private property rights. But autocratic governments are not the only source of undesirable influence. A domestic marketplace independent of state control is conducive to the establishment of democracy because it diffuses power (as the control of economic resources) away from the state: but to what extent is power evenly diffused throughout the marketplace? The relatively equal distribution of resources may arguably be a means of dispersing power; but the relatively equal distribution of private property rights is not an efficient means of doing so because it rests in the actual, not potential, ownership of resources. And a 'democracy' in which the distribution of wealth is severely unequal (and in which no political decision to address such an imbalance is permitted) can boast of only a very dubious dispersal of power overall.

It is here that the dynamics of an international marketplace become significant, but in a way which tends to alarm many participatory democrats. The discipline of international competition does indeed have an effect, but in a way which seems to increase the polarization of wealth at the same time that it increases the wealth of a society. The explanation for this is by now relatively well known: in the first place, states depend increasingly on the wealth made by the export trade of companies within their borders. Some smaller industrial countries, such as Canada, depend on exports for 40 per cent of their GNP; and developing countries on average (excluding China) have increased their exports by more than 90 per cent between 1986 and 1994 (WTO 1995: 10). In the second place, states must provide hospitable economic environments (including favourable tax deals, looser environmental restrictions, the provision of infrastructure, and so on) in order to maximize their export capacity. And, in the third place, as states' investment strategies compete to attract the most lucrative companies, there is a concomitant scaling-back of the resources devoted to programmes which address the various social needs – nutritional, health, educational, and other programmes – of the wider population. At the same time, companies' own competitive strategies involve a greater dependence upon technology and less use of labour-intensive techniques, while at the same time contracting out services to private firms in a number of countries thereby avoiding expensive labour costs.

What this means, cumulatively, is that this reconfiguration of the economy has very definitely been advantageous for some at the expense of others. In the United States, for example, the 80 per cent of 'production and non-supervisory workers' underneath the executive, managerial, and technical levels experienced a drop in average weekly earnings (adjusted for inflation) of 18 per cent between 1972 and 1995 (from $315 to $258 per week). In contrast to these rank and file workers, the real annual pay of corporate chief executives, between 1970 and 1989, rose by 19 per cent before taxes, and 66 per cent after taxes (Head 1996: 47). Given the way in which wealth is produced within the global marketplace, there is simply no reason to believe that the widening disparity between the wealthy and the poor can be addressed by increases in the total GNP of a state. 'The central problem of the 1990s', concludes Head, 'has been more the maldistribution of wealth than failure to increase overall wealth' (1996: 51).

The argument in support of the form of democracy favoured implicitly by Olson is primarily that a stable democracy is exceptionally difficult to establish and nurture in an environment of extreme poverty. Thus the process of democratization favoured by many multilateral agencies is one based upon a stable, transparent, and effective market economy. The IMF, World Bank, and World Trade Organization work in conjunction to strengthen the domestic economies and integrate them further into the international marketplace. As Chapter 7 will discuss in more detail, the concern of current democracies that developing states establish more democratic regimes is pursued by those very institutions that, formally, are strictly enjoined by their Articles of Agreement from any political influence in states' domestic affairs. Yet by pursuing a strategy of economic development characterized by the need to achieve 'good governance', the requirements of a functioning economy seem to veer very closely to some of the basic prerequisites for a stable democracy. The World Bank has, at least since 1992, articulated an economic development strategy focusing upon accountability, a clear and predictable legal framework, the wide diffusion of information, and transparency in government policy-making. 'Economic efficiency', states the Bank, 'requires that information about government policies and action be available, that major processes of economic policymaking (for example, the budget) be reasonably transparent, and that there be some opportunity for the public to affect policymaking (through, for example, comment or influence)' (1992: 40). Just as Olson suggested, it seems here that the fundamental principles for both a strong economy and a democratic regime are quite fungible indeed.

But there has also been a strong stream of objections to this account of market-based democratization. To the extent that democracy is seen as a system based most fundamentally upon the protection of private property and a firm respect for legal contracts, it neglects the representation of those who cannot effectively participate within the market. For 'the development of the market' now means very specifically the development of a globally-integrated marketplace; and the rules governing this network are ones which restrict the rules which may impede the trade of goods or services. To take advantage of the economic growth to be created through export trade, then, states must participate in the widest system of trade; and this system, governed by the rules established by the WTO, requires a high degree of economic liberalization. The WTO itself is very clear in its position that trade liberalization is a crucial component of 'the growth and development of national economies': but does this process lead to greater democratization?

The problem, argue some critics, is that the rules of international trade under the WTO are clearly neoliberal ones, rules which primarily protect private property (Robinson 1995). Strict private property rights, in turn, permit and possibly encourage the concentration of wealth within national borders by diminishing the ability of the state to take an active role in the redistribution of wealth. In the first place, an ideology of respect for private property limits the level of taxation that property owners may tolerate. More concretely, however, the mobility of capital more easily permits industries, and especially foreign enterprises, to relocate to states which are more amenable to their demands. To maximize the total wealth produced by a country, then, it is necessary to tolerate the inequalities of wealth that accrue from the normal functioning of the market.

As Adam Smith himself took great pain to point out, a freely functioning market would indeed likely result in significant disparities of income; and yet this state of inequality was to be mitigated by the fact that it led to standards of living for even the poorest workers. But Adam Smith was no democrat. He was much more sympathetic to the plight of the poor than most of his contemporary proponents acknowledge; but he was not concerned with the possible imbalances of political power that could result from such economic disparities. 'Growing income inequality', argues Robinson, 'reduces the quality of democratic politics. ' Democracy requires the ability of individuals to participate in political processes; and this, in turn, requires access to financial resources, to educational institutions, to reasonable health care. If economic resources are sources of power strong enough to constrain the ability of authoritarian governments, then such economic resources can also be used to influence citizens who have neither political nor economic resources at their disposal.

> The upshot is that the higher the levels of economic inequality, the lower the quality of democracy, and the lower the quality, the more likely it is that democratic government will fail . . . far from promoting democratization, neoliberal globalization is likely to undermine many of the vulnerable new democracies that have emerged in the last fifteen years and to reduce the quality of democracy in the countries where it survives. (Robinson 1995: 377)

Autonomy and democracy

The primary problem with accounts of democratization that depend upon the market as the key causal variable is that the dynamics of international trade seem to suggest that the distribution of wealth resulting from a strongly market-based economy may well be too distorted to permit a balanced distribution of political influence between citizens. To the extent that shifting political power from a single political elite to a set of competing economic elites is accepted as a form of 'democratization', democracy is widely achievable; but there is, at the same time, rather little to commend democracy. Yet there is another troubling aspect of a strongly market-oriented strategy of democratization, one which focuses not on the power imbalances between individuals within the polity, but on the ability of the polity itself to facilitate the life choices most important to its citizens; choices which may not simply be procured though the market.

Is there a correlation between the salubrity of democracy and the degree to which a state maintains or loses its capacity to govern in the face of the pressures exerted by international capital? There is, to begin, the reasonable observation that the nation-state was historically a prime practical precondition for the emergence of democracy: to the extent that sixteenth and seventeenth century political treaties (such as Augsburg and Westphalia) recognized the ability of geographically-based political powers unilaterally to make laws of major import (the religion of the citizenry, declarations of war or of peace), political authority clearly devolved from ultramontane absolutism to geographically-specific political authority. This not only diminished the concept of religious authority as a legitimate arbiter of political matters, but also made the state a more effective instrument for executing political decisions. The state as a geographically-limited entity with sweeping political authority within its own borders was able to accomplish two rather contradictory achievements: first, the prototypical state (in contrast to imperial rulers) generally (though not always) oversaw the interests of a relatively homogeneous population, and was able to execute decisions on behalf of a fairly cohesive population without the need to compromise its actions to meet the conflicting demands of a large and diverse populace. In the second place, rather paradoxically, a sovereign who did not have to answer to either external religious or imperial authority could execute policies that were vastly unpopular to a large portion of the population. The prime example of this, of course, was the protection of private property rights for agricultural producers in the face of a hungry populace in times of scarcity.

It was the fierce controversy over the Grain Trade in the eighteenth century which most bluntly emphasised the difference of interests that existed over the concept of private property rights. As the Physiocrats (and especially François Quesnay) argued in France through the early half of the century, the private property rights of agricultural producers had to be maintained against the cries of the hungry in order for landowners to be persuaded to reinvest in agricultural productivity. It was Adam Smith's more acute observation that private property rights had to be defended in order for the accumulation of

wealth to accrue so that capital was created to invest in manu-
facturing, where the real potential of the creation of new wealth
existed, rather than in agriculture (Hont and Ignatieff, 1983).
For, as long as consumer goods were limited in number, the tendency for workers to labour strenuously was muted in times of
plentiful foodstuffs; when consumer goods were to be had in the
marketplace, in contrast, a stable and industrious labour force
would produce goods to add wealth to the economy and, as a
result, would never lack for income to feed themselves even in
times of scarcity (when a rich nation could afford to import
food). But to break from the feudal tradition whereby the rulers
directly provided for the poor during times of need, it was essential first to establish the inviolability of private property rights
and to let the hungry go without. It was thus the existence of a
strong state which permitted the establishment of an independent market, which created in turn the conditions from
which democracy in the English-speaking world arose.

The autonomous state was instrumental to democracy both
in being able to respond effectively to the needs of its citizens
(especially in defending its territory against aggressors), and in
being able to withstand the demands of the citizenry in order to
establish the framework for an efficient market. A functioning
market system would, in turn, facilitate the emergence of
democracy through the provision of wealth and the establishment of centres of power (i.e., rights) upon which the state could
not (or, more correctly, would not be inclined to) intrude.

But if the state was historically a precondition for the emergence of democracy in the West, does the existence of an
autonomous nation state remain a precondition for democracy
to function (or to function well)? Does the process of globalization, by undermining the ability of the state effectively to
respond to the demands of the its citizens, jeopardize the allure
of democracy? The perception of a close relationship between
democracy and state autonomy is becoming increasingly
common: intriguingly, for example, Jean-Marie Guéhenno's
French publication of *The End of Democracy* (*Le fin de la
democracie*) was translated into English as *The End of the
Nation State*. The relationship between the nation-state and
democracy, for Guéhenno, is that the *raison d'etre* of the democratic nation state – what Dunn calls the imaginative appeal of
democracy (1992: 239–66) – can no longer be maintained. The
compelling and evocative force of democracy as 'the hope that

human life in the settings in which it takes place may come to be more a matter of committed personal choice and less a matter of enforced compliance with impersonal and external (and unwanted) demands' was able to develop through the enabling environment of the modern nation-state, with its increasingly sophisticated bureaucratic apparatuses, the defensive capability of its armed forces, and its protection of an economic system which could allow its citizens to live a comfortable life.

But the crux of the difficulty for democratic states now, argues Guéhenno, is that these nations 'no longer have the capacity, in a global world, of protecting the peoples whose destiny they claim to embody from the uncertainties of the outside world that have irreversibly irrupted into what used to be called their domestic affairs':

> Given competition from faraway countries, given the migration of poverty and terrorism, it has become as impossible to control the world that surrounds us as it is to ignore it. And the gulf between the nation as a locus of identity and the nation as a locus of power is formidable, for the natural temptation is to compensate with the complacent exaltation of one's identity what the nation has lost in effective power over the real. (1995: 138)

And the reason that states no longer have the ability to look after the collective interests of their citizens is due to the development of transnational forces which 'are far more powerful than are the states themselves' (*ibid.*: 3). One of the most potent of these forces is of course the global market, which greatly constrains the ability of the state to perform the function which defines its legitimacy: to permit its citizens to live the lives they wish unimpeded by external forces. But while capital and the reproduction of capital is what facilitates a great deal of this freedom to choose, wealth has become increasingly mobile, unconstrained by national borders. Taxation, however, does have a territorial basis: and it is taxation which permits states to meet the needs of its population as a collectivity. And yet, observes Guéhenno,

> if the gap between the fiscal pressure imposed on those who cannot liberate themselves from territorial constraints and those who can escape them becomes too glaring, the political coherence of the fiscal system is likely to create difficulties. One cannot for long tax workers' income three times more than income from capital. So, even where it still believes itself to be sovereign, the nation-state has

> to give in to a new constraint, which distorts the relationship that had hitherto been established, through taxes, between the citizens and the state. (*ibid.*: 11)

Thus the same force which accounts for the undermining of communist systems may well be at work in the same way within capitalist democracies. Democracy requires a certain degree of clear hierarchy for the principle of accountability to work: we must know who has given the power to whom to do what, so that we can say who is responsible for bad decisions, decisions made on our behalf, when they arise. Yet this hierarchical pyramidal structure, Guéhenno asserts, has rapidly been replaced by a structure of diffusion of power; an 'eminently fluid world' where an enormous number of important decisions are made not by those ostensibly in power but through a 'capillary-like network of microdecisions' (1995: 65) that protect against the capture of power by any one agent, making it extraordinarily difficult to hold any one agent or set of agents responsible for the decisions that are made of behalf of the citizenry.

This is precisely the objection raised by many states to the project of development based upon a strong market-led economic growth: that democracy as the accountability of the powerful by even the weakest citizens is extremely difficult, if not impossible, where a weak state becomes integrated into a powerful international economy. This devolution of democratic power to transnational corporations is said to occur in two ways: 'first, through the legal restrictions they impose on the policies that governments may adopt; and second, through the market pressures that intensifying competition for scarce private investment imposes on national and subnational governments' (Robinson 1995: 375).

The Report of the South Commission, a document written by representatives from twenty-five developing states, has noted its concerns in detail on both points. Economic growth in these states is increasingly dependent upon export trade, but regional trading blocs such as the European Community and North America are making it difficult to gain access to such large consumer markets. It is therefore imperative to join the institutional network which grants access to these markets: by the late 1980s, for example, almost one quarter of all exports from developing countries (and especially from Africa) went to the European Community (South Commission 1990: 242). But membership has its price, and the price is adherence to a number of rules which essentially keep the market sphere beyond the reach of political decision-making. Over three-quarters of the World Trade Organization is comprised of 'developing countries and countries in the process of economic reform from non-market systems'; and of these, 60 implemented trade liberalization policies during the Uruguay Round which would allow them to operate according to the stipulated trade rules of the WTO (WTO 1995: 6).

The WTO, like its predecessor, the GATT (General Agreement on Tariffs and Trade), does contain provisions to assist developing countries which may not be able to compete effectively with other WTO members: introduced originally in 1965, Part IV of GATT 1994 provides for special concessions for developing states, while the 'enabling clause', established fourteen years later during the Tokyo Round, further strengthens this practice. Nonetheless, the broader rules of membership in the WTO do require a more forceful 'hands off' policy in matters where the state had historically been able to impose its policy decisions. The WTO works on the assumption that development goals are best achieved through a system of liberal trade policies which permit the 'unrestricted flow of goods, services, and productive inputs' (WTO 1995: 7, 17). A wealthy state can, logically, achieve more political goals than a poor one; but what many developing countries point out is that if this level of wealth is achieved due to rules which restrict state activity when it interferes with the operation of the market, then no level of wealth will allow the state to play a forceful role in non-commercial areas which may be of great importance to its citizens.

There are several examples where this limitation on state activity is a matter of no little interest. One is the extent to which market-oriented policies can be restricted due to concerns for ecological salubrity. There is frequently no immediate profit to be made from sound ecological practices, and often many direct costs to be incurred by 'environmentally-friendly' programmes. Smaller states can find it difficult to oblige large corporations to observe such measures both because such an attempt would interfere the firm's 'market freedoms' and because corporations would simply threaten to relocate to a less-demanding host country. Environmental groups such as Greenpeace have therefore attempted to establish multilateral regulations for environmental protection rather than focusing on domestic governments, but have had little success to date. At the WTO's June 1996 meeting of the Committee on Trade and Environment, for example, there was little support for the attempt to give existing Multilateral Environmental Agreements any teeth by enforcing them through the use of trade measures (*Inside US Trade*, 28 June 1996, 3). This is not an issue of developed against developing countries *per se*; India, Mexico, and Brazil amongst others agreed with the United States in opposing such a policy. But without such a multilateral policy it is difficult to see how any country, and especially poorer states, would have the ability to impose such environmental restrictions on its own without offending against either agreements for liberal trade policies, or larger corporations themselves, should they develop the political incentive to do so.

Much has been made, too, of the 'human costs' of a strongly market-oriented growth policy. The attempt to establish food security while pursuing a strategy of trade in commodities is best achieved, according to many developing nations, on the basis of supply management in order to establish secure and stable remunerative prices in areas notorious for destructive boom-and-bust cycles (South Commission 1990: 247). But supply management requires clear violation of market principles, and even countries like Canada are battling to retain their ability to continue with supply management programmes in the face of charges of unfair competition from neighbouring states. Moreover, the WTO is very critical of TRIMs, in which host states can impose conditions or performance requirements upon firms doing business in these countries. Yet developing countries are concerned that a blanket restriction against TRIMs could prevent states from insisting upon such requirements as long-term investment or technology transfer which may be important in establishing their development goals:

> There are very sound economic reasons why developing countries need to regulate the inflow of private foreign investment and to subject these investments to conditions and performance requirements based on their development needs and priorities. Given the vast imperfections in both product and factor markets in most developing countries, flows of foreign investment whose volumes and pattern are determined solely by the corporate objectives of foreign investors would not produce an efficient or optimum outcome from the standpoint of capital-importing countries. (South Commission 1990: 251)

But what is perhaps the most controversial assumption underlying the WTO outlook is its apparent assumption that an economically revived state will necessarily be one in which the rewards of market participation will be liberally distributed throughout the economy. Economic liberalization, states the WTO, is 'an increasingly important component in the success of the economic adjustment programmes which many WTO members are undertaking, even though it may often involve significant transaction costs' (WTO 1995, 17). These transaction costs may be significant indeed, and there is no reason to believe that they are necessarily temporary. As Guéhenno mused, an important aspect of nations' loss of sovereignty has been the limitation of states' ability to tax the production of wealth at levels the state sees fit simply due to the mobility of capital, the difficulty regarding the attribution of added value through internal transfer of item within on corporate realm, and the competition between states for new forms of wealth creation (1995: 10).

When development is viewed as 'a process of self-reliant growth, achieved through the participation of the people acting in their own interest as they see them, and under their own control' rather than as the level of national wealth, the ability of the market to facilitate democratic development is ambivalent at best. While it is reasonable to say that a state which produces little has little to redistribute, the wealth produced under a market regime seems almost to be conditional upon not being redistributed at all. It is no doubt of little consolation that these same dynamics seem increasingly to apply even in the wealthiest democratic states. The problem is that if the appeal of democracy rests in its ability to permit people to live their lives as they wish, then a democratic state bound by the dynamics of the international market is destined to lose much of its appeal. This may well explain why so much attention in contemporary democratic thought has recently focused upon issues of culture and identity: it places the political emphasis not on redistribution but upon policies that can sit quite contentedly with market freedoms. The market does not care if a Sabbath day is Saturday or Sunday, whether workers speak French or English on a shop floor, whether women must wear modest clothing, or whether religious headgear conflicts with uniform requirements. Issues of cultural identity are areas in which the state can still impose a certain degree of control without offending the market. It is thus in making pronouncements upon issues of cultural identity that the state can reassert its role of meeting its citizens' needs and concerns and, in doing so, reestablishes the appeal of democracy in the face of states' ineffectualness in addressing the more material concerns of citizens.

And yet there is, at the same time, good reason to doubt the claim that a weakening of the nation-state leads progressively to the undermining of democracy. The causal argument, again, is this: because of the dynamics of international capital, a state is increasingly unable to meet the demands of its citizens (to provide, for example, a reasonable degree of economic security or equity). And, to the extent that the appeal of democracy rests in the sense of control that the populace feels it maintains over the state (and over its own collective destiny), a state constrained by external forces from responding to popular demands weakens both its own legitimacy and the credibility of 'democracy' as a political construct.

There are at least three challenges to this claim. The first approach is to query the extent to which 'the state', as an abstract construct, has ever been able satisfactorily to meet the demands of its citizenry in the face of external economic forces. There have, argues one historian, generally been two overarching threats to nation-states. One is the challenge to territorial integrity, and the other is the inability to 'provide the people within their territory with adequate welfare and comfort':

> It is a frequently advanced contention that free international markets, and particularly their recent expansion, necessarily undermine the foundations of the 'nation-state'. But the dangers of free international markets for nation states have been recognized as a persistently difficult problem of politics ever since their beginning. In fact, some of the characteristic features of the historical development of 'nation-states' can be more readily understood as answers to problems caused by free trade than to other types of threats. (Hont 1994: 170)

Understood historically, he notes pithily, 'the idea of the "nation-state" cannot be now in crisis, because it has always been in "crisis"' (1994: 176).

A second approach is to question the degree to which the constraints faced by modern nation states are in fact due primarily to external market factors, and to suggest that many of the economic constraints faced by democratic polities, and especially the wealthier ones, have been largely internal crises of their own making. The reduced ability to provide generous social programmes, infrastructure, and low rates of taxation is a direct consequence of the massive levels of debt that have been built up since the early 1970s; and these debt burdens, according to rational choice theorists, are a consequence of political officials spending public money as a means of ensuring their reelection, or of unaccountable bureaucrats demanding excessive budgets (see, e.g., Buchanan, 1986).

A third explanation focuses upon the possibility that, rather than states becoming less capable at providing for needs, citizens' expectations have increased unrealistically. These expectations, moreover, have fixed upon problems that an autonomous state could not hope by itself to resolve. These expectations come from numerous sources; there is, for example, a familiar political movement which 'foments excessively high political expectations, and vents its disappointment at the failure of history to live up to them on the state powers which are (in fantasy at any rate) the most concrete facilities for at least attempting to realize them' (Dunn 1994: 10). Yet there is, at the same time, a consumer-driven ethos which insists that the material quality of life can and ought to improve indefinitely; and, as most proponents of the left would point out, the unrestrained working of the market can itself incur costly social externalities (e.g., increasing levels of mechanization leading to high unemployment). Expectations are not only increasing but also shifting to different areas of concern; areas in which states may have little ability (or inclination) to affect a satisfactory result. Environmental groups, as noted above, have been very critical of the WTO's perceived propensity to constrain states' ability to impose environmental regulations domestically. But due to the very nature of ecological degradation the underlying problem to an effective solution 'is not a deficiency in domestic power but a disinclination or incapacity for effective collective action': the main challenge derives not from limited state influence as much as from 'the difficulties of securing effective and trustworthy international cooperation'.

> It is a complicated and unobvious question about many ecological issues whether or not the structure of costs and rewards of cooperation yields a clear balance of advantage for state actors to cooperate or to defect: to form binding collective agreements to restrict environmental damage to one another and abide strictly by their terms, or to participate, in the spirit of Callicles, like skulking brigands, in the complex processes of global negotiations, affix their

signatures slyly to such treaty documents as emerge from them, and resolutely ignore their terms thereafter, whenever it is more convenient to do so. (Dunn 1994: 13–14)

What, then, can be said with any certainty regarding the relationship between the international market, state autonomy, and the salubrity of democracy? It cannot be denied, in the first place, that the international market exerts tremendous demands and constraints upon the vast majority of states who desire to participate within it; and that these impositions and restrictions do pose obstacles to the ability of a state to execute decisions to the satisfaction of its citizenry. At the same time, however, it is quite naive to suggest that a golden era existed when the nation-state as an abstract political entity was able to govern with little concern to external forces. There are many ways in which governance has become easier for states: advances in computer and communications technology, bureaucratic expertise, and international cooperation have in numerous instances permitted governments greater accomplishments than they could have expected before such developments.

It is important, moreover, to keep in mind that the nation-state as an abstract does not exist. Nation-states with varying levels of wealth and influence do exist, and some will manifestly be more capable of withstanding the vicissitudes of the global market than others at various times and for different reasons. How is sovereignty to be measured? Is negotiation in the sphere of international trade evidence of a state's sovereignty, or its gradual loss of sovereignty? The assumption of a causal relationship between market and democracy, either for better or for worse, underpins much political rhetoric and, frequently, a significant degree of public or foreign policy. Like Scriptural citation, selective empirical evidence on this causal relationship can be unearthed to make a persuasive case for either position. What should be emphasized here is that how one wishes to understand the relationship between democracy and the market depends greatly upon how one chooses to interpret 'democracy'. Does the market diffuse power sufficiently to facilitate the emergence of democracy? That depends upon how much diffusion of power democracy requires: if it is sufficient that a small set of powerful competing elites exist to counterbalance each other sufficiently so that none can effectively act with impunity, and if it is sufficient that the rest of the population command a set of negative rights – and most especially private property rights – to forestall arbitrary state activity, then theorists such as Olson may be quite accurate in emphasizing the preeminent role which private property rights play in promoting and maintaining a democratic regime. But if democracy ought to be understood primarily as a system permitting even the most forlorn voice an equal opportunity to determine how her society can and ought to be governed, then considering private property to be prior to (and thus impervious to) collective political demands violates the most fundamental tenet of democratic governance.

The debate concerning the degree to which international economic forces undermine democratic governance by limiting the ability of the state to respond to citizens' demands is, in the same way, dependent upon the way in which democracy is interpreted. Those who view democracy as more than merely a decision-making process which aggregates individual interests hold that democracy is more fundamentally a system which sustains the community by promoting compromise, addressing the material and psychological or spiritual needs of the citizenry, and protecting the well-being of the polity by moderating the demands of any overinfluential group. The democratic state is not merely a broker of individual interests but is also the provider of needs and the facilitator of solidarity; and if it becomes unable to perform these functions due to external exigencies, then it loses its very *raison d'etre.*

This interpretation of democracy can of course be traced to Rousseau's eighteenth-century writings on the nature of democracy but it can, more tellingly, be found in seventeenth-century discussions of the nature of the 'nation state'. '[I]n the conceptual universe derived from the Roman political and legal heritage', writes Hont, 'civitas and natio were far from being interchangeable or intimately connected terms':

> Natio referred to a spatially or hierarchally defined group, sharply demarcated from others. Status or condition, on the other hand, was a temporally defined aspect of either individuals or communities of any size, capturing their standing in the world at a given time, and serving as a marker by which to evaluate the possible directions of change . . . The origins of the modern notion of the 'state' can be found in the process whereby the status of the civitas as a whole, understood as a respublica or commonwealth, became privileged over the status of any of its parts (including the people). (1994: 183–4)

One of the most damning critiques of the absolutist regimes of the seventeenth century was not simply that they did not provide the requisite scope of rights and liberties but, more convincing to the denizens of that era, that they could not or would not modernize to the extent needed to adjust political institutions 'to the emergence of the modern economy and modern warfare, and to the new web of social relations to which these gave rise in the eighteenth century' (Hont 1994: 191). For Abbé Sieyès, for example, a stable and secure nation able to address the fundamental needs of its citizenry required a unified and homogeneous populace bound by a constitution characterised by vertical levels of accountability. This unified and homogeneous population was 'the nation', which, as an abstract amalgamation of united wills, represented the indirect sovereignty of the people. To a large extent, then, the concept of 'democracy' is irretrievably linked to the historical development of the nation-state insofar as the modern conception of the nation-state (as opposed to a 'state' *tout court*) was legitimized by reference to the 'national will'. That Sieyès also held that 'the nation' ought to be deliberately engineered according to territory rather than cultural background is evidence of a very modern political perspective despite the lack of, even fear of, emphasis on individual consent as a necessary component of the 'nation' (Hont 1994: 192–205). Nonetheless, it is hardly surprizing that many contemporary proponents of democracy see its justification lying on the same grounds as that which originally defended the establishment of the nation-state; nor that these same exponents see such a strong link between the efficacy of the state *vis-à-vis* its citizens and the health of modern democracy.

The market, then, is commonly viewed as facilitating democracy by expanding the capacity of the state through increasing the wealth of the citizenry. Not only are individuals more content because they can gratify their particular desires through the market, but the state is through taxation able to address the social requirements not readily met through the market. Increasingly, however, it has become apparent that the means chosen to reinvigorate NICs – the market – works best by constraining the capacity of the state *vis-à-vis* the marketplace. And, as states both developed and developing face social problems that arise despite (and in response to) a vigorous market, an achievable democracy becomes thinner and more unsatisfactory. To the extent that the rewards of a robust economy accrue to a smaller and smaller proportion of the populace, any form of 'democracy' is undermined by the resentful and acrimonious fragmentation of the citizenry. To the extent that democracy is assumed to exist through the consent of the people, it is hardly surprizing that many of 'the people' should choose to be uncooperative when they perceive that such a system, 'democratic' or not, promises little for them except a continual stream of peremptory threats.

In response to this dilemma has emerged a school of thought which attempts to regain a sense of social solidarity. Some form of market mechanisms may be important to a viable democracy; but so too, according to this account, is a sense of social rapport without which a market ultimately undermines the invisible bonds upon which democratic cooperation precariously sits. This was Rousseau's point (and also, to an extent, Tocqueville's); and this was a warning quickly forgotten in the easy assumption of ever-increasing wealth smoothly distributed to all. A chastened generation is now revisiting this point. From the World Bank's cautious development strategies incorporating the idea of 'governance' (World Bank 1989, 1992, 1994), to the discussions of the British Left regarding 'stakeholder capitalism' (Hutton, 1995), an attempt is being made – with varying degrees of enthusiasm – to temper the fragmentary tendency of the market with a strategy of social solidarity under the banner of a reinvigorated democracy. In the wake of state-driven and market-driven theories of development, then, come those based upon the reanimation of 'civil society'. What is this account, and how theoretically coherent is it? Much hope has been placed in the various formulations of democratization *via* civil society: but can this emphasis upon civil society deliver democracy from the intemperance of the marketplace?

6

Civil society

> To invoke the need for community spirit . . . is essentially an admission that concrete ways of dealing with the respective problems have not yet been discovered – community spirit is called upon as some deus ex machina. What is actually required to make progress with the novel problems that a society encounters on its road is political entrepreneurship, imagination, patience here, impatience there, and other varieties of virtu and fortuna – I cannot see much point (and do see some danger) in lumping all of this together by an appeal to Gemeinsinn.
> (Albert O. Hirschman 1994: 216)

Genealogy and usage

The focus upon both the market and civil society as strategies for democratization has been a reaction to the abysmal and disheartening performance of state-led development throughout the 1960s and 1970s. And as the 'sociological counterpart of the market in the economic sphere and to democracy in the political sphere', suggests White, 'it is a valuable analytical complement to the tired old "state-market" dichotomy' (1994: 375). But how useful is this focus upon civil society as a means of either theorizing about, or strategizing toward, democratization? Both activists and academics have been placing a great deal of attention on this subject; and major development documents by such bodies as the World Bank and the Organization for Economic Cooperation and Development (OECD) have increasingly articulated their positions in terms of the importance of civil society.

Interestingly, this emphasis upon civil society is not limited to developing states: it is a concept increasingly arising in discussions about the dismal and apathetic state of democratic participation in contemporary western states as well (e.g., Putnam 1995; Sandel 1996). Other theorists are more ambivalent: 'I want to join', wrote Michael Walzer, rather wistfully, 'but I am somewhat uneasy with, the civil society argument' (1991: 303). This 'civil society argument' thus dominates much contemporary political debate within both political theory and comparative politics; and is perhaps indicative of a positive trend towards an increasingly normative investigation of development issues. The 'civil society argument' is in this way both a normative claim and an analytical argument; it holds that 'men and women actively engaged – in state, economy, and nation, and also in churches, neighbourhoods, and families, and in many other settings too' (*ibid.*) is both a good thing in and of itself, and also the best strategy to remedy a number of the political ills that plague contemporary polities.

Why one would wish to join those espousing this position is evident: normatively, it seems to capture all that is virtuous and benign in political life; analytically, it avoids the need to incorporate the faceless and imperious state or corrupt, inefficient, and unrepresentative political parties as agents of political change. Whether one ought to trust one's more benevolent instincts and champion 'civil society' is a far more intellectually fraught issue. '[W]e are convinced that the recent reemergence of the 'discourse of civil society' is at the heart of a sea change in contemporary political culture', write Cohen and Arato. 'Despite the proliferation of this "discourse" and of the concept itself, however, no one has developed a systematic theory of civil society' (1992: 3). The authors are certainly correct to note the ubiquity of the concept. Unfortunately, however, the task of 'theorizing civil society' is ultimately impossible. This is not to say that political events cannot be explained by looking at non-state agents: merely that the class of non-state agents is so tremendously wide and varied, and the supporting explanatory variables so complex and diverse, that any attempt to find a 'theory' to fit all of these cases could only do so at the cost of making that theory descriptive or exegetical at best, and puerile or fatuous at worst.

The discussion in this chapter will not directly be a critique of Cohen and Arato's theorization of civil society (although their work is one of the most comprehensive and energetic attempts at such a task). Rather, I wish to look more broadly at many of the issues involved in theorizing civil society *per se*.

This first section is a short discussion of how, and why, the term has come to be used so widely and with such enthusiastic hope. Adam Ferguson, in the late eighteenth century, and both Tocqueville and Hegel, in the early nineteenth, made the idea of a civil society a central part of their own theories of political life. Part of the current perception of novelty regarding the term may possibly be due to the fact that it is generally used by comparativists who, due to the increasing fragmentation and categorization of political science, are simply not expected to be conversant with the penetralia of (until recently) unfashionable or obscure political philosophers. While understandable, this does mean that some of these philosophers' more sobering observations have remained undiscussed and unappreciated. More recently, of course, the ultimately successful struggle against authoritarian regimes in eastern Europe, the concern with the lack of civic spirit and moral bonds in western democracies, and the failure of state-led development in many non-industrialized countries have all given the idea of civil society a more timely resonance.

The second section in this chapter will discuss a number of conceptual objections to the term. Can 'civil society' be defined in a sufficiently clear and precise manner to be usefully employed as an analytical term? Are the functions of civil society explicit, or do diverse interests have contradictory conceptions of what the purpose of this 'political space' is for? Is civil society organized or spontaneous? Political or apolitical? Can we apply the term to non-liberal societies at all? And what of the ubiquitous normative undertone of even the most analytical of accounts? 'Civil society' generally connotes 'civility in society', an understanding not always present when the definition fits many less virtuous organizations (the mafia, it has frequently been observed, meets the prerequisites of numerous definitions of civil society quite well). Finally, are the political implications of such a focus upon civil society fully considered? Tocqueville and Hegel, amongst others, articulated some of the potential costs of attaining a thriving civil society: are contemporary theorists as candid?

There is, as historians of political thought point out, a very clear distinction between 'modern' and 'premodern' conceptions of civil society. The term, as it was used by Aristotle, or Cicero, or even Kant, was synonymous with political society: both referred to a 'pattern of public social life' in which citizens discussed matters important to the community. Civil society was indistinguishable from political society because, as Riedel (1984: 139) points out, social life was by its very nature political. In feudal society, writes Gellner,

> [t]here is only one social order, political and economic. There is no talk of Civil Society as distinct from the state: there is only overlapping, identical political hierarchy and economic specialization, mutually reinforcing each other. Political rank and economic function are firmly welded, and one entails the other. The political subject is also the peasant, the owner of the land is also the ruler and judge. (1994: 55)

By the seventeenth century, the nascent Industrial Revolution in Britain, along with constitutional limitations upon the monarchy, permitted the evolution of a class whose economic strength gave it a certain degree of autonomy from the crown. Adam Ferguson, whose *Essay on the History of Civil Society* was published three years before his more illustrious colleague's treatise on the *Wealth of Nations*, acknowledged the evident separation between the rulers (or warriors) and civilians, and worried that a political/military class separate from a distinct body of civilians could potentially 'create the danger of a takeover by the former', which might well 'destroy the benign order which had itself engendered the separation' (Gellner 1994: 63).

But the most pivotal historical figure in the development of the concept of civil society is G. W. F. Hegel, who clearly differentiated between 'civil' and 'political' society in his *Philosophy of Right*. For Hegel, explains Riedel,

> the expression 'civil' gains a primarily 'social' content as opposed to its original meaning and is no longer taken to be synonymous with 'political' as it was in the eighteenth century. It now names only the 'social' position of the self-supporting citizen within the state which has become absolute politically, and which from its side grants society its own centre of gravity, and sets it free as 'civil'. (1984: 139)

It is important to remember that Hegel was especially concerned not to protect individuals from the state but rather to mitigate the forceful development of individualism which he could discern in the political developments in Britain, France, and America. While he approved the substantive improvements in the character and well-being of individual citizens in the nineteenth century, he argued that they could only be secured and developed within a very specific social and political context. To recreate within a state the respect and recognition that generally existed between family members, argued Hegel in his 1824–5 lectures, it was necessary to concentrate upon the civil associations which could simultaneously 'tear the individual from his family ties' and reinforce the virtue of reciprocating dignity at a much broader level. Civil society, then, acted as a stepping stone from family life to the 'ethical entity' of the modern state; like the market itself, it was a means of teaching individuals how (and why) all individuals within the state were to be seen as agents of respect and dignity.

Taylor (1991) argues that Hegel's account of civil society is in essence a combination of Lockean and Montesquieuean ideas. Locke, while still employing civil society in its traditional, pre-modern sense, nonetheless clearly articulated the argument that an association of free citizens acting to preserve their economic interests existed prior to the establishment of a formal political order. Montesquieu, while less suspicious than Locke of a strong monarchy, still presumed the need for a resilient network of social organizations to hold the monarchy in check. But this synthesis, argues Taylor, meant that the Hegelian formulation of civil society contained certain contradictions evident in much modern usage of the term.

One of the most common tensions manifest in contemporary uses of the concept can be found in the many functions which civil society is to perform. Theorists currently engaged in 'bringing civil society back in' generally do not clearly articulate precisely the functions which this institution is to perform, and often assume that one achievement (such as a limited state) will occasion others (such as civic virtue). The former generally emphasizes the utility of a network of strongly-rooted grassroots organizations in minimizing the need (or the power) of state authority; while the latter attends to the salubrity of a community itself. Bendix has labelled the former 'Anglo-American' term *Zivilgesellschaft*, in distinction to Hegel's own *bürgerliche Gesellschaft* (1990: 143, 148); and the two are frequently used interchangeably by various groups with their own political agenda.

As Cohen and Arato (1992: 31–6; 58–69), amongst others, observe, the ubiquity of the term 'civil society' is closely linked with the growth of intellectual opposition by eastern Europeans to communist authority through the 1970s and 80s. The concept 'civil society', declared Bendix, became a polemical slogan opposed to Communist Party 'dictatorship' (1990–91: 143).

These intellectuals (including Michnik and Kolakowski, in addition to the better-known Sakharov and Solzhenitsyn), like Locke, see civil society both as a separate entity morally prior to the state and, like Tocqueville, view civil society as a means of strictly containing the power of the state. This approach, as Isaac (1993) notes, seems also to hold an intellectual debt to the (especially Russian) anarchists, including Tolstoy, Bakunin, Kropotkin, and Goldman.

Cohen and Arato (1992: 48–58) also note that recent Latin American transitions can be explained by examining the political role of 'civil society'. As O'Donnell and Schmitter describe, for example, '[t]rade unions, grass-roots movements, religious groups, intellectuals, artists, clergymen, defenders of human rights, and professional associations all support each other's efforts toward democratization and coalesce into a greater whole which identifies itself as "the people" (1986: 54)' But Cohen and Arato look less closely at other (less successful) fields of development. In Africa, for example, 'civil society' has been far less robust than in Latin America for a number of reasons, including both the pattern of colonialism and the specific nature of pre-colonial African cultures (see, e.g., Bayart 1986; Hutchful 1995–6). The focus in African development, then, is generally not to investigate the ways in which an existing civil society confronts and mitigates state power, but rather to determine how a viable and stable civil society can be established at all (e.g., Fatton 1992; World Bank 1989). The concerns here address not only questions of power balances between state and citizenry, but also the quality of relationship between the citizens themselves.

In contrast to Latin America, emphasis in Africa following independence from colonial administration was placed upon the state as the agent most capable of quick, intense economic transformation. An unpalatable paradox became apparent as the state, the only agent powerful enough to control the contestation of specific group interests within the newly independent polities, became more than willing to use the resources at its disposal for its own purposes (see the World Bank 1992; Chabal 1986). The current response has thus been upon 'building the capacity' of the society itself to secure economic development with reasonable distribution of rewards, without relying excessively upon a too-often corrupt state administration (e.g., World Bank, 1989; although cf. Jeffries, 1993). This approach encourages aid donors (both bilateral and multilateral) to utilize their resources to strengthen the more organized non-state groups in order to nurture the production of domestic goods and services, to construct efficient means of redistributing social resources and, less explicitly, to consolidate popular bases of political opposition to the state.

To return to Bendix's terminology, it is the establishment of a 'bürgerliche' society, rather than an 'Anglo-American' model, which is the object of Africanists, in contrast to Latin American specialists. The irony here is that contemporary Anglo-Americans themselves are increasingly more concerned with the quality of social relations than simply the balance of power between state and citizenry. The Cold War has been won; Locke is the victor. But the Lockean society held together by a common desire to protect private property has also been viewed more recently as dismayingly superficial. Thus a disparate collection of Anglo-American philosophers including Charles Taylor, Michael Sandel, Michael Walzer, Alasdair MacIntyre, and Robert Bellah have written pensive works concerned not, like their eastern European counterparts, with the overwhelming power of the state *vis-à-vis* its citizens, but with the nature of citizenship itself.

Sandel has labelled the distinction one of liberal freedom, which entails 'a neutral framework of rights within which people can choose their own values and ends', versus 'republican' freedom, which 'requires a formative politics, a politics that cultivates in citizens the qualities of character that self-government requires' (1996: 58). Rosenblum (1994) has similarly divided civil society into a triptych of 'democratic' civil society, which schools the citizenry in the skills of public deliberation; 'mediating' civil society, necessary to inculcate the virtues of 'civility, sociability, and responsibility'; and 'elective' civil society, which encourages and accommodates the 'incongruity and movement' necessary in a tolerant and pluralistic political culture. And Taylor discusses the 'two rather different kinds of hope' which arise from those articulating the term civil society: '[t]he one moves towards the norm of self-determination; the other towards the goal of marginalizing the political' (1991: 131).

Both political theorists and public policy officials, as well as political activists, have evinced an ardour for a term that seems, despite its considerable age, to have recently acquired a great deal of novelty and relevance. The question remains, however, whether the concept has gained such popularity by virtue of the analytical resonance it imparts, or simply because more discriminating ideas have been tried and found wanting. In sum, the issue is whether the concept of civil society is 'indispensable' because it promises 'a theoretical framework that can anchor what is in the end a common discussion across boundaries' (Cohen and Arato 1992: 69); or whether 'the basic concept appears to be riddled with so many ambivalences that good reasons to hope for this are few' (Honneth 1993: 22).

Conceptual and analytical objections

Locating 'civil society'

The difficulties in articulating a precise definition of 'civil society' mirrors, unsurprisingly, the debates during the 1980s (especially within neomarxist theory) regarding the specific nature of 'the state' (see, e.g., Carnoy 1984). One way of avoiding this difficulty is simply to depict civil society as 'those dimensions of social life which cannot be confounded with, or swallowed up in, the state' (Taylor 1991: 117). And, while theorists such as Taylor begin their discussions with such a loose designation in order to explain precisely why it is so difficult to define clearly, most writers never proceed beyond such general definitions as 'all civil institutions and organizations which are prior to the state' (Honneth 1993: 19) or 'those human networks that exist independently of, if not anterior to, the political state' (Isaac 1993: 356).

Most accounts stress some aspect of 'civil society' over others: Walzer's, for example, emphasizes the inherent sociability of such a sphere:

> The words 'civil society' name the space of uncoerced human association and also the set of relational networks – formed for the sake of family, faith, interest, and ideology – that fill this space . . .
> The picture here is of people freely associating and communicating with one another, forming and reforming groups of all sorts, not for the sake of any particular formation – family, tribe, nation, religion, commune, brotherhood or sisterhood, interest group or ideological movement – but for the sake of sociability itself. For we are by nature social, before we are political or economic beings. (1991: 293, 298)

Other accounts, in contrast, focus on the natural self-interestedness of human beings: 'Civil society is the system of interactions which is established and sustained when people act self-interestedly but independently in a community' (Drydyk 1991: 457).

Much of the literature regarding theories of the state pointed out the surprising difficulty in distinguishing precisely what the state *is* from what it is not. In the first place, our societies are comprised of bodies, agencies, and institutions which have some governance functions but which are not elected, such as the judiciary, the police force, and the bureaucracy. Professional associations perform regulatory functions, but are generally seen to be self-regulating. There are in addition an increasing number of quasi-autonomous non-governmental associations (quangos) and parastatals, such as housing authorities or crown corporations, as well as public services such as universities and health workers. Many of the 'autonomous civil associations' discussed by theorists utilizing 'civil society' are also funded directly by the state (such as government-subsidized women's umbrella organizations, or cultural associations); others (such as religious or charitable organizations) are funded indirectly by the state through tax relief.

Finally, because of the way we use the term 'state' in international relations to mean a relatively self-contained entity, legally distinct from other states, it is easy to think of 'the state' as a unit completely separate from 'civil society'. But when referring specifically to domestic politics, it is important to keep in mind that 'the state' is comprised of individuals who themselves make up some part of 'civil society': politicians, military officers, and bureaucrats frequently belong to churches or clubs or cultural associations as individuals; and thus do not always make decisions of behalf of 'the state' that are purely divorced from the interests of 'civil society'. For example, in many African states, as Hutchful points out, 'subaltern elements in the state structure, such as junior civil servants and even military other ranks, are often actively involved in the struggle for democracy and accountability and thus should be regarded as an important component of civil society' (1995–6: 71). Despite their drawbacks, sophisticated neomarxist theories at least recognized that the composition of 'state' and 'civil society' was a complex relationship rather than a clear opposition, the question being the extent to which the state worked on behalf of a particular class (e.g., Poulantzas 1969; Miliband 1970, 1973.)

More recently, civil society has been used to refer not only to that which is not the state, but also to that which is not part of the economy. While many authors are content to conceive of civil society as a social sphere in which individuals interact with each other 'in a series of overlapping relationships and associations – communal, civic, religious, economic, social, and cultural' (Mirsky, 1994: 4), others choose to define their civil society exclusive of the economy. Cohen and Arato refer to 'a "third realm" differentiated from the economy and the state (what we call "civil society"' (1992: 18). This definition is becoming increasingly popular with theorists who choose to use the term (e.g., Dean 1991: 379); partly because the term has been increasingly employed by the Left as a means of rejuvenating socialism in the west and, somewhat paradoxically, partly because the concept is also favoured by traditional moral conservatives (as opposed to neoliberals) who see consumerism and the exigencies of the market as destructive to social bonds.

But if it is difficult to ascertain what is 'not the state', it is even more perplexing to determine what is 'not the economy'. A large number of autonomous civil associations frequently lobby the government for changes in management of the economy even if they themselves have no direct impact on the economy: trade unions, for example, are frequently seen as key actors in processes of democratization (as in South Africa: see, e.g., Adler and Webster, 1995). And, to the extent that 'civil society' is most commonly used by development theorists interested in processes of democratization, by ignoring corporate actors in authoritarian regimes one dismisses one of the most forceful loci of opposition to well-entrenched state power (e.g., MacIntyre 1990). Moreover, market exchanges occur continuously in most people's daily lives; the market pervades 'civil society'. Do individuals step out of the sphere of civil society and into a different environment every time they execute a market transaction? Or only 'relevant' transactions? Which transactions are relevant? Can we really distinguish 'the economy' from what goes on in 'civil society'?

Cohen and Arato attempt to resolve this definitional difficulty by following Claus Offe in noting that 'economic activities in the substantive sense are (at least in part) included in civil society, but economy as a formal process is outside of it' (1992: 75): 'while we also differentiate the economy from civil society, we differ from the pluralists in that we do not seal off the borders between them on the basis of an allegedly sacrosanct freedom of contract or property right' (ibid.: 20). In other words, it would seem, 'civil society' does not generally involve 'the economy', although it does occasionally and on certain issues (although we are not told clearly in which instances and on what occasions). Rather than making it more useful analytically such a distinction makes the concept in question much less helpful. But why is it important to be so clear about political concepts that are, by their very nature, so unsettled and amorphous?

Conceptualizing power

Words, wrote one professor of moral philosophy, are like tools: we must endeavour to clean them occasionally (Austin 1961: 129). If we do not, then they do not perform their functions as well as they might. And (despite the possible objections of some postmodernists), as political scientists are concerned with identifying and explaining the nature of power, they require tools that will allow them to do so with some precision.

Walzer, as noted above, conceives civil society as the sphere of 'uncoerced' behaviour between individuals (1991: 293). But if this is the case, actual manifestations of 'civil society' are rare indeed. This is one of the most uncompromising weaknesses of the concept: those who use the term seem to shuffle between conceptions of what civil society is and what, ideally, it could be. And, while there is good reason to talk about what the exemplar of 'civil society' would be, such a usage cannot be used as an analytical term to investigate the political role that civil society does in fact play. This is partly because, as I have already noted, there is no clear agreement regarding what function 'civil society' should have. But the problem is also due to a failure to investigate the nature of power within civil society . This could, in turn, be due to the hasty dichotomization of 'state' from 'civil society', the assumption being that all things political belong in the former sphere, with the latter remaining an environment of cooperation and good will.

Recent theorists of 'civil society' have suggested that we utilize a tripartite distinction of 'state', 'civil society', and 'political society'. 'The concept of political society' write Cohen and Arato, 'thus includes the public sphere as its major dimension, but, given the stress on conflict (and negotiation and compromise), it is not entirely reducible to it. ' (1992: 38) But what does it mean to separate 'political' (non-state) society from 'civil' society? Must we take this to mean that the myriad groups and organizations within the latter sphere are not fraught with their own indigenous form of politics? Most people who have been an active participant in any voluntary association will probably attest that, regardless of how morally earnest the organization may be, contestations of power and authority will likely be found not too far underneath the surface (Anthony Trollope's chronicles of Barset being an excellent example). Surely one of the most profound victories of feminist theory from the 1960s on has been the acceptance of a much broader definition of 'power' than that practiced by formal political groups. Power is no longer simply seen as the ability of A to make B do or abstain from an activity but also, less tangibly, the ability to define the political agenda or the ability to shape others' interests with their approval and support (e.g., Lukes 1974). Power suffuses and pervades most instances of social interaction; frequently it is benign and tolerable, but often it is not. By making a distinction between 'political' and 'civil' society, we must either accept that the groups comprising civil society are not affected by the exercise of power (a conclusion manifestly unpalatable to those concerned with the politics of race, class, and gender); or we must grant that the politics that do inform these civil associations are simply less important than the 'formal' power relations in 'political society' (a suggestion that is probably equally unacceptable to those concerned with the 'politics of difference').

Another manifestation of the confusion regarding the conceptualization of power in civil society is the disparity of opinion regarding the extent to which the groups comprising this sphere must, to merit the definition, either be 'spontaneous' or 'well organised. ' Many theorists stress the almost anarchical nature of civil society, emphasizing the lack of structure and organization. 'Membership in this kind of voluntary civil association', writes Tamás, 'is nothing but a "discreet" series of disjointed political acts. Institutions in a civil society are shapeless congeries of decisions between mutually consenting private persons; in other words, they are not institutions' (1994: 217). Similarly, Isaac (1993) discusses civil society as a collection of self-contained, present-oriented, self-limiting groups that are 'more or less spontaneously formed'; while Gellner (1991: 303) insists that civil society must be large, powerful, and organized: '[a]n atomized or powerless residue would fail to qualify.'

It is understandable that each individual instance of 'civil society' could have its own specific manifestation and dynamic of power. But if this is the case, then to what extent can power within civil society be *theorized* at all? And if it cannot be theorized adequately, then to what extent ought it to play a pre-eminent analytical role in a discipline concerned explicitly with the determination of patterns of power? Some particularly thoughtful theorists have attempted to show how the concept of civil society can remain useful even while acknowledging its diverse interpretations: White, for example, argues that '[r]ather than trying to solve the problem of clarity by adopting a restrictive notion of "civil society, " it may make more practical sense to adopt an approach which tries to come to terms with this breadth rather than defining it away' (1994: 379). He then presents a working definition of civil society as 'an intermediate associational realm between the state and family populated by organizations which are separate from the state, enjoy autonomy in relation to the state and are formed voluntarily by members of society to protect or extend their interests or values' (*ibid.*: 379); and proceeds to explain the various manifestations of civil society depending upon the 'terms of its relationship to the broader socio-economic structure in which it is embedded' (*ibid.*: 386). While this flexible approach works adequately as a means of describing the political relations in any given context, it does not work as a viable basis upon which to 'theorize' civil society as a strategy for democratization because, as I argue below, it does not permit a clear account of causality to emerge.

Normative connotations

The idea of civil society is unrepentantly grounded within the history of liberal thought. As the European state grew in power and complexity so too grew articulate opposition to its influence; the political theory of the eighteenth and nineteenth centuries – from Ferguson and Locke to Tocqueville and Marx – was an ongoing attempt to articulate a convincing account of the legitimate boundaries of state power. But while the original conceptualization of civil society was rooted in western political development, it is a term that is increasingly being applied to non-western contexts. Yet to what extent can it – or ought it – to be applied to manifestly non-liberal states?

It was perhaps the development and utilization of civil society by eastern European intellectuals, with no little success, which led theorists of democratization enthusiastically to apply the term to those instances where equally authoritarian regimes practiced similarly stringent politics. But eastern Europe, despite its varied political histories, still has much greater an affinity to liberalism than most other non-liberal states and especially, as Gellner argues, than with Muslim states, where the society,

> has a very strong commitment to the faith which defines it, and little, if any, powerful longing for civil society, for a set of religiously neutral institutions counterbalancing the state. In the struggle of the networks, violation of the faith is a weighty but not always decisive consideration which can be invoked against any one of them. To sum up, there is a plethora of faith and little craving for civil society. (1991: 328)

But Norton disagrees, arguing that 'the lineage of the concept should be largely irrelevant': 'Applying the concept in the Middle East is not an exercise in imposing alien social values on the region any more than exploring aspects of religiosity can be construed as proselytizing' (1993: 212). But there are two different ideas at work here, which may account for the disagreement between Norton and Gellner and, it would seem, value judgements pervade both approaches.

The first type of subjective claim being inferred in the use of 'civil society', and perhaps the reason that Gellner wishes to discount the utility of the term at all, is that, to the extent that 'civil society' is (in its broadest definition) that which is completely outside of the purview of the state, there is an implicit assumption that there *ought* to be a sphere that is outside of the purview of the state. According to Islamic religious codes the political leaders are also those who oversee religious behaviour, a practice that informs private life very profoundly. In other words, it is in theory impossible to make clear divisions between 'the personal' and 'the public' simply because Islamic societies are not based upon the liberal principles which hold such a division to be important. Those holding Gellner's position, then, would argue that looking for a foreign concept like a private/public split is, notwithstanding Norton's objection, indeed a form of 'proselytizing'. For, if it is not in fact important, then why look for it?

Defenders of Norton's position, however, would likely point out that women's movements, business associations, organized labour, and other groups often critical of government policy simply do, in practice, exist. To the extent that these theorists do hold a point of view distinct from that of the official position, it is possible to apply a purely analytical and neutral concept of 'civil society' to them. To such an extent these theorists are correct: but such analyses generally contain a different type of implicit value judgement in the types of groups which they are willing to classify under the rubric of 'civil society'. Norton, for example, accepts only those groups which chafe under 'repression at the hands of the state' (1993: 205); and other theorists too seem willing only to classify those groups as part of 'civil society' if they have a political agenda of which the theorist himself approves.

While some (such as Walzer) are happy with an account of civil society that focuses largely upon groups whose primary function is the simple human desire for sociability (bridge clubs and baseball teams), more often political scientists desire only to focus upon those associations which have specific political objectives. Isaac (1993: 359), for example, defines civil society as self-constituted voluntary associations 'that are organized to resist specific injustices'; while Cohen and Arato are drawn by a vision of civil society as 'self-limiting democratizing movements seeking to expand and protect spaces for both negative liberty and positive freedom and to recreate egalitarian forms of solidarity without impairing economic self-regulation' (1992: 17).

But conceptualizing civil society as only those groups whose aim is the achievement of morally appropriate goals does render the idea unapologetically subjective and, as such, unfit to do much analytical work. The mafia might, for example, be justifiably excluded from the groups making up 'civil society' (on the grounds, perhaps, that this organization involves economic transactions); but the same cannot be said of the Ku Klux Klan or Hitler Youth. And, while these groups may be a rather extreme examples, there are more difficult examples (such as Real Women or International Socialism) which provoke widely differing responses about their moral suitability as legitimate groups for civil society. The question, of course, is what criteria, other than moral subjectivity, can be applied to distinguish between groups that are part of 'civil society', and those which are not.

The conceptual difficulties, again, are that theorists frequently use the notion of civil society as an ethical ideal interchangeably with the concept of civil society as an analytical

construct; and that the various (and often contradictory) functions of 'civil society' are not articulated. If we choose to
analyze the political dynamics of a society by using a definition
of civil society which only incorporates those associations
which we feel have morally credible objectives, then our
account of the political relations within that society become
equally subjective (i.e., it becomes an account of the extent to
which that society can conceivably achieve a political state of
which we morally approve). And, while some writers are quite
content to articulate their ethical standards clearly from the
outset, others are not so forthcoming.

Even those who are quite clear that 'civil society' is a good
thing are often confused about why it is so. Again, this confusion has its roots in the contradictory genealogy of the term
itself. And, while those who wrote about civil society in eastern
Europe generally were concerned about the overwhelming
power of the state, and while those who focus upon civil society
in industrial democracies frequently address the apathy and
nihilism of modern urban life, it is less clear how civil society
is to be construed outside of these two areas. Indeed, some states
weathering economic and cultural devastation as well as political repression no doubt suffer both malignancies equally.
Unfortunately, the aims of each of these conceptions of 'civil
society' are not always without contradiction; and the expression of 'meaningfulness', as we see in occasional outbreaks of
nationalist venom, is not always one which seeks to mitigate
the unbridled exercise of power.

Consideration of the implications

The enthusiasm for 'civil society' throughout the 1990s both as
an analytical device to understand why things happen and, more
commonly, as an ideal model of political life leaves much
unsaid. Part of the reason for this silence regarding the potential
costs to be incurred with such an uncritical emphasis upon the
concept is because, as noted above, there is little willingness to
investigate the various dynamics of power within the sphere of
'civil society'. (And one of the reasons that such dynamics are
not rigorously investigated is because they vary so considerably
from situation to situation, a point discussed more fully below.)
This objection is made with some force by G. M. Tamás, who
notes that, like communism, 'the myth of civil society is a tale
of a noncoercive political order' (1994: 216). The voluntary

associations comprising civil society are both contractual and impermanent; but this absence of coercion means that each of these contractual acts is 'a new affirmation of individual will, a new commitment and a new beginning'. They are also acts requiring 'a sustained effort of the will. ' And, while the description of civil society thus far may seem rather reminiscent of anarchist thought, argues Tamás, it also has much in common with the more idealist aspects of Marx's writings:

> Civil society is conceived as a regulative idea that can be approached asymptotically by continuously reducing the power of the state, of tradition, and of economic necessity. If this picture reminds the reader of communism, he is on the right track. Impermanent contractual obligations as the rule of civil society spell out the end to alienation that was held by Marx to mean the interchangeability of social roles, the end to the rigidity of belonging to social groups that – like castes – monopolize social functions (thought, toil, battle), making them unavailable for members of the out- groups, severely limiting our 'substantive' freedom. (1994: 217)

It may be objected that this is account is both extreme and alarmist, and that Tamás' assertion that 'Eastern Europe – *und morgen die ganze Welt* – has reinvented Communism' (*ibid.*: 218) depends upon a rather selective understanding of the nature of civil society. The very focus upon civil society and governance, as advocated by the major multilateral aid agencies, for example, rests precisely upon political accountability and respect for the rule of law, admittedly two quite bourgeois notions. But Tamás' account does underscore the naive and potentially dangerous faith in the bucolic and benign character of a 'political space' free of domination by either state or market, even though it is precisely through either the state or the economy that groups and individuals generally find themselves best protected. Legal strictures to prevent harassment and discrimination on the basis of 'difference' requires at least some state presence in civil society; while individuals who fear persecution due to some aspects of 'difference' find that a substantial degree of economic clout is often one of the best means of limiting the distress others can impose. Like Adam Ferguson, Alexis de Tocqueville was well aware that an independent civil society had its own negative dynamics. In addition to his observation that fellow citizens could be just as ruthless as a corrupt state, Tocqueville worried that the very success of a thriving social sphere could lead to a political apathy that might

vest too much power in the hands of those who had little intention of using it benignly. Current accounts of civil society do
assume that individuals will zestfully contribute to the political
fabric of a society but fail to recognize, as Tocqueville did, that
the more successfully apolitical organizations fulfil the social
functions of interaction between individuals, and the less of a
political threat facing them, the less motivation there is for
people to participate in the stresses and irritations of democratic politics.

Hegel too assumed that citizens in the ethical State would be
active both socially and politically; but he was willing to
acknowledge forms of political motivation that strike most
modern liberals as unethical as well as unpalatable. One could,
for example, achieve what theorists such as Walzer and Cohen
and Arato like to call 'strengthening solidarity' and 'making
connections' by emphasizing the danger faced by the polity as a
whole. Warfare, on this account, might be a useful and salubri-
ous situation in moderation, because it defines common
purpose and stresses the virtue of self-sacrifice for the common
good. War was, for a nineteenth-century Prussian, simply part
of the business of politics; and the desire for a Kantian world
peace was more a sign of naivety and weakness than of ethical
consistency. But it does raise an issue for us that ought to be
addressed with a certain degree of brutal honesty: to what
extent does the creation of 'egalitarian forms of solidarity'
within a society depend upon the creation of a threatening
Other against which such bonds can be nurtured and defined?
Most theorists espousing the reinforcement of civil society tend
to believe, like Rorty, that the fear of those different from us is
remediable by gradually and gently exposing ourselves, as a
society, to those dissimilar from ourselves (Rorty 1989: 196).
What empirical evidence we have, however, seems to favour
Hegel's account of the development of solidarity as much, if not
more, than Rorty's.

Contemporary liberals are, no less than communitarians,
recognizing the intangible force with which cultural ties sit
athwart more traditional liberal principles of universality and
individualism. Their concern, as noted above, is more upon the
recreation of 'meaningfulness' in social life than it is upon mit-
igating the power of the state in modern politics. These thinkers have much evidence at their disposal, for blood ties and the
protection of traditional customs seem in so many instances to

be more worth fighting for than the sedate principles of due process and political accountability. But the very resonance of such trends must also raise the question of the extent to which the achievement of one comes possibly at the expense of the other. This is not, of course, to assert that the two trends are mutually exclusive: it is merely to suggest that neither are they natural allies. The hope that the comfortable feeling of inclusiveness can be achieved without deliberately excluding others may not be ill founded, but it will probably require a large amount of work and a larger portion of caution.

Lack of causal clarity

The problem with 'civil society' as an analytical concept, or even as a political ideal, is not that it is undertheorized, but that it is overtheorized. It leaves out very little. Let us look at the vision of civil society that is articulated as a desirable political objec-tive: '[t]he task', write Cohen and Arato, 'is to guarantee the autonomy of the modern state and economy while simultane-ously protecting civil society from destructive penetration and functionalization by the imperatives of these two spheres' (1992: 25). This is no small order. What does it mean to 'protect' civil society from 'destructive penetration'? Does it assume that some network must exist, impervious to state power, or does it mean that a network consisting of a certain set of moral virtues (egalitarian, polite, nurturing) remains autonomous from state authority? But how can a civil sphere that must remain subject to the laws of the state stay autonomous from it? And how do we achieve a society characterized by 'civility' if the state is barred from using its authority? Must we guilelessly assume that, once the distorting influences of State and Economy are removed, people will be able to relax and treat each other with the respect, kindness, and dignity that is their due? Such a claim is not novel: it is, after all, what sat at the heart of Marx's vision of a stateless society. Articulating a vision of what we would, ideally, like our society to be can be useful, as it acts as a measure of what we have already achieved, and how far we have to go. But to assume that such a scenario is a readily achievable political task, without explaining precisely how such behaviour is to be accomplished, makes such an account more of a statement of faith than a work of theory.

But if the concept of civil society as a political ideal is both descriptively vague and politically feckless, the use of civil society as an analytical instrument is futile. To utilize a term that defies clear description in order to theorize about achieving an impossibly romantic situation in numerous political contexts that bear little or no resemblance to each other is a brave intellectual task. Grappling with the popularity of Freudian psychoanalysis and marxist theory after the First World War, Karl Popper wrote that the problem with various theoretical analyses was that 'these theories appeared to be able to explain practically everything that happened within the fields to which they referred': if one looked hard enough for corroborating evidence, one would inevitably find it (1963: 34–5). To count as a theory with analytical integrity, continued Popper, it must 'forbid certain things to happen. The more a theory forbids, the better it is'. This was because the vaguer the theory, the more proponents 'were able to explain away anything that might have been a refutation of the theory had the theory or prophecies been more precise' (*ibid.*: 36–7).

What are proponents of 'civil society' attempting to achieve? There is, as noted above, the declaration that a strong civil society is simply a good thing; generally for the same reasons that we hold democracy, accountability, due process, and the respect for human dignity to be good things. But there are also analytical objectives that are not quite so readily articulated. The first of these is the assumption that the act of strengthening civil society will either diminish or prevent authoritarian government; and the second is that reinforcing the bonds of civil society will simply make people happier and more 'fulfilled' individuals. This will lead them to perform their duties as citizens in a heartier and more engaged way which will, in turn, maintain a stable and productive society. But what would count as evidence against either of these claims? To be useful as an analytical term, proponents of 'civil society' must be able to reply to three objections.

1. *The definition is too ambiguous.* As discussed above, Cohen and Arato, who claim to have written the most thorough treatment of the term, dissect civil society (1992: 38) into two components, civil society ('the space of social experimentation for the development of new forms of life, new types of solidarity, and social relations of cooperation and work') and political society ('the space in which the autonomy of groups and the articulation of conflict among them are defended and the discussion and debate of collective choice occur'). These on their

own do not leave out very much; but then Cohen and Arato go on to say that they intend 'to use both conceptions and at times to combine them', both in terms of their normative and analytical dimensions (*ibid.*: 80). Moreover, while civil society is the 'third realm' differentiated from both the economy and the state, the term ought, they write, to include 'economic activities in the substantive sense', at least 'in part' (*ibid.*: 75). Given the enormity of the entity considered here as 'civil society', it would be surprising to find anything that such a concept could not explain. Nonetheless, one might choose to adopt White's strategy of employing a deliberately broad definition of civil society in order to apply the term to a wide range of possible contexts. What are the possible objections to this approach?

2. *Causal relationships are circular or misidentified.* When 'civil society' is defined so broadly, the distinction between agent and subject becomes blurred, often to the point where any relevant analytical distinction is lost altogether and the causal relationship becomes circular. If the point of identifying civil society as an analytical construct is that it can be used to change the political nature of the polity in question, then saying that 'reinforcing the vibrancy of certain civil associations will make our state stronger and more stable' is simply saying that 'making civil society stronger and more stable will make our society stronger and more stable', and this does not provide any utility as the basis for social policy at all. 'State' here is used interchangeably between 'the collection of citizens who make up a geopolitical entity whose autonomy is recognized by other states' and 'the collection of powerful individuals who make the crucial decisions affecting the polity as a whole'; while 'civil society' is used interchangeably between 'the collection of citizens who make up a geopolitical entity whose autonomy is recognized by other states', and 'individuals who are subject to the power of political decision-makers'. Who is acting upon whom to achieve what? And how are they doing so? The problem with this construction as a tool for analysis is that 'strengthening civil society' is both the strategy to *achieve* a particular goal, and the goal *itself*.

But the problem is not simply that the causal forces and the subjects of causation are employed in a circular construction of causality: it is also that civil society is simply assumed to be the causal agent rather than potentially the subject of some other causal force. A significant example of this confusion between subject and agent is Robert Putnam's much-lauded 1993 book contrasting northern and southern Italy. Entitled *Making Democracy Work*, the book argued that '[d]emocratic government is strengthened, not weakened, when it faces vigorous civil society' (Putnam 1993: 182). More than merely an analysis of Italian politics, this thesis has been applied by Putnam to other societies (and most pointedly, to the United States) to argue for the vital necessity of revitalizing the social groups outside of the formal domain of the state (Putnam 1995). Yet, as Sidney Tarrow (1996) has pointed out, all Putnam has done is to show that northern Italy has both a notable tradition of lively civic participation and a strong economy. Not only does Putnam not persuasively show that the former has caused the latter, argues Tarrow, but he seems to assume that policy performance is a reasonable measure of democracy. Careful readers are left confused over who has caused what to occur, and why. Did a weak tradition of civic participation lead to a stagnant economy in the South or, as Tarrow suggests, was the dual manifestation of poor economy and weak civil society itself a product of structural factors (such as the historical trend of exploitative governments)? The end result of misidentifying the causal relationship is, as Tarrow writes, too often a policy which attacks the symptoms rather than the cause of economic and social undevelopment. And what, finally, is the role of democracy in all this? Putnam assumes that strong civic activity leading to a strong economy is a sufficient manifestation of democracy (even though both variables could also describe a populist form of fascism). Notwithstanding the title of Putnam's book, concludes Tarrow, it has little to say about democracy (1996: 395, 396).

3. *Falsifiability is impossible.* We can, suggests White, think about civil society as comprising a number of different sectors, each constellation of sectors being dependent upon the specific context under scrutiny. Each of these different sectors 'have different power resources at their disposal', and thus 'different sectors of civil society can be expected to have different sets of norms about the political relationship between state and society and the yea or nay of democracy would depend on the interaction between these sectors' (1994: 385). This may indeed be a reasonable account of the relationship between civil society writ large and the process of democratization, but it does not permit a particularly clear explanation of why things occur.

'Civil societies', declares White, 'contain inequalities and domination and the resolution of any competitive game between components of civil society depends heavily on its internal balance of power' (*ibid.*: 385). But this formulation could explain any outcome, thus 'proving' the utility of civil society as an explanatory variable. The logical construction follows this pattern: why did event X occur? Because group A in civil society is more powerful than group B in civil society. How do we know that it was this particular balance of power which caused the event to occur? Because the outcome of event X was that group A prevailed over group B. 'The strength of group A in civil society' is both the causal variable, and the evidence of the relevance of this causal variable. Thus to say that 'the "civil society" factor may be more or less influential depending on the current and evolving balance of power' (*ibid.*: 386) is not necessary inaccurate; it is merely unhelpful.

This is the same logical formulation employed by Nicos Poulantzas in his analysis of the state, a model which enjoyed no little popularity amongst neomarxists throughout the 1970s and 1980s. Poulantzas attempted to explain political outcomes by looking at the relative balances of power between various factions within the state; but, again, the outcomes themselves were used as 'proof' that given balances of power were the causes of these very outcomes (Poulantzas 1978). Regardless of what the outcome happened to be, it was used as evidence to support Poulantzas' theory that the relative balance of power between state factions could be used to explain any political event. Thus, in the same manner, a broad and flexible definition of civil society avoids the problem of numerous descriptions of what 'civil society' is, but only at the cost of making it into an overly accommodating concept.

If the point of 'civil society' is that it can be used as a political strategy to change the polity in an identifiable way, then is it possible to determine after the fact whether a particular strategy focusing upon 'civil society' has in fact not been successful? Probably not; simply because we are not clear what is to cause what, and what would constitute proof of this causal link. If we can successfully bolster the autonomy of certain non-state groups, for example, then we have already achieved that which we have sought to attain: the autonomy of non-state groups (i.e., a 'strengthened civil society'). And even if we chose to define our terms, our strategy, and our objectives more precisely than proponents of 'civil society' strategies commonly do, we are still faced with the possibility that failure can be explained away in a number of different ways that protect the strategic utility of the term 'civil society'.

Analytical ambiguity and political applications

If civil society is such an intellectually unsatisfying term, then why is it being used so enthusiastically by such powerful and august bodies as the World Bank and OECD? Many trends in abstract vocabulary are zealously shared by intellectuals within relatively self-contained academic circles, but far fewer are employed so regularly and indulgently in the political realm as the term 'civil society'. The most convincing testament of the popularity (and ambiguity) of the concept, however, must be the observation that institutions so frequently accused of upholding an unrepentantly liberal-capitalist agenda are, ironically, using an idea that has been so recently espoused most energetically by intellectuals on the Left as a means of reinvigorating socialism (e.g., Keane 1988). But analytical ambiguity can, unsurprizingly, be a considerable political virtue, and especially so in consensus politics where agreement is more readily assured when parties are not always clear on what it is that they have agreed. And, despite socialist intellectuals' 'rediscovery' of the Gramscian focus upon civil society as a locus of 'non-totalizing political activity', the concept is also being used by multilateral agencies essentially as an attempt to impose 'liberalism' on client states, for better or for worse, without the need to call it liberalism.

A focus on 'civil society' has permitted institutions such as the World Bank to emphasize such principles as the accountability of the state to its citizens, and the desirability of due process and transparency in all government activity. The World Bank's 1989 document *Sub-Saharan Africa: From Crisis to Sustainable Growth* was the first attempt to concentrate upon measures 'that foster grassroots organization, that nurture rather than obstruct informal sector enterprises, and that promote non-governmental and intermediary organizations' (World Bank 1989: xii). Its subsequent 1992 document *Governance and Development* looked more systematically at 'popular participation in the design and implementation of projects' (World Bank,

1992: 25–8) but did not refer explicitly to 'civil society' as either an operational category or an analytical construct. Only with the publication of *Governance: the World Bank's Experience* two years later was the term used systematically and continuously, as it was in the OECD's *Participatory Development and Good Governance* (OECD, 1995) and *Our Global Neighbourhood*, the final report of the Commission on Global Governance (1995). That the main thrust of the World Bank's governance project is to provide a more auspicious environment for market activity (see, e.g., World Bank 1994: 58) should not be lost in the numerous references to 'limiting state power' and 'strengthening civil society'. The author will not engage here in a discussion of the extent to which this ought or ought not to be a primary objective of such institutions; but it is rather ironic that documents arguing the merits of 'transparency' should be so coy about their own objectives. A more detailed discussion of the political motivations for various international actors to subscribe to an account of democracy strongly influenced by this 'civil society discourse" will follow in Chapter 7.

'Civil society' has been the object of interest to sociologists far longer than it has for political scientists, and Cohen and Arato's long discussion of the concept, with their especially sympathetic utilization of Parsons' theories, is evidence of this long-standing relationship. But the main distinction between the related disciplines of sociology and political science is that the latter is far more focused than the former upon the manifestation and the dynamics of power. Sociologists have, admittedly, been far more receptive to the now-standard observation that relations of power are very importantly present in most human interactions, and not simply within the formal spheres of political power. But political scientists have an equally long-standing concern with the specific institutions and processes through which power is to be contained and moderated. It may be this very overlap between disciplines which could explain why a concept of such limited analytical use to political scientists (as opposed to the political utility of the term to specific political actors) is nonetheless used with such increasing enthusiasm. Those who do hold the term in some esteem either do not have a clear conception of the dynamics of power within the political sphere upon which they focus, or else they are too willing to generalize from specific instances in which certain elements of 'civil society' have had considerable political success.

It is simply too easy to articulate a vision of a stable and autonomous civil society without explaining how, precisely, this is to be achieved. 'How', asks Kumar, 'does civil society protect itself against the state? Must its independence rest simply upon the disinterested benevolence of the state – a most insecure basis?' (1993: 386). And if the power of the state is indeed effectively curtailed, then what mechanism keeps those individuals with a great deal of (non-state) power accountable to those who do not? It was not only fear of the State's influence which led early Americans to construct the democratic institutions which impressed Tocqueville so much; it was also fear of non-state institutions such as the Church. America was settled by those fleeing religious persecution as well as political oppression, a fact lost on those who frequently uphold 'the church', with its modern homespun connotations, as the civil association *par excellence.*

In sum, the concept of 'civil society' is overused, overrated, and analytically insubstantial. But does it nonetheless contain a modicum of intellectual utility? There is, as just noted, the political utility of ambiguity that permits a greater degree of consensus; but, less cynically, the idea of civil society does perform a powerful normative function in its espousal of the value of a cohesive polity characterized by the lack of excessive state control. It is, as Isaac (1993) writes, useful in its ability to keep 'the spirit of revolt' alive. It reminds citizens that we cannot depend too passively upon the state for some of the social qualities we value most, and that we have a collective right to prevent political leaders from controlling too many aspects of our lives. 'Civil society' is a shorthand way of expressing the principle of limited government; and its use flags interlocutors to the normative stance we assume.

But that is its most significant function. Analytically, any 'theory of civil society' simply cannot work: it is too vague, too ambiguous, and too riddled with contradictions to provide any useful theoretical insight. We can use the term as an arbitrary definition; we can declare that certain specific organizations work in a certain way within a certain context to achieve a particular political outcome. But this term cannot regularly be used in the same way to impart the same analytical observations in a variety of political and social contexts, simply because 'civil societies' are so vastly different in diverse instances. Those who use the term are declaring that 'support for resistance against the state can be found outside of the state' (and, usually, that 'it is a good thing that support for resistance against the state can be found outside of the state'.) But neither of these statements is particularly complex, and neither requires a 'theory' of civil society to be understood. To say that 'civil society can serve as a locus of protest against the state' is to say nothing more than that 'the people can serve as a locus of protest against the state'. The truth claim of this statement is not in dispute; merely its analytical profundity.

Charles Taylor (1991) has suggested that retrieving our historical understandings of civil society in all their richness and complexity can help us better to theorize about human rights; and this utilization of 'civil society' (as a tool to understanding concepts that *can* be usefully theorized) is the best example of a non-normative analytical application of civil society currently offered by the literature on the subject. But, as comparativists, what we need is not a theory of civil society but a theory of power dynamics within civil society, or between civil society and state; and these power dynamics will simply be too distinct (at any but the most superficial level) in each case to be of much intellectual interest. What happened in Poland is not what happened in Peru, and neither will be of much use in trying to understand what is happening in Nigeria. We may well choose to theorize about, say, the role of trade unions, or churches, or international NGOs in the process of democratization; but to call each one a comprehensive theory of 'civil society' *per se* is a very selective account of civil society. Indeed, such a theorization could easily be constructed without any reference to the term civil society at all.

The muddle over the way we currently tend to use 'civil society' has its explanation in a number of factors: the limitations of the state, both theoretically and politically; the achievements of specific social organizations in a number of different polities; the complex and contradictory historical lineage of the concept; and even a moral glibness or timidity in our failure to insist upon a rigorous investigation of such manifestly desirable concepts as 'democracy' or 'civil society' or 'meaningful identity'. But we must learn not confuse the claim that 'this is a good thing' from the claim that 'this, then, must be a good way to understand things'. Some have claimed that intellectual discourse is too permeated with cynicism and despair; in this case, however, analytical rigour seems too clouded by hope.

III

Pursuing democracy:
political debates

7

The politics of definition

In acting to promote democratization, the United Nations is not trying to persuade States to imitate others or borrow extraneous political forms or to democratize simply to please certain Western States. On the contrary, and I should like to repeat this here, no one has a monopoly on democracy. Democracy can, and should be assimilated by all cultures. It may take many forms, depending on the characteristics and circumstances of peoples. Democracy is not a model to be copied from certain States, but a goal to be attained by all peoples.
(Boutros Boutros-Ghali 1995: 110)

Inflating democracy

In 1989 an American civil servant piqued the intellectual community with the simple but provocative claim that liberal democracy was the global culmination of a long historical progress toward the most desirable system of governance possible (Fukuyama, 1989). He was certainly correct in his observation that more support for democracy exists worldwide than ever before. But his assertion rested importantly upon the glib assumption that democracy was so prevalent because of its moral superiority, rather than because the meaning of 'democracy' had been broadened well beyond its earlier, more limited, connotations.

If we believe that democracy, as the ability of people collectively to lead their lives as they see best, is simply a good thing, then it might seem intuitively that democracy ought to be 'assimilated by all cultures' and thereby, as Boutros-Ghali suggests, 'to take many forms, depending upon the characteristics and circumstances of peoples'. But this is fundamentally to misunderstand the nature of, and possibilities inherent in, the idea of democracy. The expansion of 'democracy' is similar to the discussion surrounding 'citizenship' in the mid-twentieth century: with the advantage of hindsight, we can see the simple flaws in T. H. Marshall's argument that the concept of 'citizenship' could (and would) expand to incorporate many different dimensions (political, economic, social) as polities progressively became wealthier and more enlightened. In like manner, many contemporary proponents of democratization believe that 'democracy' can expand indefinitely – and without contradiction – to be all good things to all people.

Widening the interpretation of democracy solves little, and only exacerbates existing difficulties. This book has argued that two interpretations of democracy have undeservedly gained an especial import: those based upon private property rights, and those focused on differential cultural rights. But, as sections one and two illustrate, neither philosophical coherence nor causal certainty exist with sufficient force in either case to give these rights the political force with which they are frequently imbued. This chapter will discuss why, politically, the currency of democracy has become inflated. There are good political reasons for accepting accounts of democracy that are both philosophically and causally suspect. Are there better reasons to reject them?

Underlying theoretical tensions

While countless explanations for the expansion of the meaning of democracy could be identified, the two principal variables responsible for the current dilation of interpretation are the recent interest in the epistemological tensions underlying the term, and the political dynamics characterizing the 'new world order'. Any investigation of political phenomena must begin with an attempt to understand the conceptual or ideological terrain upon which political structures are made or actions are executed. And, as Chapter 2 described, the 'western' conception of democracy itself is, and has been throughout its development, philosophically ambiguous and frequently contradictory. There is, quite simply, no monolithic account of what democracy is (or ought to be); and the ability to state with confidence that 'this is democracy, and that is not' in certain instances does not necessarily provide clarification regarding more ambiguous cases. That such ambiguity exists does not, however, justify expanding the term indefinitely.

There are, again, substantial differences in accounts concerning both the *structure* and the *function* of democracy. In its simplest formulation, democracy entails institutions which oblige governors to be accountable to the governed. This leaves a tremendous amount unsaid. What form does this mechanism of accountability take? It is generally agreed to take the form of a system of voting in which decisions are made according to majority rule. But the ambiguity arises in the specific processes which govern this system: who gets to vote? what type of voting is used? how large a majority is required? and what do we mean by 'free' and 'fair' elections in specific contexts? (see, e.g., Wiseman 1993: 443–4). A more politically fraught issue still concerns which issues are to be subject to democratic voting, and which are prior (or simply off limits) to community decision-making. The most common tension historically has been the extent to which a workable democratic system depends either upon a system of private property that is not subject to the caprices of the majority, or upon a system of private property that is ratified collectively.

Along with the principle of majority rule which protects a system of political accountability is a corollary which stipulates some form of protection for minorities against the vicissitudes of majority will. This has generally been expressed as a system of rights which exist, in theory, independently of (or prior to) political decision-making. But because the normative justification of this concept of 'rights' rests historically upon a Christian formulation of natural law and divine intent, it has become difficult to offer a convincing justification of rights that does not, at the very least, depend upon some set of culturally specific values (such as the estimation placed upon human dignity or freedom). And even if we can establish a theoretically convincing account explaining why rights exist, we are still left with much philosophical work to be done in identifying *which* rights, in particular, ought to be respected (and which have 'trumps' over what others).

The ambiguity underlying the structures required before a polity can be identified as 'democratic' is mirrored in the equivocal understanding of what the *function* of democracy should be. Again, to borrow David Held's (1987) typology, most accounts of democracy can be placed on a spectrum that runs from 'developmental' to 'protective' models. Exponents of the former work on the assumption that the purpose of democracy is to provide a context in which individuals' skills and capacities are nurtured and improved, while supporters of the latter model hold that the function of democracy is to provide an environment that provides the highest amount of (equal) negative liberty for all. What individuals chose to do with this liberty, or whether they choose to utilize it for any particular purpose at all, is completely up to them.

The history of western political thought does not immediately provide support for either account over the other; in most western democracies one can generally find examples of both types of reasoning. A jurisdiction may maintain, for instance, that one's freedom of speech must be upheld despite the unpalatable nature of one's words (thereby defending negative rights); yet insist, at the same time, that gambling or drinking ought to be banned because too many people who cannot afford to gamble or drink nonetheless do so (i.e., violating negative rights in the interests of the individual whose rights are thus affected). Inconsistency is hardly novel in practical politics; and ambivalent attitudes underlying public policies merely illustrate the equivocal understanding of the proper function of democracy in conjunction with the free play of everyday politics.

But there is yet another theoretical tension underlying discussions of democracy which is a particularly contemporary debate. This is the politicization of epistemology, in which the meanings and definitions of words themselves become the focus of controversy. The ability to interpret events and to ascribe meaning is, in this account, seen as a significant source of power; those who must accept others' definitions thereby illustrate their weakness in the relationship of power. Emerging from this body of thought (frequently but not always bearing the label of postmodernism), an increasingly vocal number of advocates has asserted that western voices have 'captured' or distorted developing cultures by describing the nature of reality in a way that works to the advantage of the former: science is a superior form of rationality; structural adjustment policies lead to healthier states; democracy is a better form of governance; and so on. The problem, claim the dissenters, is that such arguments are informed by particular cultural assumptions and values; and by redescribing 'reality' in *their* own terms nonwestern states can challenge or undermine the hermeneutic power of dominant states.

Critics of the postmodern position generally view these arguments regarding the conflicting interpretations of reality as ephemeral and generally inconsequential. Power is not a matter of interpretation; power exists, they argue, quite independently of how it is described. Whether an invading army is successful hardly depends upon how 'state sovereignty' is described; an inefficient and corrupt economy will lead to poverty whether or not capitalism is deemed to be an artificial and arbitrary social construct; and the absence of human rights can facilitate a nasty political environment regardless of whether 'rights' are a culturally-specific reification or not.

This counterposition leads critics of realism to respond, in turn, that beliefs and values themselves produce a 'reality' that serves concretely to limit action: a high public debt may indeed disadvantage a state's economy, they acknowledge, but that is only because of the structure of the international economy, a constraint that is not at all 'natural' but rather the product of arbitrary assumptions regarding the primacy and sanctity of private property, the limitations of national boundaries, and so on. While I do not wish to examine this debate at length, it is worthwhile to underscore the degree to which epistemological and ontological issues are playing an increasingly visible role in the study of international relations. Understanding the nature of the changing global order, writes one international relations specialist, entails understanding that 'realities are not self-evident and that all "realities" are to a certain extent theorized':

> In this sense, the 'reality' of global order is constituted partly by the knowledge structures that prevail in the configuration of production, consumption, and exchange structures of the global political economy, as well as in the political structures associated with the concepts of sovereignty and the state. Knowledge structures are integral to understanding and explaining contemporary processes of historical change. (Gill 1994: 76)

This epistemological debate, which has been a staple of political theory at least since the publication of Wittgenstein's *Philosophical Investigations* (1953), has become an increasingly vociferous component of both international relations and comparative politics. And 'democracy' has been a locus of such definitional ambiguity not only because of its messy historical evolution in western political thought, but also because certain intellectual trends within international relations have stressed the political importance of imposing upon key political terms a meaning distinct from the one utilized by dominant actors. The rationale for this, again, is that by refusing the received interpretation of consequential terms, political actors refuse to validate the values and assumptions 'built in' to the term. Thus, for example, by constructing a unique meaning for 'democracy' a state can actively choose which component part of democracy it values (e.g., popular participation) rather than passively acknowledge those aspects (e.g., private property rights) which it does not. Whether this practice establishes epistemological and political independence, or merely engenders confusion, is a matter of no little debate. But it is, nonetheless, within this particular constellation of theoretical tension that the globalization of democracy is occuring; and it is within this abstract environment that the substantial political constraints must be considered.

The 'new world order'

Just as the process of democratization began gathering momentum in the late 1970s, one person noted wryly, 'consensus had been achieved on the improbability of democratic political development outside of the North Atlantic basin' (Remmer 1995: 103). What changed? Three of the variables most frequently cited to account for the flourishing of democracy globally include the end of the cold war, which undermined the legitimacy of marxist (and single-party) political regimes; severe economic stagnation, which precipitated the emergence of structural adjustment programs overseen by the IMF; and the 'rise of increasingly organized and vocal pressure groups' that sought 'the liberalization of their respective political and economic systems' (see, e.g., Schraeder 1995: 1160).

These events may account for the emergence of 'democratization' (understood quite broadly as the weakening of authoritarian systems), but they do not themselves explain why the *interpretation* of democracy began to expand so widely. The inflationary expansion of democracy can perhaps be addressed by examining four particular characteristics of the 'new world order'.

1 *Theoretical modelling.* As the plethora of authoritarian regimes of the 1970s began to be replaced by political systems that diffused power more widely than those they succeeded, theorists increasingly began to accept that no single set of variables could be found to explain democratization (e.g.,

Huntington, 1991). Certain variables (such as the market) might be necessary but not sufficient; other variables (church, unionization, education) might be of great importance in some cases and of little consequence in others. Yet those accounts of democratization which focused on specific causal relationships were critiqued for not including variables which seemed to be relevant in other instances; while accounts (like Huntington's) which attempted judiciously to cover all possible bases were criticized for lacking a strong theoretical framework that could deal consistently with such a large number of empirical cases. 'What can only be described as a loose conceptual framework, based on the simple addition of factors', wrote one reviewer, 'does little to organize in a more or less systematic fashion the empirical detail from a mass of cases' (Munch 1994: 357, 369).

It is this frustration with causal modelling which, in the academic sphere, has prompted a much greater tolerance for the way in which 'democracy' or 'democratization' is understood. Unable to identify conclusively the causal relationship governing the emergence or consolidation of democratic regimes, the theoretical trend has been to acknowledge that 'democracy' is a distinct phenomenon in each country. Diverse political constraints and opportunities in each instance have created slightly different democracies: the reason that there is no 'one model' of democratization is that there is no 'one model' of democracy. The assumption, never clearly articulated, seems to be that of a Wittgensteinian model of 'family resemblances', with each case having some variables in common with other democratic regimes, but no narrowly defined variables being common to all. Remmer's 1995 review of 'new theoretical perspectives on democratization', for example, cites approvingly the strengths of recent theoretical approaches to suggest 'new ways of understanding political democracy'. These accounts, she notes, 'begin with the assumption that political democracy is not *the* political system of a particular level or historical pattern of development but a consensual framework or cooperative equilibrium that may be achieved in a variety of ways, involve various types of institutional arrangements, levels of competition, and popular participation, and generate very different types of outcomes' (1995: 111).

Thus one of the reasons that democracy is increasingly broadly defined is that the theorists themselves, rather than rebuking political actors for their cavalier usage of the term,

encourage a more flexible and less discriminating understanding of democracy. Notwithstanding the epistemological
battles noted above, the expansion of the term by theoretical comparativists is generally a conceptual rather than
political phenomenon. Regardless of intent, however, the
definitional loosening of democracy is inherently a political
matter, as specific political actors espouse their own renderings
of the term for unrepentantly political reasons. Who are these
actors, how do they conceptualize democracy, and what are
their motivations?

2 *State actors and the preservation of sovereignty.*
Individual states have a manifestly political interest in
reconceptualizing democracy for their own interests, both to
protect their sovereignty *vis-à-vis* other states and to protect the
influence of domestic administrations against encroachment
from autochthonous challenges. State-specific interpretations
of democracy are by no means always examples of opportunis-
tic political behaviour: political culture, history, geography and
other variables clearly play a role in the establishment of democratic systems. Very rarely will one established democracy ever
take the same form as any other: even the English-speaking
democracies such as Britain, the United States, Canada and
Australia manifest quite distinct varieties of democratic
governance; and the distinctions between these and European
democracies are wider still. (One notable point of difference
between the latter, for example, is the attempt to ensure that
'individual rights are carefully balanced in constitutional law
against responsibilities to the community' (Fukuyama 1995: 31;
Bail 1994, unpublished).) Historical and institutional variables
are also important in understanding the different approaches to
democratic governance across the Atlantic: because of the
legacy of European fascism, for instance, modern European
states have, unlike the United States, been more wary of emphasizing electoral mechanisms of democracy to the detriment of
social and economic participation (Whitehead 1986: 14–17).

Yet these nations have made concerted efforts since the post
war years to define democracy in a way that would clearly distinguish them, as a group, from states which rejected democratic norms. 'To be preserved from the temptations of
pseudo-democracy', writes Whitehead, 'it would be necessary to
agree on clear and inflexible criteria for distinguishing between
fraudulent imitations and the real thing' (1986: 12). Both the

North Atlantic Treaty Organization (NATO) and the Council of Europe (in 1949) and the European Economic Community (EEC) (in 1962) established ground rules for membership that required, at least in principle, adherence to democratic criteria. Yet strategic considerations were even from the beginning deemed preeminent to purely ideological ones; and NATO, after considerable discussion, permitted the membership of countries such as Portugal, Greece and Turkey which could at that point in time only be considered to fit the democratic criteria with a great deal of imaginative manipulation. The EEC, with an interest in keeping membership exclusive, had less need to resort to such creativity (*ibid.*: 13).

Current attempts both to restrict and to expand the definition of democracy are similarly informed by states' desires to include or exclude themselves, or others, from strategic blocs: increasingly, as Chapter 5 outlines, the opportunity cost for not becoming involved in trade networks arguably exceeds the cost of membership. This, at a very superficial level, explains the political inclination of nonliberal states to accept the rhetoric of democratic discourse in the first place. But concurrent with the need to participate in a global community to reap the rewards of either trade or aid is the fear that such participation restricts the exercise of state sovereignty. Yet sovereignty is a tricky conceptual term, one which contains a number of distinct connotations; and states which tentatively adopt democratic norms generally attempt to balance them against the preservation of 'sovereignty' in its various manifestations. The three types of sovereignty which are most often the focus of concern are state autonomy *vis-à-vis* other states; governmental control over the citizenry; and cultural independence as an organic unit.

The first of these, a concern with external sovereignty, is based upon the claim that, to the extent that democracy depends upon a state capable of meeting the basic physical demands of citizenship such as security, stability, and the establishment of a minimal standard of living, the establishment of a stable state is prior to the protection of certain civil rights. This claim, prevalent in African states since independence, argued that certain abstract democratic rights were dependent upon 'the achievement of such overriding goals as economic development, the eradication of poverty and disease, and the development of stable and effective government' (Wiseman 1993: 442). '[T]he centrality of democracy in the present historical context', argues one Tanzanian theorist, 'lies precisely in the fact that it expresses, or constitutes, an ideology of resistance and struggle of the large masses and popular classes of the people . . . Can a liberal perspective on democracy in Africa be anything else but compradorial?' (Shivji 1991: 82, 80). The claim that a state must become robust before it can usefully establish democratic rights has become largely discredited by the propensity of national elites to design legal codes to their own advantage indefinitely. Yet the disrepute of such states has nonetheless coincided with the increased concern by established democracies regarding precisely the same phenomenon: perceived limitations upon the ability of states to act freely in their citizens' behalf due to various external constraints.

Concern for the 'internal sovereignty' of a state, in contrast, addresses the fear that the government may lose control of the population to the detriment of order, good government and, more cynically, the political advantage of the ruling elites. Thus Singapore's Lee Kuan Yew expressed his apprehension that 'western-style democracy' would have such deleterious effects as encouraging permissiveness, social instability, and economically irrational decision-making (Fukuyama 1995: 24). The main objection to 'western' democracy is often that the values perceived to be 'inevitable by-products' of liberalism contribute to the disintegration of the social order:

> moral relativism, materialism, the denial of any kind of spirituality, a proud disdain for everything suprapersonal, a profound crisis of authority and the resulting general decay, a frenzied consumerism, a lack of solidarity, the selfish cult of material success, the absence of faith in a higher order of things or simply in eternity, an expansionist mentality that holds in contempt everything that in any way resists the dreary standardization and rationalism of the technical civilization. (Havel 1995: 7)

This concern for the erosion of authority has its western equivalent in conservative writers apprehensive about the loss of moral (and political) order in their respective societies. But this anxiety is qualitatively distinct from the third focus: the concern for the preservation of deeply-rooted cultural norms, which addresses the importance of *identity* rather than *authority*. While the two may well be linked (e.g., a clear sense of traditional identity can reinforce traditional forms of authority), a secure sense of identity is increasingly seen as a both a personal and political objective in and of itself. More specifically, what is contested is what is required for an strong sense of dignity. Fukuyama's famous claim that 'there is a universal tendency of human beings to seek recognition of their dignity through a political system that allows them to participate as adult human beings' (1995: 32) is no doubt at least partially true: the democratic discourse of the past century, combined with an increasing degree of international awareness, has established the normative ground rule that individual dignity ought to be respected. What is much more problematic is the second half of Fukuyama's claim: that the political requirement of dignity is political participation. It is precisely the question of *what it means to respect individuals* that is the primary cause of disagreement regarding the nature of 'democracy' as it moves into the second millennium.

The village woman in Bangladesh who affirms that heaven is under the feet of her husband, the cleric who insists that Muslim women must be veiled to protect their honour, or the Javanese farmer who sees dignity resting in the traditional hierarchy of his society all provide clear conceptions of individual dignity completely independent of individual participation in the political process. Even within the history of western political thought, the conception of Platonic justice with its emphasis upon dignity arising within proper hierarchical ordering shows that the conception of dignity is not merely grounded upon political participation. Precisely what 'human dignity' depends upon is, according to many, a culturally independent variable resting primarily on cultural self-determination rather than upon an imported political construct such as 'rights'. National sovereignty is thus required to protect the specific cultural rendering of human dignity unique to each society. The expansion of what democracy means, or ought to mean, is in this way causally understood as a desire by non-liberal states to protect their autonomy; and their wish to preserve this sovereignty in turn has at least three different justifications, all of which have similar manifestations in liberal societies themselves.

3 *The new role of Bretton Woods institutions.* The 'new world order', to the extent that it is an identifiable entity at all, is a combination of a reconfigured international system and the actors which must learn how to adjust to these supranational forces. The most important actors are generally states, although increasingly a number of transnational organizations

are seen to play key roles in facilitating or constraining the behaviour of states. And of these organizations, the most influential *vis-à-vis* developing countries are powerful economic bodies (such as the World Bank, the IMF and, increasingly, the WTO) as well as a number of international development NGOs. As noted briefly in Chapter 6, the proliferation of policy documents from international financial institutions which focused upon 'good governance' rather than 'democratic government' as an overarching policy objective has become quite pronounced. By 1989, the World Bank had, in its remarkable document on Sub-Saharan Africa, stated that '[a] root cause of weak economic performance in the past has been the failure of public institutions. Private sector initiative and market mechanisms are important, but they must go hand-in-hand with good governance – a public service that is efficient, a judicial system that is reliable, and an administration that is accountable to its public' (1989: xii). Broader policy documents emphasizing good governance followed. These included *Governance and Development* (World Bank, 1992) and *Governance: The World Bank's Experience* (World Bank, 1994); as well as *Development and Good Governance*, a 1995 OECD paper, and *Our Global Neighbourhood*, a 1995 report published by the UN's Commission on Global Governance. What accounts for this fascination with good governance and the concurrent reticence concerning 'democracy' *per se* ? A simple answer is that 'democracy' became too political a term to be employed usefully. A more complex answer, however, is that states' interests in widening the moral criteria of political legitimacy coincided with the international agencies' own more immediate institutional interests.

In an article written three years after the publication of *Sub-Saharan Africa: From Crisis to Sustainable Growth* (World Bank, 1989), one of that report's co-authors wrote that democratization could not be achieved merely by reconfiguring national institutions, and that 'Africa will only emerge from its current difficulties if it can progressively remodel its institutions to be more in tune with the traditions, beliefs, and structures of its component societies' (Landell-Mills, 1992: 544–5). The intellectual justification of this move toward 'good governance' rather than 'democratization' as a policy objective was therefore to 'deepen and broaden civil society' in order to establish 'strong, inbuilt systems of political and bureaucratic accountability' (*ibid.*: 552). And the means to nurture civil society were fourfold:

> (1) by facilitating the dissemination of information; (2) by strengthening the rule of law; (3) by expanding education, so that there are more people able both to understand what is happening and to articulate clearly the interests of the groups to which they belong in a language understood by the state bureaucrats; and (4) by generating surplus resources in cash or kind to support associational activities without compromising their autonomy. (*Ibid.*: 552)

This strategy seemed to embody both causal sense and political diplomacy. Given clear evidence that imposing 'democratic' institutions upon a populace uncertain how to use them was not working, a policy of 'empowering groups throughout society to both voice their concerns and take direct action to achieve their ends' meant establishing a more participatory politics, which would lead to greater public accountability 'and hence more basic democracy' (*ibid.*: 563). Politically, intranational agencies could avoid charges of ideological imperialism by showing that they were sensitive to the cultural particularities of specific nations.

But 'good governance' as an institutional strategy was subject to a great deal of criticism by those who argued that it was merely a means of window-dressing the liberal, capitalist nature of these institutions' *real* intentions. In the first place, as Williams and Young argue, this 'construction of governance' rests upon a number of very liberal assumptions, including the presumption of a neutral state, a public sphere independent of government involvement, and a conception of autonomous selfhood with 'modern patterns of behaviour' (1994: 99). And, in the second place, good governance is viewed as a strategy designed primarily to facilitate the establishment of stable capital investment. The 'crisis of governance', in Schmitz' view, was a means for the World Bank to explain why its policies so often did not have the intended effect: rather than pinpointing 'adverse conditions, unfair markets, or inappropriate economic reforms', according to this account, the problem was reconceptualized as the 'lack of proper institutional capacity to manage necessary processes of adjustment' (1995: 68):

> The eventual resort to 'governance' was driven by a recognition that something had to be done to forestall this impending crisis of the [neoliberal] development model, not by a sudden desire to welcome democratic change. . . the burgeoning demands for democratic

> development had somehow to be contained within a controlled and
> superordinate 'good governance' regime which could then be
> counted on to deliver 'political sustainability' for neoliberal politics.
> (*ibid.*: 73)

What, then, does governance mean? While one interpretation
focuses specifically upon administrative and managerial definitions, it can also include 'an insistence on competitive democratic politics' (Leftwich 1993: 606) or the 'popular participation
and "empowerment" of the poor', including people's rights
'freely to choose their own modes of development' (Schmitz
1995: 73). But while the critics of governance as an administrative paradigm argue that 'governance' is little but a tepid and
impoverished account of legitimate political authority, the
same critics fail to provide a similarly convincing argument of
how it is that 'competitive democratic politics' or 'empowerment of the poor' can exist *without* such a stable administrative
framework. 'In the absence of the establishment of relatively
autonomous government institutions committed to a national
"public interest"', writes Jeffries (1993: 20), '"democratic" politics is likely to exacerbate rather than reduce problems of
corruption, wastefulness and short-sighted economic policy
formulation.'

There exists, moreover, the question of how popular
participation can be coordinated and the distribution of power
brokered in an environment where the rules concerning what,
precisely, 'fair participation' is are not clearly delineated. The
'citizen empowerment' model seems to be based loosely on phenomena such as the demonstration at Tiananmen Square, where
over a million individuals congregated seemingly spontaneously
with the same political objectives. But a political system cannot
depend too heavily upon this form of spontaneous organization,
or the good will of its citizens, or upon traditional forms of
authority in a modern world to establish the ground rules for the
just allocation of political power. What 'democracy' attempts to
do ideally is to set out the minimal parameters of agreement
regarding what the fair distribution of power ought to be; and
what policies of 'good governance' attempt to do, ideally, is to
prevent some interests from manipulating others. It is *possible*
that the governance strategy is merely a smokescreen for capitalist interests; but it is also arguable that, whether or not this was
the deliberate intent, a policy of sound administrative governance is nonetheless necessary to execute and to moderate

between interests. But if one chooses to argue that the protection of a neoliberal ideology is not the only, or even the preeminent, explanation for the adoption of 'governance' policies by international agencies, then how could one explain why such an imprecise term as governance has been accepted?

There is no question that institutions such as the World Bank and the IMF are defending a liberal capitalist development paradigm. Both institutions are quite clear that this is precisely the approach which they endorse, and both institutions contend, further, that this is the best way to improve the well-being of developing states. They may, of course, be quite wrong in this claim; there is no lack of critical voices articulating such a point (see, e.g., Brand 1993). But given how candid they are on this position, it is rather difficult to believe that they would feel the need for a cloak of rhetoric which the discussion about 'governance' is supposed to provide. It is doubtful that the governance strategy is a form of window-dressing used either by the World Bank or the IMF to distract anyone from their ulterior motive of capitalist development, simply because this 'covert intention' is (for better or for worse) unapologetically transparent.

A slightly different explanation for the emphasis upon governance might simply be found in the institutional interests of the World Bank and IMF (as distinct from the ideological interests of those who have ultimate control over these institutions). To understand the behaviour of the two most influential financial institutions upon developing states (although the WTO is itself increasingly the most influential international financial institution (IFI) for a number of increasingly robust developing economies), one must understand the relationship between the World Bank and the IMF since the mid-1970s, as well as the way in which the international context of this relationship has shifted.

The dynamic, essentially, is this: the IMF, created primarily to oversee a monetary system based on fixed exchange rates, has found a niche of relevance as a development bank. But this, of course, was the reason for the creation of the World Bank, which is increasingly being displaced by private commercial banks. And, to maintain *its* particular relevance in the current context, the Bank has chosen to define its *raison d'etre* as the establishment of 'softer' development targets (health care, education systems, and other 'capacity building' structures) that orthodox economic policy neglected.

The period following the end of the Second World War was characterized by a stark dearth of global investment capital: except for the United States, most states were unable to supply such funds, while the private markets themselves remained too 'small and cautious' to be effective in providing substantial levels of investment capital. It was in order to address this shortage that the IMF was initially established (see Owen, 1994: 98). Formally, the role of the IMF was threefold: to oversee the fixed exchange rate system, to provide short-term support to countries facing financial difficulties, and to promote currency convertibility as a means of fostering international trade. But none of these objectives have much relevance in the contemporary global economy: '[t]he breakdown of the Bretton Woods system of fixed exchange rates in the early 1970s, the removal of capital controls and, most important, technological and financial innovation have transformed global finance' (Minton-Beddoes, 1995: 124).

The IMF has thus become largely irrelevant to the industrialized states, which neither utilize its funds nor feel bound to heed its policy advice due to the abundance of private capital markets. At the same time, however, the IMF has been playing an increasingly prominent role *vis-à-vis* developing states. By 1981, when a major recession lowered developing states' foreign exchange earnings and thus their ability to service their debts, the IMF took the lead in coordinating and providing loans for these countries. A decade later, the IMF was also heavily involved in reorganizing the financial systems of the formerly communist states of eastern Europe. Since this time the functions of the IMF are the provision of long-term financial support, technical support, and subsidized loans; it has managed to forge for itself 'a central coordinating role – cajoling banks toward providing insolvent countries with new money in return for improved economic policies' (Minton-Beddoes, 1995: 127). But this, as the *Economist* has observed, is 'not just a far cry from its original mandate, but also much too close to the functions of the World Bank' (23 July 1994: 18). The postwar decades have shown that the nature of development programmes is extremely complex and requires a longer-term focus. For the IMF to be effective in its new role in the developing world, it cannot depend upon isolated, short-term economic contracts to fulfill the development agenda. This is reflected in the enormous amount of criticism levied at the IMF 'for having an excessive short-term horizon and [for] concentrating too much on cutting budget deficits and controlling credit while neglecting the core issues that affect a country's capacity to produce goods and services' (Minton-Beddoes 1995: 129). The IMF, in brief, can only reinforce its own relevance by usurping the more traditional functions of the World Bank.

As the IMF has gradually taken over the duties of the World Bank, the Bank itself has shifted *its* focus. The original mandate of the World Bank was to provide longer-term project loans for specific infrastructure investment. But in the half-century since its creation, this role has been overtaken by private markets: in 1993, for example, World Bank lending to developing countries was close to $24 billion, while private capital levels reached over $88 billion (*The Economist*, 23 July 1994: 73). In the soul-searching that has pervaded the remaining Bretton Woods institutions on their fiftieth anniversary, the World Bank has been groping for a means of differentiating itself from the IMF. And the obvious solution has been to cede focus upon fiscal matters proper to the IMF (and to private capital markets), and to help bolster the public sector, focusing upon health, education, and infrastructure projects. 'It will be a long time', noted a Co-Chairman of the United States' Bretton Woods Commission, 'before the private markets can finance the health and education programs that the World Bank now supports in poor and rapidly growing developing countries' (Owen 1994: 106).

This has not been a sudden change in direction for the World Bank. Throughout the 1980s a number of documents emerged based upon the premise that sound economic development cannot occur solely by imposing drastic constraints upon the economy at the top: rather, according to this view, a broad base of people must 'effectively participate in the design of the strategies that affect their lives' (Gibbon 1992, 215). Thus, even before the 'governance'-oriented documents of the 1990s, international agencies such as the United Nations International Childrens Emergency Fund (UNICEF) and the International Labour Organization (ILO) (as well as a number of state aid agencies) had presented this 'new approach' which was later incorporated into World Bank programmes such as the Programme to Mitigate the Social Costs of Adjustment (PAMSCAD) in 1987 (together with the United Nations Development Programme (UNDP) and the

African Development Bank); the 1990 African policy-reform document *Making Adjustment Work for the Poor*; and the Social Dimension of Adjustment programme along with its successor, the Social Dimension of Development (Gibbon 1992). The World Bank's future, to a large extent, thus depends upon its ability to move away from its traditional focus upon state-run projects, and to work towards a cooperative strategy with NGOs which 'increasingly shape the environment in which both multilateral development banks and for-profit financial institutions must work' (Owen 1994: 107); a strategy that has attempted to involve a much larger proportion of the population in development strategies. The World Bank's emphasis on governance, in other words, has been a result of its attempt to define a role for itself in the 'new world order'.

4   *The new role of non-governmental organizations.* It is quite arguable that the push from the 1980s on for greater democratization has been in part a consequence of the scope and influence of the global network of NGOs. But it is no less arguable that the increasing strength of these NGOs is also responsible for the expansion of the way in which democracy is interpreted. For if the IMF and the World Bank have their own ulterior motives in pursuing the strategy of 'governance', either for ideological or institutional reasons, so too do NGOs have their own rationale for utilizing a very broad and indefinite conception of democratization.

The majority of development NGOs must work within a context structured by the political agenda of both industrialized and developing states. Throughout the 1990s there has been much pressure in many industrial democracies to transfer their overseas development policies from state-directed agencies to more independent NGOs. NGOs, it is argued, are more flexible, decentralized, and autonomous than state-run agencies; they can respond more quickly and more efficiently to the needs of people in developing countries (see, e.g., Clark 1991: Sandbrook and Halfani 1991; Edwards and Hulme 1992). Thus donor states ought to subsidize these agencies rather than use the state arm of international development. This policy generally fits well with the neoliberal assumption that states ought to contract services out to the private sphere. But is it more *democratic*?

Nossal has argued that delegating development policy to NGOs 'far from being democratic, instead entrenches and institutionalizes access to the policy making process that is limited to the few' (1995: 39):

> the conflation of a closed policy process with an *undemocratic* policy tends to mask a thorny analytical problem; it is rarely explained by critics of the foreign policy process precisely why an open policy making process is necessarily more *democratic* than a closed one. Rather, it tends to be accepted as an article of faith that there is a link between open policy making systems and democratic policy making. (*Ibid.*: 35)

NGOs may well be more efficient in their ability to achieve a myriad objectives with a minimum of bureaucratic obstacles. They may be more sympathetic to the less well off, and they may have a wider knowledge base than state agencies. A great deal of literature exists arguing precisely this point and, to a large extent, it underpins the 'civil society' approach to development noted in Chapter 6. Yet it is not clear why, despite the generally honourable intentions of these organizations, they are more democratic. To the extent that a donor state formulates its international development policy through wide consultation with a number of parties involved in development work, 'this is little more than policy making by elite invitation, where groups are actively sought out by state officials for participation in policy making' (*ibid.*: 38–9).

NGOs frequently argue that their effectiveness, as well as their integrity, depends upon the fact that they are autonomous and unanswerable to governments. This arm's-length relationship preserves their independence and their efficiency; and yet, to the extent that transparent mechanisms of accountability between NGOs and the government which funds them do not exist, the participation of NGOs in a state's international development programme hardly seems the epitomization of democratic governance. But NGOs continue to argue that international development is best achieved through 'multi-stakeholder working groups' rather than by 'short-sighted, ill-informed, and easily manipulated' public opinion (Canadian Council for International Cooperation, quoted in Nossal 1995: 40). The argument seems to be that a less accountable process within the donor country is more than amply justified by the claim that NGOs are frequently more accountable to the client population in developing states than government agencies can be. 'There is, in other words', concludes Nossal, 'no consensus on what constitutes democratization of the policy process'. (*ibid.*: 41)

Why the parameters of democracy must be tightened

Democratic criteria, writes Carew, ought to be reconfigured better to fit underdeveloped societies: '[d]efining the problem this way allows for a new focus which primarily entails the reconstruction of democratic theory to render it applicable to "underdeveloped" and ethnically diverse societies (1993: 37).' The sentiments underlying such declarations are themselves laudable; they illustrate the desire for culturally-specific obstacles to be removed to make the practice of democracy more attainable for the widest possible variety of countries. But the caution raised in this book is the concern that the transformation of democracy into such a plastic concept destroys its capacity to achieve precisely that which makes it valuable to us.

What *has* made democracy so valuable? Two answers are frequently given, but both are misleading. The first, and more honourable of the two, suggests that democracy promotes the virtues of tolerance, diversity, fairness, and respect. This may be true in a superficial way, insofar as these values will most likely be reinforced in a society where respect and toleration are already practised. Yet, as an increasing number of failed experiments with democratic institutions have illustrated, these values must to a large extent exist prior to the establishment of a viable democracy; and, as we have seen in centuries of stable hierarchical societies, a sense of social justice and respect for individual citizens can themselves exist independently of democracy.

The second answer concerning the value of democracy is less estimable, but perhaps more widespread. That is the claim that a democratic system permits more opportunity to amass more wealth. And, while this perception may well be the motivating force for a great number of democratic proponents, the causal evidence is too sobering to reach any firm conclusions:

> All that can be said with complete confidence is that it is easy to understand why economic failure and constitutional disruption often reinforce each other, and why economic success and democratic constitutional continuity likewise help to foster one another where either proves protractedly available. With representative democracy, as with capitalist development, nothing succeeds quite like success, and nothing fails as comprehensively as failure. (Dunn 1992: 255)

Democracy is first and foremost a process, a system; and what is most valuable about this particular process is its capacity to achieve a balance between two rather contradictory ends: the maintenance of stability and order, on the one hand; and the diffusion of power, on the other.

The argument for the continual modification of liberal democracy is that western processes and institutions have not always worked well outside the western context because they fail to accommodate traditional values and conventions. Yet these same traditional customs themselves cannot be sustained without modification because the context of governance itself is continually changing. The shifting patterns of accumulation and distribution, the establishment of a geographically-bounded state system, and the proliferation of technology are factors which have irreplaceably distorted the balance of traditional customs of governance. Traditional practices cannot be protected *by* a modern state simply because the state *itself* changes the political relationships within a polity. A modern state has the capacity to carry out enormously intrusive actions, and the concept of 'universal human rights' thus becomes necessary in the modern world to address this potentially frightening imbalance:

> the search for an indigenous legal foundation for human rights becomes paradoxical in that it has to be 'erected'. . . within the confines of the state, whose alien and transplanted, but essentially unalterable, structures have rendered the local tradition impotent as a source of authentically traditional, political assertions . . . The question remains whose authenticity are we asked to restore, who would make this judgment, for what political purpose, and at what cost? (Afshari 1994: 251)

Precolonial Africa, for example, had its own form of accountability with 'symbolic depth', 'a common language of deep accountability', and 'indigenous conventions of high-political restraint'. This relationship of political responsibility was to a large extent dependent upon the very absence of a sovereign territory: traditional chiefdoms had little concentration of force to use against their citizens; polities were largely based not on the exercise of power but upon social cooperation. An unpopular or irresponsible king would find his subjects not confronting him but turning their backs on him: the lack of state borders, the relative availability of resources throughout the continent, and the ability for most families to produce for themselves what they needed meant that emigration could itself act as a very efficient check upon the abuse of power (Lonsdale 1986: 139, 144, 146). But state boundaries now palpably exist, and are protected with no little vigour. Assuming that traditional customs of accountability can survive in a context where the traditional 'checks and balances' have *not* is very much to romanticize tribal societies without understanding the traditional dynamics of political accountability, where they existed at all.

There is, in addition, a high level of trans-cultural migration which makes this 'common language of deep accountability' of traditional cultures increasingly impossible. In 1969, in a famous paper, Joel Feinberg asked why it was that the concept of individual moral rights were necessary at all. He presented the hypothetical town of 'Nowheresville' which functioned in a very civilized manner using a moral code (such as the Ten Commandments) without reference to individual moral rights. What, if anything, was missing from this society? Why were such rights necessary at all? Feinberg suggested that what the idea of individual moral rights imparts is a respect for individuals *qua* individuals that is absent in any context lacking such rights; but he admits that Nowheresville might, nonetheless, be a very pleasant society in which to live notwithstanding its conceptual deficit. Yet if Feinberg were a political scientist facing the twenty-first century, rather than a legal theorist writing in the middle of the twentieth, he might have recognized that his description of Nowheresville depended implicitly upon the assumption of a homogeneous and stable society underpinned by a traditional structure of authority and personal mores which all citizens implicitly understood and respected (Feinberg 1979 [1969]).

Again, this portrait of an enduring and homogeneous society is one rapidly becoming unrecognizable. How, then, do we address problems of power and accountability where a common moral language of political responsibility is not intelligible to all? The only reasonable solution is a system ensuring a dispersal of power and the protection of individuals both from the state and each other. The objective of democracy in a contemporary world is not the propagation of one particular view of 'the good' as much as it is an attempt to find a way for individuals and cultures with different sets of values to function in a world of increasing globalization. If there is a conception of a 'good' at all, it is of an international sphere in which diversity can be accommodated with a minimum of confrontation and antagonism. This vision does, of course, make two very definite assumptions: first, that the individuals and groups involved will *want* to live together with some degree of cooperation; and second, that they will agree to tolerate some degree of diversity in values and customs rather than feel the need to impose their own upon others (for a more philosophical account of this see Barry 1995).

This last point, of course, seems to be philosophical fly in the ointment. For if we cannot impose any conception of the good on others, then how can we justify our demand that other states must become democratic to be legitimate? The answer is that democracy is, quite simply, the best method we have to prevent the accumulation of political power; and that it is the accumulation of political power in any polity which prevents us from understanding what the preferences of 'the people' in any nation happen to be. If we have good reason to believe that each person in a system we deem to be unpalatable does in fact prefer it, then we must accept their decision as a group of self-determining individuals. But that is not the argument which is generally presented: rather, it is a state government (or self-styled 'representatives of the people') which articulates 'the will of the people'. Yet, unless we can be sure that 'the people' themselves have unflinchingly chosen this government to represent their views (and that they are free to change their minds) there is no good reason at all to believe that the government does in fact accurately represent the views of its people. And if the people *have* clearly chosen this government as their representative in a fair, open, and systematic process, then this government is, by definition, at least minimally 'democratic'. *That* is why 'democracy' is both a reasonable measure of legitimacy and a reasonably 'impartial' political construct.

This is of course not to say that western conceptions of liberal democracy are faultless. On the contrary, there is in many such accounts too facile a toleration for a different type of power: private property. The two most powerful threats to democracy as a means of diffusing power are claims to private property and cultural legitimacy. Like many superb pharmaceuticals, what is therapeutic in measured doses is toxic in unlimited ones. A strong support for democracy which asserts that private property rights are prior to and untouchable by political agreement is both philosophically inconsistent and ultimately destructive to the distribution of political power that democracy attempts to maintain. This is *not* to assert that private property rights are inherently oppressive and must thereby be eliminated; it is simply to remind us that private property rights must be seen, philosophically and politically, as a means to a particular end; and when it becomes apparent that they no longer fulfill that function, they cannot retain their political and legal preeminence.

In the same way, cultural constructs cannot be permitted to trump the function of democracy as a means of diffusing political power. To say that certain cultural groups must be exempt from democratic criteria because 'that's the way they've always done it' is both potentially pernicious and theoretically incoherent. Historical patterns of governance are themselves not evidence that those situated in such patterns necessarily agree to them; and using such traditional forms of governance as proof that there *is* consensus on its legitimacy is logically unintelligible. To say that what 'a people' want is definitionally the same as saying what each person within the community desires is a particularly vicious and ubiquitous form of logical error known as the 'fallacy of decomposition': the interests of the political representatives *cannot simply be assumed to be* the interests of each member of the group.

The argument that democracy is illegitimate and destructive to societies or cultural groups which traditionally have used 'consensus-based' forms of decision-making generally fails because such proponents simply assert that consensus exists without offering any proof for their claims (beyond the argument that such systems seemed to 'work well' before European colonial powers disrupted them) . This is not to hold that a consensus-based system could never be a plausible alternative to an institutionalized form of representative democracy. But it is to argue that the onus of proving that a system is truly consensual rests upon proponents of such a system. Writing under house arrest in 1994, Aung San Suu Kyi wrote that identifying the sources of power is crucial because it:

> decides who has the means of imposing on a nation or society their view of what constitutes culture and development and who determines what practical measures can be taken in the name of culture and development. . . The 'national culture' can become a bizarre graft of carefully selected historical incidents and distorted social values intended to justify the policies and actions of those in power. (1994: 13–14)

Democratic legitimacy and the power of definition

Democracy is, ultimately, just a word. Why ought we to be concerned at all about the way in which it is used? We should be concerned because our language – specifically, our 'normative vocabulary' – is very closely related to our acceptance or rejection of political acts and institutions. When attempts are made to modify or transform our normative vocabulary, we are being asked by a political agent – whom Skinner calls 'the innovating ideologist' – to reconsider the way in which our current political relations are structured. 'It is essentially by manipulating this set of terms', writes Skinner, 'that any society succeeds in establishing and altering its moral identity' (1974: 112).

> This being so, the task of the innovating ideologist is a hard but an obvious one. His concern, by definition, is to legitimate a new range of social actions which, in terms of the existing ways of applying the moral vocabulary prevailing in his society, are currently regarded as in some way untoward or illegitimate. His aim must therefore be to show that a number of existing and favourable evaluative-descriptive terms can somehow be applied to his apparently untoward actions. If he can somehow perform this trick, he can thereby hope to argue that the condemnatory descriptions which are otherwise liable to be applied to his actions can in consequence be discounted. (*Ibid.*: 112)

This, for the reasons noted above, is precisely what is occuring within the current discussion of democracy. What we must ask ourselves is whether we wish to accept both these changes, and their consequences.

Why has democracy increasingly become the measure of legitimacy throughout the world? It has served as this standard both for what it facilitates, and what it prevents. It is perceived to promote stability, security, prosperity, and, above all, the ability to live as one chooses. In like manner, it inhibits the possibility of domination from a foreign 'other'. The paradox of democracy in the global sphere, however, is that democracy in certain contexts *itself* becomes the foreign 'other'. The issue then becomes whether we ought to accept that democracy should *not* be the arbiter of legitimacy, or whether the idea of democracy should be expanded to incorporate limitless cultural features (as many, including the former Secretary-General of the United Nations, have argued), or whether a narrower conception of democracy is the best starting-point with which we have to work.

There is little except apathy or unbridled sensitivity to commend jettisoning democracy completely. There is, of course, the infinite regress involved in the declaration that political credibility ought to be built upon respect for individual consent (*why* individual consent?); but there is correspondingly little upon which to defend any other schema of legitimation. Unless we *all* share the belief that God's word is preeminent, or that our physical needs are prior to our free agency, or that the protection of an organic community is prior to the desires of its component members, there is no reason to accept that any other legitimizing principle ought to be acknowledged. Some degree of consensus must exist as widely as possible in order for any claim of legitimate rule to function:

> in the absence of any independent moral law, fundamental rights must rest upon such a consensus. However, a comparable scenario for group rights is not easy to describe. The circumstances of the privileged and the disadvantaged are different in significant ways that make it difficult to promote general consensus on the comparisons that support the extension of rights to groups. (Simpson 1997: 54)

But could one then not simply argue that, as such consensus can only exist in culturally-similar groupings, each grouping itself ought to determine its own legitimizing principles? Two problems arise here. First, what is *meant* by the claim that each grouping should be responsible for their choice of governance? If each individual gives their express acceptance of a system at regular intervals, then the system is already essentially 'democratic'. And if by 'self-determination of a peoples' one means that the most powerful individuals in a society can impose their own beliefs on the rest with no proof of the citizens' own consent except for the lack of continual political foment, then very little distinguishes the 'moral' claims of such a polity from the sheer exercise of brute force.

Second, contemporary political relations are such that discussions about the internal rules of appropriate political procedure cannot be divorced from discussions about appropriate political behaviour between groups. If a minimal set of political norms cannot be established to judge conduct *outside of* or *between* 'culturally-distinct groups', then simple political power will, by default, become the operative principle. Thus principles of legitimacy cannot depend solely upon internally-accepted cultural norms, but also upon the reflective consideration by all of what it would be fair for people of disparate beliefs to accept. This condition is the underlying point of 'democratic' legitimacy: as long as disagreement on substantive points exists, agreement may at the very least be reached on the procedural principle that each party has a right similar to every other that their particular norms be respected to the extent that it does not interfere with any other's. There will, of course, be hard cases where conflicts will arise, and these will have to be sorted out according to their unique circumstances. But this does not detract from the claim that a universal 'neutral space' is, for the most part, the simplest principle upon which to establish a workable point of agreement between distinct parties. The conceptualization of 'neutral space' is, admittedly, a tricky concept that may be impossible to achieve concretely. But the alternative bases of legitimate government are even more intricate and less persuasive. Clinging to the status quo of traditional forms of governance alone is an unmitigated exhibition of romanticism as long as the technological and organizational capacity of the modern nation state has the potential of controlling and subjugating its citizenry.

Democracy is, most fundamentally, the measure of political legitimacy due to its ability to minimize, better than any other *contemporary* alternative, the capacity of some individuals systematically to oppress others. There is, of course, the question of why this itself should be the standard of a legitimate government; yet that is intrinsically a question of why we ought to be moral at all, and this is an issue as old as politics itself. At the very least, we should heed the lessons of recent political transitions (no less than those of political philosophers) and remember that any contemporary system requires the willing acceptance of its members to function well: and, possibly, to function at all.

References

Adekanye, J. 'Bayo (1995), 'Structural adjustment, democratization and rising ethnic tensions in Africa', *Development and Change*, 26, 355–74.

Adler, Glenn and Eddie Webster (1995), 'Challenging transition theory: the labour movement, radical reform, and transition to democracy in South Africa', *Politics and Society*, 23 (1), 75–106.

Afshari, Reza (1994), 'An essay on Islamic cultural relativism in the discourse of human rights', *Human Rights Quarterly*, 16, 235–76.

Aidoo, Akwasi (1993), 'Africa: democracy without rights?', *Human Rights Quarterly*, 15, 703–15.

Allison, Graham and Robert Beschel (1992), 'Can the United States promote democracy?', *Political Science Quarterly*, 107 (1), 81–98.

Anderson, Benedict (1983), *Imagined Communities*, London: Verso.

Bail, Florian (1994), 'Justice, property, and the privatization of East Germany', unpublished.

Ball, Terence, James Farr and Russell Hanson (eds) (1989), *Political Innovation and Conceptual Change*, Cambridge: Cambridge University Press.

Barnard, F. M. (1965), *Herder's Social and Political Thought*, Oxford: Clarendon Press.

Barry, Brian (1989), *Theories of Justice*, London: Harvester-Wheatsheaf.

Barry, Brian (1995), *Justice as Impartiality*, Oxford: Clarendon.

Bayart, Jean-François (1986), 'Civil society in Africa', in Patrick Chabal (ed), *Political Domination in Africa*, Cambridge: Cambridge University Press, 109–25.

Beetham, David (1994), 'Conditions for democratic consolidation', *Review of African Political Economy*, 60, 157–72.

Beetham, David (1995), 'What future for economic and social rights?', *Political Studies*, 43, 41–60.

Beetham, David (1996), 'Market economy and democratic polity', paper presented at the conference on 'The Emergence of Civil Society', Centre for the Study of Democratisation, Warwick University, Coventry, UK.

Bendix, Reinhard (1990–91), 'State, legitimation and "civil society"', *Telos*, 86, 143–52.

Berman, Marshall (1995), 'Modernism and human rights near the millennium', *Dissent*, Summer, 333–41.

Bird, Graham (1996), 'The International Monetary Fund and developing countries: a review of the evidence and policy options', *International Organization*, 50 (3), 477–511.

Blum, J., R. Cameron and T. G. Barnes (1966), *The Emergence of the European World*, Boston: Little, Brown.

Boldt, Menno (1993), *Surviving as Indians: The Challenge of Self-Government*, Toronto: University of Toronto Press.

Boutros-Ghali, Boutros (1992), *An Agenda for Peace*, New York: United Nations.

Boutros-Ghali, Boutros (1995), 'Global prospects for United Nations', *Aussenpolitik*, 11, 107–14.

Brand, H. (1993), 'The World Bank, the Monetary Fund, and poverty', *Dissent*, Fall, 497–504.

Bratton, Michael (1989), 'The politics of government–NGO relations in Africa', *World Development*, 17 (4), 569–87.

Braybrooke, David (1968), *Three Tests for Democracy*, New York: Random House.

Bromwich, David (1995), 'Culturalism, the euthanasia of liberalism', *Dissent*, Winter, 89–106.

Buchanan, James (1986), *Liberty, Market, and State*, Brighton: Wheatsheaf.

Burke, Edmund (1968 [1790]), *Reflections on the Revolution in France*, ed. Conor Cruise O'Brien, London: Penguin.

Carew, George Munda (1993), 'Development theory and the promise of democracy: the future of postcolonial African states', *Africa Today*, 4, 31–53.

Carothers, Thomas (1995), 'Democracy promotion under Clinton', *The Washington Quarterly*, 18 (4), 13–25.

Chabal, Patrick (ed) (1986), *Political Domination in Africa*, Cambridge: Cambridge University Press.

Chandhoke, Neera (1995), *State and Civil Society*, Sage: New Delhi.

Clark, John (1991), *Democratizing Development*, London: Earthscan.

Cohen, Jean L. and Andrew Arato (1992), *Civil Society and Political Theory*, Cambridge, Mass.: MIT Press.

Commission on Global Governance (1995), *Our Global Neighbourhood*, Geneva: Commission on Global Governance.

Cowie, L. W. (1977), *Sixteenth-Century Europe*, Edinburgh: Oliver and Boyd.

Cox, Robert (1995), 'Civilizations: encounters and transformations', *Studies in Political Economy*, 47, Spring, 7–31.

Dahl, Robert (1971), *Polyarchy: Participation and Opposition*, New Haven: Yale University Press.

Dahl, Robert (1989), *Democracy and its Critics*, New Haven: Yale University Press.

Dean, Jodi (1992), 'Including women: the consequences and side effects of feminist critiques of civil society', *Philosophy and Social Criticism*, 18 (3), 379–406.

Diamond, Larry (1992), 'Promoting democracy', *Foreign Policy*, 87, Summer, 25–46.

Diamond, Larry, Juan Linz, and Seymour Martin Lipset (eds) (1989), *Democracy in Developing Countries*, Boulder: Lynne Rienner.

Dirlik, Arif (1994), 'The postcolonial aura: third world criticism in the age of global capitalism', *Critical Inquiry*, 20, 328–56.

Doyle, Michael W. (1983), 'Kant, liberal legacies, and foreign affairs', *Philosophy and Public Affairs*, 12 (3), 205–35.

Dryzek, John S. (1996), *Democracy in Capitalist Times*, Oxford: Oxford University Press.

Dunn, John (ed) (1978), *West African States: Failure and Promise*, Cambridge: Cambridge University Press.

Dunn, John (ed) (1992), *Democracy: The Unfinished Journey*, Oxford: Oxford University Press.

Dunn, John (1994), 'Introduction: crisis of the nation state?' *Political Studies*, 42, 3–15.

Dworkin, Ronald (1996), *Freedom's Law: The Moral Reading of the American Constitution*, Cambridge, Mass.: Harvard University Press.

Edwards, Michael and David Hulme (eds) (1992), *Making A Difference: NGOs and Development in a Changing World*, London: Earthscan.

Ekins, Paul (1992), *A New World Order: Grassroots Movements for Global Change*, London: Routledge.

Elster, Jon (1986), 'The market and the forum: three varieties of political theory', in Jon Elster and Aanund Hylland (eds), *Foundations of Social Choice Theory*, Cambridge: Cambridge University Press, 102–32.

Fanon, Franz (1963), *The Wretched of the Earth*, trans. Constance Farrington, New York: Grove Press.

Fatton, R. (1992), *Predatory Rule: State and Civil Society in Africa*, Boulder: Lynne Rienner.

Feinberg, Joel (1979 [1970]), 'The nature and value of rights', in David Lyons (ed), *Rights*, Belmont, Calif.: Wadsworth, 78–91.

Fierlbeck, Katherine (1994), 'Economic liberalization as a prologue to democracy: the case of Indonesia', *The Canadian Journal of Development Studies*, 15 (2), 151–69.

Fowler, Alan (1991), 'The role of NGOs in changing state-society relations: perspectives from eastern and southern Africa', *Development Policy Review*, 9, 53–84.

Frank, Andre Gunder (1975), *On Capitalist Underdevelopment*, Bombay: Oxford University Press.

Frankl, Viktor (1985 [1959]), *Man's Search for Meaning*, New York: Washington Square.

Fukuyama, Francis (1989), 'The end of history?' *The National Interest*, Summer, 62.

Fukuyama, Francis (1992), *The End of History and the Last Man*, New York: Free Press.

Fukuyama, Francis (1995), 'Confucianism and democracy', *Journal of Democracy*, 6 (2), 20–33.

Geddes, Barbara (1994), 'Challenging the conventional wisdom', *Journal of Democracy*, 5 (4), 104–18.

Gellner, Ernest (1991), 'The civil and the sacred', in Grethe B. Peterson (ed), *The Tanner Lectures on Human Values*, 12, Salt Lake City: University of Utah Press.

Gershman, Carl (1993), 'The United Nations and the New World Order', *Journal of Democracy*, 4 (3), 5–16.

Gibbon, Peter (1992), 'The World Bank and African poverty, 1973–91', *The Journal of Modern African Studies*, 30 (2), 193–220.

Gilbert, Alan (1992), 'Must global politics constrain democracy?', *Political Theory*, 20 (1), February, 8–37.

Giliomee, Hermann (1995), 'Democratization in South Africa', *Political Science Quarterly*, 110 (1), 83–103.

Ginzberg, Ruth (1989), 'Feminism, rationality, and logic', *American Philosophical Association Newsletter on Feminism and Philosophy*, 88 (2), 34–9.

Glendon, Mary Ann (1991), *Rights Talk: The Impoverishment of Political Discourse*, New York: Free Press.

Grant, Judith (1987), 'I feel therefore I am: a critique of female experience as the basis for a feminist epistemology', *Women and Politics*, 7 (3), 99–127.

Green, Thomas Hill (1986), *Lectures on the Principles of Political Obligation*, ed. Paul Harris and John Morrow, Cambridge: Cambridge University Press.

Guéhenno, Jean-Marie (1995 [1993]), *The End of the Nation-State*, Minneapolis: University of Minneapolis Press.

Guinier, Land (1993), 'Groups, representation, and race-conscious districting: a case of the emperor's clothes', *Texas Law Review*, 71, 1589–642.

Guinier, Land (1994), *The Tyranny of the Majority*, New York: Free Press.

Haack, Susan (1995), 'Multiculturalism and objectivity', *Partisan Review*, 62 (3), 397–405.

Haack, Susan (1996), 'Science as social? Yes and no', in Jack Nelson and Lynn Hanfinson Nelson (eds), *A Dialogue on Feminism, Science, and Philosophy of Science*, Dordrecht, The Netherlands: Kluwer.

Habermas, Jürgen (1983), *The Theory of Communicative Action*, trans. Thomas McCarthy, Boston: Beacon Press.

Habermas, Jürgen (1996), *Between Facts and Norms*, trans. William Rehg, Cambridge, Mass.: MIT Press.

Harding, Sandra (1991), *Whose Science? Whose Knowledge?*, Ithaca: Cornell University Press.

Havel, Václav (1995), 'Democracy's forgotten dimension', *Journal of Democracy*, 6 (2), 3–19.

Hawthorn, Geoffrey (1994), 'The crises of southern states', *Political Studies*, 42, 130–45.

Hayek, Friedrich (1960), *The Constitution of Liberty*, Chicago: University of Chicago Press.

Head, Simon (1996), 'The new, ruthless economy', *New York Review*, 29 February, 47–52.

Healey, John and Mark Robinson (1992), *Democracy, Governance and Economy Policy*, London: Overseas Development Institute.

Held, David (1987), *Models of Democracy*, Cambridge: Polity Press.

Held, David (1991), 'Democracy and globalization', *Alternatives*, 16, 201–208.

Held, David (ed) (1993), *Prospects for Democracy*, Cambridge: Polity Press.

Held, David (1995), *Democracy and the Global Order*, Cambridge: Polity Press.

Herman, Margaret and Charles Kegley (1995), 'The political psychology of "peace through democratization"', *Cooperation and Conflict*, 20 (1), 5–30.

Hill, Christopher (1964), *Puritanism and Revolution*, New York: Schocken Books.

Hill, Christopher (1966), *The Century of Revolution, 1602–1714*, New York: Norton.

Hill, Christopher (1980), *Intellectual Origins of the English Revolution*, Oxford: Clarendon Press.

Hill, Christopher (1972), *The World Turned Upside Down*, London: Penguin.

Hirschman, Albert O. (1981), *Essays in Trespassing*, Cambridge: Cambridge University Press.

Hirschman, Albert O. (1994), 'Social conflicts as pillars of democratic market society', *Political Theory*, 22 (2), 203–18.

Hobbes, Thomas (1968 [1651]). *Leviathan*, ed. C. B. Macpherson, Harmondsworth: Penguin.

Hobhouse, Leonard (1964 [1911]), *Liberalism*, Oxford: Oxford University Press.

Hobsbawm, Eric (1983), 'Inventing traditions', in Eric Hobsbawm and Terence Ranger (eds), *The Invention of Tradition*, Cambridge: Cambridge University Press, 1–14.

Hobsbawm, Eric (1996), 'Identity politics and the left', *New Left Review*, 217, May/June, 38–47.

Holloway, Richard (ed) (1989), *Doing Development: Governments, NGOs, and the Rural Poor in Africa*, London: Earthscan.

Holmes, Stephen (1993), *The Anatomy of Antiliberalism*, Cambridge, Mass.: Harvard University Press.

Honneth, Axel (1993), 'Conceptions of "civil society"', *Radical Philosophy*, 64, Summer, 19–22.

Hont, Istvan (1994), 'The permanent crisis of a divided mankind: "contemporary crisis of the nation state" in historical perspective', *Political Studies*, 42, 166–231.

Hont, Istvan and Michael Ignatieff (1983), *Wealth and Virtue*, Cambridge: Cambridge University Press.

Hume, David (1955 [1748]), *An Inquiry Concerning Human Understanding*, ed. Charles Hendel, Indianapolis: Bobbs-Merrill.

Hume, David (1970 [1777]), 'Essays, moral and political', in Henry D. Aiken (ed), *Hume's Moral and Political Philosophy*, Darien, Conn.: Hafner Publishing, 293–386.

Huntington, Samuel P. (1991), *The Third Wave: Democratization in the Late Twentieth Century*, Norman and London: University of Oklahoma Press.

Hutchful, Eboe (1995–96), 'The civil society debate in Africa', *International Journal*, (51) 1, Winter, 54–77.

Hutton, Will (1995), *The State We're In*, London: Vintage.

Ihonvbere, Julius O. (1995) 'From movement to government: the movement for multi-party democracy and the crisis of democratic consolidation in Zambia', *Canadian Journal of African Studies*, 29 (1), 1–25.

Isaac, Jeffrey (1993), 'Civil society and the spirit of revolt', *Dissent*, Summer, 356–61.

Jeffries, Richard (1993), 'The state, structural adjustment and good governance in Africa', *Journal of Commonwealth and Comparative Politics*, (31) 1, 20–35.

Johansen, Robert (1991), 'Real security is democratic security', *Alternatives*, 16, 209–42.

Jung, Courtney and Ian Shapiro (1995), 'South Africa's negotiated transition: democracy, opposition, and the new constitutional order', *Politics and Society*, 23 (3), 269–308.

Kamrava, Mehran (1993), 'Conceptualising third world politics: the state-society seesaw', *Third World Quarterly*, 14 (4), 703–16.

Kotzé, Hennie (1995), 'The state, civil society, and democratic transition in South Africa', *Journal of Conflict Resolution*, 39 (1), 27–48.

Krasner, Stephen (1992), 'Realism, imperialism, and democracy: a response to Gilbert', *Political Theory*, 20 (1), February, 38–52.

Krasner, Stephen (1992), 'Economic interdependence and independent statehood', in

Robert H. Jackson and Alan James (eds), *States in a Changing World*, Oxford: Clarendon Press.

Kumar, Krishan (1993), 'Civil society: an inquiry into the usefulness of an historical term', *British Journal of Sociology*, 44 (3), 375–401.

Kymlicka, Will (1989), *Liberalism, Community, and Culture*, Oxford: Oxford University Press.

Kymlicka, Will (1995), *Multicultural Citizenship*, Oxford: Clarendon Press.

Kymlicka, Will (1996), 'The good, the bad, and the intolerable: minority group rights', *Dissent*, Summer, 22–30.

Landell-Mills, Pierre (1992), 'Governance, cultural change, and empowerment', *Journal of Modern African Studies*, 30 (4), 543–67.

Lawson, Stephanie (1993), 'Conceptual issues in the comparative study of regime change and democratization', *Comparative Politics*, January, 183–205.

Leftwich, Adrian (1993), 'Governance, democracy and development in the Third World', *Third World Quarterly*, 14 (3), 605–24.

Locke, John (1965 [1689]), *Two Treatises of Government*, ed. Peter Laslett, New York: Mentor.

Longino, Helen (1992), 'Essential tensions – phase two: feminist, philosophical, and social studies of science', in Ernan McMullin (ed), *The Social Dimensions of Science*, Notre Dame: Notre Dame University Press, 198–216.

Lonsdale, John (1986), 'Political accountability in African history', in Patrick Chabal (ed), *Political Domination in Africa*, Cambridge: Cambridge University Press, 126–57.

Lukes, Steven (1974), *Power: A Radical View*, London: Macmillan.

Lukes, Steven (1993), 'Five fables about human rights', *Dissent*, Fall, 427–37.

Lyotard, Jean-François (1984), *The Postmodern Condition: A Report on Knowledge*, trans. Geoff Bennington and Brian Massumi, Minneapolis: University of Minnesota Press.

MacIntyre, Alasdair (1988), *Whose Justice? Which Rationality?*, Notre Dame: University of Notre Dame Press.

MacIntyre, Andrew (1990), *Business and Politics in Indonesia*, St Leonards, Australia: Allen and Unwin.

Mackinnon, Catherine (1987), *Feminism Unmodified: Discourse on Life and Law*, Cambridge: Cambridge University Press.

Macpherson, Crawford Brough (1962), *The Political Theory of Possessive Individualism*, Oxford: Oxford University Press.

Macpherson, Crawford Brough (1983 [1965]), *The Real World of Democracy*, Montreal: CBC Enterprises.

Mahmud, Sakah S. (1993), 'The state and human rights in African in the 1990s: perspectives and prospects', *Human Rights Quarterly*, 15, 485–98.

Mansbridge, Jane, J. Roland Pennock and John W. Chapman (eds) (1977), 'The limits of friendship', *NOMOS XVI: Participation in Politics*, New York: New York University Press.

Mardjana, Ketut T. (1993), 'Public enterprise in Indonesia', *The Indonesian Quarterly*, 21 (1), 49–72.

Marshall, T. H. (1964) *Class, Citizenship, and Social Development*, New York: Doubleday.

McKay, Derek and H. M. Scott (1983), *The Rise of the Great Powers, 1648–1815*, London: Longman.

Mendus, Susan (1992), 'Losing the faith: feminism and democracy', in John Dunn (ed), *Democracy: The Unfinished Journey*, Oxford: Oxford University Press, 207–20.

Minow, Martha (1990), *Making All the Difference: Inclusion, Exclusion, and American Law*, Ithaca: Cornell University Press.

Minton-Beddoes, Zanny (1995), 'Why the IMF needs reform', *Foreign Affair*, 74 (3), 123–33.

Mitchell, William (1983), 'Efficiency, responsibility, and democratic politics', in J. Roland Pennock and John W. Chapman (eds), *NOMOS XXV: Liberal Democracy*, New York: New York University Press, 343–73.

Mittelman, James (1996), *Globalization: Critical Reflections*, Boulder: Lynne Rienner.

Morgan, Clifton T. (1993), 'Democracy and war: reflections on the literature', *International Interpretations*, 18 (3), 197–203.

Munck, Geraldo (1994), 'Democratic transitions in comparative perspective', *Comparative Politics*, April, 355–75.

Nagel, Thomas (1973), 'Rawls on justice', in N. Daniels (ed), *Reading Rawls*, New York: Basic Books, 1–15.

Nasr, S. V. R. (1995), 'Democracy and Islamic revivalism', *Political Science Quarterly*, 110 (2), 261–85.

Nel, Philip (1995), 'Transition through erosion: comparing South Africa's democratisation', *Aussenpolitik*, 1, 82–93.

Norton, Augustus Richard (1993), 'The future of civil society in the middle east', *Middle East Journal*, 47 (2), Spring, 205–16.

Nossal, Kim Richard (1995), 'The democratization of Canadian foreign policy: the elusive ideal', in Cameron, A. Maxwell and Maureen Appel Molot (eds), *Democracy and Foreign Policy*, Ottawa: Carleton University Press, 29–43.

Nozick, Robert (1974), *Anarchy, State, and Utopia*, New York: Basic Books.

Nussbaum, Martha (1994), 'Feminists and philosophy', *New York Review*, 20 October, 59–63.

Nyang'oro, Julius E. (1992), 'The evolving role of the African state under structural adjustment', in Nyang'oro and Shaw (eds), *Beyond Structural Adjustment in Africa*, New York: Praeger, 11–27.

Nyang'oro, Julius E. and Timothy M. Shaw (eds) (1992), *Beyond Structural Adjustment in Africa*, New York: Praeger.

O'Connor, James (1973), *The Fiscal Crisis of the State*, New York: St. Martin's Press.

O'Donnell, Guillermo (1978), 'Reflections on the patterns of change in the bureaucratic-authoritarian state', *Latin American Research Review*, 13, 3–38.

O'Donnell, Guillermo and Philippe C. Schmitter (1986), *Transitions from Authoritarian Rule: Tentative Conclusions about Uncertain Democracies*, Baltimore: Johns Hopkins University Press.

OECD (1995), *Participatory Development and Good Governance*, Paris: OECD.

Offe, Claus (1984), *Contradictions of the Welfare State*, ed. John Keane, Cambridge, Mass.: MIT Press.

Okin, Susan M. (1989), *Gender, the Public and the Private*, Toronto: University of Toronto Press.

Olson, Mancur (1993), 'Dictatorship, democracy, and development', *American Political Science Review*, 87 (3), 567–75.

Owen, Henry (1994), 'The World Bank: is 50 years enough?', *Foreign Affairs*, 73 (5), 97–108.

Pateman, Carole (1970), *Participation and Democratic Theory*, Cambridge: Cambridge University Press.

Peceny, Mark (1995), 'Two paths to the promotion of democracy during U.S. military intervention', *International Studies Quarterly*, 39, 371–401.

Pitkin, Hanna (1967), *The Concept of Representation*, Berkeley: University of California Press.

Popper, Karl (1968 [1962]), *Conjectures and Refutations*, New York: Harper Torchbooks.

Potter, David (1993), 'Democratization in Asia', in David Held (ed), *Prospects for Democracy*, Cambridge: Cambridge University Press, 355–79.

Prakesh, Gyan (1992), 'Postcolonial criticism and Indian historiography', *Social Text*, 31/32, 8–19.

Przeworski, Adam (1991), *Democracy and the Market*, Cambridge: Cambridge University Press.

Przeworski, Adam and John Sprague (1986), *Paper Stones: A History of Electoral Socialism*, Chicago: University of Chicago Press.

Putnam, Robert D. (1993), *Making Democracy Work: Civic Traditions in Modern Italy*, Princeton: Princeton University Press.

Putnam, Robert D. (1995), 'Bowling alone: America's declining social capital', *Journal of Democracy*, 6 (1), January, 65–78.

Rawls, John (1971), *A Theory of Justice*, Cambridge, Mass.: Belknap Press.

Rawls, John (1993a), 'The law of peoples', *Critical Inquiry*, 20, 36–68.

Rawls, John (1993b), *Political Liberalism*, New York: Columbia University Press.

Remmer, Karen (1995), 'New theoretical perspectives on democratization', *Comparative Politics*, October, 103–22.

Riedel, Manfred (1984), *Between Tradition and Revolution: The Hegelian Transformation of Political Philosophy*, Cambridge: Cambridge University Press.

Robinson, Ian (1995), 'Globalization and democracy', *Dissent*, Summer, 373–80.

Robinson, Pearl T. (1994), 'Democratization: understanding the relationship between regime change and the culture of politics', *African Studies Review*, 31 (1), 39–67.

Robison, Richard (1986), *Indonesia: The Rise of Capital*, Sydney: Allen and Unwin.

Robison, Richard (1988), 'Authoritarian states, capital-owning classes, and the politics of newly industrializing countries', *World Politics*, 1, 41.

Rorty, Richard (1993), 'Human rights, rationality, and sentimentality', *The Yale Review*, 81 (4), 1–20.

Rosenau, James (1996), 'The dynamics of globalization: toward an operational formulation', paper presented at the annual meeting of the International Studies Association (San Diego, Calif.: 18 April).

Rosenau, Pauline Marie (1992), *Post-Modernism and the Social Sciences*, Princeton: Princeton University Press.

Rosenblum, Nancy (1994), 'Civil societies: liberalism and the moral uses of pluralism', *Social Research*, 61 (3), Fall, 539–62.

Russett, Bruce, *et al.* (1993), *Grasping the Democratic Peace: Principles for a Post-Cold War World*, Princeton: Princeton University Press.

Ryan, Alan (1994), 'Self-ownership, autonomy, and property rights', *Social Philosophy and Policy*, 11 (2), 241–58.

Sacks, Oliver (1989), *Seeing Voices*, Berkeley: University of California Press.

Sandel, Michael (1982), *Liberalism and the Limits of Justice*, Cambridge: Cambridge University Press.

Sandel, Michael (1996), *Democracy's Discontent*, Cambridge, Mass.: Belknap Press.

Schmitz, Gerald (1995), 'Democratization and demystification: deconstructing "governance" as development paradigm', in Gerald Schmitz and David Moore (eds) *Debating Development Discourse*, London: Macmillan, 54–90.

Schraeder, Peter (1995) 'Understanding the "Third Wave" of democratization in Africa', *The Journal of Politics*, 57 (4), 1160–8.

Schumpeter, Joseph (1942), *Capitalism, Socialism and Democracy*, New York: Harper and Row.

Shin, Doh Chull (1994), 'On the third wave of democratization', *World Politics*, 47, 135–70.

Shivji, Issa G (1991), 'The democracy debate in Africa: Tanzania', *Review of African Political Economy*, 50, 79–91.

Shklar, Judith (1989), 'The liberalism of fear', in Nancy Rosenblum (ed) *Liberalism and the Moral Life*, Cambridge: Cambridge University Press, 21–38.

Shrag, Peter (1994), 'California's elected anarchy', *Harper's*, 289 (1734), 50–9.

Simmons, John (1992), *The Lockean Theory of Rights*, Princeton: Princeton University Press.

Simpson, Evan (1997), 'Rights thinking', *Philosophy*, 72, 29–58.

Skinner, Quentin (1978), *The Foundations of Modern Political Thought*, vol. 1, Cambridge: Cambridge University Press.

Smith, Adam (1970 [1776]), *The Wealth of Nations*, Harmondsworth: Penguin.

South Commission (1990), *The Challenge to the South: The Report of the South Commission*, Oxford: Oxford University Press.

Stimson, Shannon and Murray Milgate (1993), 'Utility, property, and political participation: James Mill on democratic reform', *American Political Science Review*, 87 (4).

Suu Kyi, Aung San (1995), 'Freedom, development, and human worth', *Journal of Democracy* 6 (2), 11–19.

Tamás, G. M. (1994), 'A disquisition on civil society', *Social Research*, 61 (2), Summer, 205–22.

Tamir, Yael (1993), *Liberal Nationalism*, Princeton: Princeton University Press.

Tarrow, Sidney (1996), 'Making social science work across space and time: a critical reflection on Robert Putnam's *Making Democracy Work*', *American Political Science Review*, 90 (2), 389–97.

Taylor, Charles (1989), *Sources of the Self: The Making of the Modern Identity*, Cambridge, Mass.: Harvard University Press.

Taylor, Charles (1991), 'Civil society in the western tradition', in E. Groffier and M. Paradis (eds), *The Notion of Tolerance and Human Rights: Essays in Honour of Raymond Klibansky*, Ottawa: Carleton University Press, 117–36.

Taylor, Charles (1992), *Multiculturalism and 'The Politics of Recognition'*, ed. Amy Gutmann, Princeton: Princeton University Press.

Thompson, Mark (1993), 'The limits of democratisation in ASEAN', *Third World Quarterly*, 14 (3), 469–84.

de Tocqueville, Alexis (1945 [1835]), *Democracy in America*, New York: Vintage.

Tuck, Richard (1979), *Natural Rights Theories*, Cambridge: Cambridge University Press.

Tully, James (1980), *A Discourse on Property*, Cambridge: Cambridge University Press.

Tully, James (ed) (1988), *Meaning and Context: Quentin Skinner and his Critics*, Cambridge: Polity Press.

Tully, James (1995), *Strange Multiplicity*, Cambridge: Cambridge University Press.

Wade, Robert (1990), *Governing the Market*, Princeton: Princeton University Press.

Waldron, Jeremy (1988), *The Right to Private Property*, Oxford: Oxford University Press.

Waldron, Jeremy (1994), 'The advantages and difficulties of the Humean theory of property', *Social Philosophy and Policy*, 11 (2), 85–123.

Walker, R. B. J. (1991), 'On the spatiotemporal conditions of democratic practice', *Alternatives*, 16, 243–62.

Walzer, Michael (1991), 'The idea of civil society', *Dissent*, Spring, 293–304.

White, Gordon (1994), 'Civil society, democratization and development (I): clearing the analytical ground', *Democratization*, 1 (3), 375–90.

Whitehead, Laurence (1986), 'International aspects of democratization', in O'Donnell, Guillermo, Philippe C. Schmitter, and Laurence Whitehead (eds), *Transitions from Authoritarian Rule: Comparative Perspectives*, Baltimore: Johns Hopkins University Press, 3–46.

Williams, David and Tom Young (1994), 'Governance, the World Bank and liberal theory', *Political Studies*, 42, 84–100.

Wiseman, John A. (1993), 'Democracy and the new political pluralism in Africa: causes, consequences, and significance', *Third World Quarterly*, 14 (3), 439–49.

Wittgenstein, Ludwig (1953), *Philosophical Investigations*, trans. G. E. M. Anscombe, Oxford, Basil Blackwell.

Wolff, Robert Paul (1965), 'Beyond tolerance', in Robert Paul Wolff, Barrington Moore Woolf, Jr. and Herbert Marcuse (eds), *A Critique of Pure Tolerance*, Boston: Beacon Press.

World Bank (1989), *Sub-Saharan Africa: From Crisis to Sustainable Growth*, Washington, D.C.: World Bank.

World Bank (1992), *Governance and Development*, Washington, D.C.: World Bank.

World Bank (1994), *Governance: The World Bank's Experience*, Washington, D.C.: World Bank.

World Trade Organization (1995), *Trading into the Future*, Geneva: WTO.

Young, Iris Marion (1989), 'Polity and group difference: a critique of the ideal of universal citizenship', *Ethics*, 99, 250–74.

Young, Iris Marion (1990), *Justice and the Politics of Difference*, Princeton: Princeton University Press.

Young, Robert (1978), 'Dispensing with moral rights', *Political Theory*, 6, 63–74.

Žižek, Slavoj (1991), *Looking Awry*, Cambridge, Mass.: MIT Press.

Index